BRAAAIIIINNNSSS!

ROBERT SMITH?

BRAAAIIINNNSSS!

FROM ACADEMICS
TO ZOMBIES

UNIVERSITY OF OTTAWA PRESS
OTTAWA

uOttawa

The University of Ottawa Press acknowledges with gratitude the support extended to its publishing list by Heritage Canada through its Book Publishing Industry Development Program, by the Canada Council for the Arts, by the Canadian Federation for the Humanities and Social Sciences through its Aid to Scholarly Publications Program, by the Social Sciences and Humanities Research Council, and by the University of Ottawa.

Library and Archives Canada Cataloguing in Publication

  Braaaiiinnnsss! : from academics to zombies / Robert Smith.

Includes bibliographical references.
ISBN 978-0-7766-0770-2

  1. Zombies. I. Smith, Robert, 1972 Oct. 28- II. Title: Brains.

GR581.B73 2011   398.21   C2011-906504-5

Design by Sandra Friesen
Chapter title page illustrations by Jakub Dolejš

∞

PRINTED AND BOUND IN CANADA

CONTENTS

To my zombie students, Phil, Ioan and Joe, without whom
this book could not possibly exist.

INTRODUCTION

ROBERT SMITH?

When it started, it was so small nobody noticed. At first. But then reports began to surface in different places, few of them believed at the time. Quickly, far more quickly than anyone thought possible, the news began to spread. First locally, then globally. In a matter of days, the story was everywhere: a professor at the University of Ottawa had created a mathematical model of zombies. Soon there was a second wave to the epidemic: the professor had a question mark in his name. That too spread around the globe.

For several weeks in the summer of 2009, mathematical modelling of zombies was one of the biggest news stories in the world. It spawned print and radio interviews, podcasts, TV features and documentaries. Coincidentally, it happened at the same time as the publication of *Pride and Prejudice and Zombies*, so it seemed as though zombies were everywhere.

The best thing about the media attention was that it raised awareness of my academic field—mathematical modelling of infectious diseases—among people who had no idea that such a thing is possible. Mathematics is essentially a language

i

that's extremely rigorous and systematic. If you can translate a real-world problem into the language of mathematics, then you have access to a system of logic that's completely robust. You then do your mathematical analysis and any conclusion you find is 100 percent true, based on the premise. The premise might not be true—in fact, almost certainly it won't be, any more than a map is a true representation of streets—but your conclusion is solid. You can then go back and improve your premise by comparing the outcome with what you know from the real world. This requires being an expert in math, but also in biology. If you have the know-how, then it's incredibly powerful and very rewarding.

The zombie model was the perfect illustration of this process. You take the "biology" (in this case a zombie outbreak) and try to understand the underlying mechanisms involved (zombies can infect susceptible humans or raise the dead, but they can also be killed by humans). You translate that into mathematics (using differential equations, which are mathematical engines of change, telling you how things move in time) and come up with a conclusion: zombies will take over the world. You compare your conclusion with data (in this case by watching movies and playing video games) and maybe refine your model (to include, for example, a latent period of infection). Once you have the model, you can alter it to include other factors: quarantine, potential cure, more aggressive attacks.

Usually, I study infectious diseases, such as HIV and malaria. The process allows us to consider big questions for which there might not even be data yet. If there is an HIV vaccine, can it make things worse? (Answer: Yes, unless it lowers the viral load sufficiently.) Can spraying inside houses in malaria-endemic areas control the disease? (Answer: Yes, but global warming will make this progressively harder.) Can we spend our way out of the AIDS epidemic if we spend all the available money at once? (Answer: Yes, but we need to act quickly.)

I mention all this because this is as close to mathematics as this book will get. So, mathphobes, you can breathe more easily.

It all started because I was teaching a course in mathematical modelling of infectious diseases. The students had to do a project and I told them they could model any disease they liked. When a group came to my office and suggested zombies, they thought I'd shoot the idea right down. But I loved it! Zombies are the perfect way to illustrate disease modelling. At the end of the course, I so enjoyed their project that I rewrote it for publication in an academic book. This amused me and I thought no more of it.

Six months later the book came out, just as I decided to present the chapter at an academic conference (the Society for Mathematical Biology annual meeting in Vancouver, Canada). I was scheduled to do the last talk in the last session on the last day of the conference, so I thought it would be nice to finish with an amusing topic.

The response was incredible: I've never attended a talk (let alone given one) where the question period went on longer than the talk itself. Everyone laughed in the right places (except for one poor soul who'd never heard of zombies and thought this was a real disease). Distinguished professors in their seventies asked insightful questions about drug resistance to the cure. And, crucially, a blogger from the *Globe and Mail* (Canada's national newspaper) found out about it and wrote a story for the online version of the paper.

National Geographic had interviewed me the week before after seeing the book's table of contents. Among mathematical models of HIV, malaria and tuberculosis, the chapter on zombies stood out like a decaying, undead thumb.

From those two stories, the chapter began to get attention. First it was tweeted about. Then blogged. The *Globe and Mail* decided to run a print version. A few other Canadian newspapers also picked it up. Then it hit Wired.com and that was the point at which the tsunami was unleashed.

"Science Ponders 'Zombie Attack,'" BBC News, United Kingdom, 18 August 2009 (the number one story for forty-eight hours).

"What's the Best Way to Fight Zombies? Someone Did the Math," *Wall Street Journal,* United States, 18 August 2009.

"Mathematicians Use Zombies to Learn about Swine Flu, *Toronto Star,* Canada, 18 August 2009.

"Who Will Win in Human, Zombie War?," National Public Radio,
United States, 20 August 2009.

"Forget Swine Flu—Could We Cope with a Plague of the Undead?,"
Daily Mail, United Kingdom, 26 August 2009.

"How to Survive a Zombie Invasion," *Hungry Beast,* ABC TV, Australia,
2 December 2009.

"Tiedemiehet pohtivat zombien hyökkäystä," *Iltalehti,* Finland,
18 August 2009.

I think the appeal of zombies lies in the fact that they're so
primal. They represent two fundamental fears that we have as
humans: being eaten by a predator and dying from an infectious disease. Although they're not technically a disease, they
have the hallmarks of one, so we can learn a lot from thinking
about them in the same way.

Zombies allow us to explore our fundamental fears in a safe
way. When confronted with an actual predator, we're unlikely
to have much of a chance. Weapons provide the illusion of comfort, which is why they're so intrinsically associated with zombies, but that's really only because we like to think we could
fight off a predator with guns. In reality, shooting something
that's moving is incredibly difficult and shooting a moving
creature in a specific area such as the head is all but impossible. And the nasty thing about zombies is that it doesn't matter
how many you kill; there are a thousand more on their way.

The particularly gruesome twist that zombies offer is that
they're a deathly parody of the living. You might shoot a polar
bear coming at you without a second thought, but would you
shoot your grandma? Maybe, but if you pause to think about
it, you'd soon be a zombie snack. That's a deliciously complex
spanner in the zombie machine: almost by definition, those
of us who think and have compassion will likely be the first to
go, leaving behind only the bloodthirsty and those incapable
of empathy. So, even if some of us survive, civilization has already lost the war.

Disease is so terrifying because it takes away even that illusion of control. You can be struck down without warning and

there's very little you can do about it. Little wonder we seize onto perceived differences with such fervour: if you can cast someone suffering from a disease into a fundamentally different camp, then you give yourself the illusion of protection.

What's more, the most successful diseases aren't the fast ones, such as Ebola. They're fast, but they're too fast, burning themselves out too quickly. If your entire village will be dead before anyone can reach the next village, then the disease doesn't have a good chance of spreading. Instead, like zombies, the most successful diseases are the slow ones: those whose initial signs we ignore or those that don't show symptoms for a long time. Combine that with moral panic and you have a recipe for the perfect epidemic. Little wonder HIV/AIDS has done so much damage.

In fact, the best defence against zombies is our brains. Zombies might be unstoppable, neither needing sleep nor lacking in numbers, but we have the one thing they don't: intelligence. We can electrify fences, build moats, construct walls. To do this, of course, we need each other, because our society has become so interdependent that few people are generalists anymore. The thing zombies fear more than anything else is braaaiiinnnsss.

Which brings me to this collection. Covering feminism, archaeology, political science, biology, law, musicals, library science, education, biomechanics, history, landscape architecture and criminal intelligence, the essays assembled here show that zombies have infested every aspect of our lives. Unlike most academic collections, this book has been written with the interested non-expert in mind.

The theme of this collection is "academics on zombies." The remit is to do for your field what I did for mine: showcase its power for non-academics using zombies as a hook. Not everyone who wrote for this collection is an academic, for we also wanted to examine some broader takes on zombies. Contributors range from senior professors, postdocs and graduate students, to writers, comedians and zombie historians.

Academics bring a particular thoughtfulness to a topic, one that comes not with the soundbite of a politician or the utter conviction of the secretly insecure, but the willingness to question and consider ideas over and over until every aspect is understood. It's important to situate your argument in the field, so existing literature allows context to be built. A crucial part of academia, often overlooked, is the ability to communicate those ideas to the next generation of thinkers.

This book is part of our fight against zombies. The best weapons we have are our brains. It's time to unleash them.

ACKNOWLEDGEMENTS

Chapters 3, 4, 8, 9, 11, 12, 14, 15, 16, 17, 19 and 20 were peer reviewed. I'd like to thank Mike Aloisio, Brad Ault, Matt Bailey, Diem-My Bui, Brigid Cherry, Mike Delorme, Sarah Groenewegen, Julia Gruson-Wood, Nancy Halifax, Kim Hutchinson, Ummni Kahn, Kathleen Kern, Tracy Kivell, Marina Levina, Natasha Patterson, Jen Rinaldi, Tara Rodgers, Gina Rosich, Daniel Schmitt, Anthony Wilson and Holly Weimar for generously offering their time and expertise. I'd also like to thank Shoshana Magnet, Kristina Donato, Kristin Downey, Daniel Ma, Phil Munz, Ioan Hudea, Joe Imad, Richard Salter, Graeme Burk, Lars Pearson, Alison Kealey and George A. Romero for advice and assistance. I am grateful to Esmond Harmsworth, Eric Nelson, Jessica Clarke, Marie Clausen and Michael O'Hearn for valuable for valuable discussions and for steering this project in the right direction when needed. Most importantly, I am extremely grateful to all the authors of the chapters within for their excellent contributions and for their continued passion for zombies.

FITTING THE THEORY TO THE FACTS

JOHN SEAVEY

It's been repeated in so many summaries, analyses and discussions that it almost feels like a litany; anytime you read about the film *Night of the Living Dead* you'll read this: "No explanation is ever given for the zombie uprising." The more complete texts briefly bring up the repeated mentions of a mysterious "radiation" from outer space in the film, but only to scoff at them. After all, as Jonathan Maberry pointed out in *Zombie CSU: The Forensics of the Undead*, there's absolutely no form of radiation that can produce the effects we see on screen. Therefore, we can safely dismiss radiation as the cause and look to some sort of biological agent, such as a virus or parasite. Right?

Except that.... Well, I hate to spoil the fun, and I'll try to do it only once here at the beginning before returning to the extremely enjoyable game of examining a zombie outbreak as if it were a real possibility. Basically, there's no virus or parasite that can produce the effects we see in George A. Romero's films either. This is because they're made up. Radiation was the cause in the 1960s because it was the era of nuclear paranoia, and back then radiation was a mysterious, invisible, terrible force that seemed to be able to do just about anything, much like genetic engineering today, which is why modern zombies are always the result of lab-created superviruses. (Which is why Sam Raimi changed the spider that bit Peter Parker from a radioactive bug to a genetically engineered one. But that's a whole other topic.)

We like the biological hypothesis because it seems more plausible to modern eyes; now that we know what radiation can and can't do, it no longer seems like a believable way to accomplish the impossible. We need a more outlandish field of pseudoscience to produce our technobabble. (One can assume that in a hundred years zombies will need to be the product of nanotechnology or some sort of bizarre quantum mechanics effect. "He's Schrödinger's Corpse: Half-alive! Half-dead! Always hungry for the flesh of the living!")

But if there's one thing that the long, contentious history of science has taught us, it's that we can't choose to accept or dismiss a theory simply because we like or dislike its aesthetics. The fundamental criterion of the value of a scientific theory is how well it fits the facts as we know them. A theory that fails to conform to the data, no matter how elegant, must be wrong. As Sherlock Holmes put it, "It is a capital mistake to theorize in the absence of facts. One begins to fit the facts to the theory, rather than the theory to the facts."

So how well does a biological explanation fit the facts of the Romero films? (For the purposes of this chapter, I will consider the films *Night of the Living Dead, Dawn of the Dead, Day of the Dead, Land of the Dead* and *Diary of the Dead.* Romero has helmed a sixth film, *Survival of the Dead,* but at the time of writing it was in limited release and unavailable to me for viewing.)

The biological explanation certainly seems to fit on first examination. We have plenty of second- and third-hand evidence that a bite or scratch from a zombie produces an illness lasting several days and finally culminating in death and resurrection as a zombie. As one scientist puts it in *Dawn of the Dead,* "The people it kills get up and kill!" We have a first-hand example right off the bat as little Karen Cooper in *Night of the Living Dead* dies of a zombie bite and gets up to go after her parents.

In *Dawn of the Dead,* we see an even better-documented

case as Roger (played by Scott Reiniger) slowly succumbs to a fatal bite and rises from his deathbed as a zombie. A second, somewhat ambiguous, case happens in *Day of the Dead*: Miguel Salazar (played by Anthony Dileo Jr.) is bitten, but amputation seems to slow the infection and his gruesome death at the hands of a horde of zombies leaves us uncertain about whether or not he would have turned. (In the original draft of the screenplay, Romero unambiguously states that it's a parasite causing the outbreak, but the line never made it on screen, and the final version of the film is drastically different from his original conception in many respects.)

Even in Romero's later films, we see plenty of evidence that bites cause zombification. In *Land of the Dead*, John Leguizamo's Cholo is bitten and the wound is treated as a death sentence (though several gunshot wounds no doubt contribute to his death). Given that the characters in *Land of the Dead* have become very familiar with zombies, we can assume that Leguizamo's reaction is more than just a guess. And *Diary of the Dead*, though it returns to much earlier in the outbreak timeline, does contain one more clear case of death by zombie bite and subsequent resurrection.

But to take this evidence and decide, based on it, that it must be a biological agent causing the zombie outbreak is to fit the facts to the theory. If you start with the certainty that the zombie outbreak must be caused by a virus (or bacterium, or parasite, or other tiny living thing), then watch the series, you'll find evidence to confirm your viewpoint. But if you watch it without that preconception, you'll notice other things as well.

Significantly, you'll notice that the outbreak is global. (Indeed, "outbreak" isn't a very good term for it at all; it doesn't break out from any one place.) *Diary of the Dead* provides the clearest evidence, via the characters' use of the internet to monitor the situation and to make their voices heard, that the dead began to get up everywhere, all at the same time. Even before that, though, Romero clearly intended his zombie uprising to be worldwide. The television announcer in *Night of the Living Dead* speaks of it as a nationwide crisis, affecting cities from Miami to Pittsburgh all at once. Only the limits of Romero's characters' abilities to find out about events beyond their immediate surroundings (and the limits of his budgets) prevent us from seeing how Uganda, China and Australia deal with their own hordes of walking dead.

This is an important piece of evidence. One of the key elements of epidemiology is the establishment of a vector of transmission: How does the disease get from one victim to the next? It cannot be via the bite or scratch of an infected individual, not in Romero's zombie movies. Too many victims crop up in too many places too quickly. The characters who die of zombie bites in his films die over the course of several hours to several days, with visible symptoms of physical and mental deterioration that would be impossible not to spot. In *Night of the Living Dead,* the first sign that something is wrong is the hordes of walking dead wandering around looking for people to feast on. Dozens, hundreds, even thousands of zombies pop up (entirely off screen, given Romero's budget) in the course of a single night, but none of the characters has heard about thousands of people sickening and dying anywhere.

· And if the zombie outbreak isn't spread by a bite, then how is it spread? The living characters in Romero's films all seem to be perfectly healthy; they can sprint around, engage in gunfights and full-throated arguments about what room to barricade themselves in, and even design and build giant armoured personnel carriers. There's certainly no sign of someone spontaneously sickening and dying from a zombie germ of any sort, let alone one that's worldwide. In fact, it's a bit difficult to tell, since each film is only one piece of a larger mosaic that we can't see, but it looks as if the initial uprising didn't affect any living beings at all. An airborne virus that only affects corpses, moving through the body without the benefit of a working circulatory system, starts to sound less believable than space radiation.

But we still have all those troublesome bits of data described above. A zombie bite causes death followed by resurrection. That has to point to something transmitted by the bite as the key, doesn't it? Perhaps not. The on-screen evidence is ambiguous, but Romero certainly implies several times over the course of the series that, though a bite is fatal, any death without brain trauma will result in resurrection as a zombie.

Night of the Living Dead describes a scene in which a medical cadaver wakes up in the cold room, but we're not shown the scene and thus can't be sure of the cause of death. Later in the film, Helen Cooper is stabbed repeatedly with a trowel and gets back up as a zombie, but the film cuts away between her death and resurrection, allowing some question about whether her daughter also nibbled on her a bit. (*Land of the Dead* has a sequence unambiguously proving that any corpse will get up as a zombie, for a suicide victim reanimates while still dangling from the ceiling; unfortunately, the scene was cut and hence can't be used as evidence.) No single scene from the film shows a resurrection without a bite, but all of them taken together hint strongly at the possibility.

It's a bit frustrating not to have a definite answer, because it's an important distinction: if you reanimate after any type of death, whether by bite or not, then the bite can't be the cause of reanimation. In fact, there's a very plausible explanation for "death by zombie bite" that doesn't involve any mythical supervirus that reanimates corpses, one that we have already observed in nature.

The Komodo dragon, a large reptile found in the South Pacific, enjoys feasting on carrion as much as on live meat. In fact, this is one of its main hunting strategies; its mouth is septic, filled with bacteria from consuming rotten meat and laceration of the gingival tissue in its mouth. The bite of a Komodo dragon generally produces a festering, gangrenous wound that usually causes death from the infection, even if the victim survives the attack. (There have been reports of bite victims dying weeks later, even with professional medical treatment.) This is a survival strategy for the Komodo dragon, of course; once it bites an animal, it's guaranteed a meal sooner or later, even if it's not exactly what you'd call fresh.

So a bite from a creature whose mouth is septic can produce a slow death from a festering wound, sometimes taking hours or days, even with modern antibiotics and medical techniques. Sound familiar? As Harry Cooper says in *Night of the Living Dead*, "Who knows what those things are carrying?" Let's face it, it would take a lot more than Listerine to clear the germs out of the mouth of someone who's been dead for a couple of weeks.

5

So the "disease" theory falls apart. There's no clear vector of transmission, no timeline for infection or spread of the epidemic, probable asymptomatic cases, and an alternative explanation involving opportunistic diseases for the case studies we do have. Whatever is causing the dead to get up and walk, it doesn't involve a germ.

What, then, does it involve? Well, let's look at what we know. It's a simultaneous outbreak worldwide, causing all corpses to get up and walk and all living humans from that point on to resurrect as soon as they die. That points to something that can affect the entire planet simultaneously, something capable of passing through the planet to work on corpses on the other side. Something with an extraterrestrial point of origin, most likely, or something non-directional.

Amusingly enough, space radiation really does fit the facts best. For all that everyone insists Romero didn't really intend radiation to be the culprit, clearly it was what he was thinking about when he co-wrote the screenplay for the first film, and it's the scenario he was working from when he wrote the subsequent films. Other zombie films might be all about the super-virus, but the *Dead* films? Space radiation.

It's silly, of course. We can make it less silly by engaging in some high-grade technobabble; perhaps the radiation is actually an exotic particle stream that stimulates the growth of a benign, anaerobic tumour in the human brain. When the living person's brain cells die from lack of oxygen, the anaerobic tumour takes over key motor functions, allowing the person to continue with some form of "life." This smaller tumour-brain doesn't work as well, leading to the traditional zombie shamble, moan and hunger for living flesh. But, really, that's pretty silly too.

Ultimately, a zombie uprising is an absurd concept. It's an inversion of all the natural laws, the dead doing things (such as walking and eating) that dead people don't do. No scientist is ever going to make a flesh-eating zombie (I hope) and trying to find a "realistic" explanation for a horde of walking corpses is like trying to divide by zero.

So why bother? For the same reason we do lots of intellectual exercises: it strengthens our mental muscles. When we explore the consequences of fictional ideas, we become better at thinking through the implications of a hypothesis. If we can answer the "what if?" question Romero poses, then we might become better at answering some of the questions reality throws at us.

And the key to that, as any good scientist will tell you, is unbiased observation. If the *Dead* films have anything to teach us, then maybe it's that we should collect our facts first, then look for an explanation, rather than the other way around. Maybe it's that our preconceptions can blind us to alternative explanations and that we need to open our minds as well as our eyes.

Or maybe it's just that, no matter what created a zombie, a bullet between the eyes puts it down. Yeah. Probably that.

REFERENCES

Conan Doyle, Sir Arthur. 1887. *A Study in Scarlet.*

Maberry, Jonathan. 2008. *Zombie csu: The Forensics of the Undead.* Citadel Press.

Romero, George A., dir. 1968. *Night of the Living Dead.* Walter Reade Organization, USA, 96 minutes.

———. 1978. *Dawn of the Dead.* United Film Distribution Company, USA, 126 minutes.

———. 1985. *Day of the Dead.* United Film Distribution Company, USA, 102 minutes.

———. 2005. *Land of the Dead.* Universal Pictures, USA, 93 minutes.

———. 2007. *Diary of the Dead.* Weinstein Company, USA, 95 minutes.

———. 2009. *Survival of the Dead.* United Film Distribution Company, USA, 90 minutes.

WHAT FEMINISM HAS TO SAY ABOUT WORLD WAR Z

JEN RINALDI

I'm woefully impractical. With World War Z coming, I have done little to strategize about provisions, am ill prepared when it comes to barricades and couldn't handle a gun to save my life, quite literally. Ever the feminist, though, I am indignant over what will constitute this eventual zombie horde, and how both the spread of the virus and zombie-human engagement will play out in a patriarchal culture.[1] In the event of World War Z,

1 It is possible that patriarchy would cease to exist if we had such a drastic paradigm shift as a zombie outbreak. Indeed, as long as there are no human beings to reinforce patriarchy, since patriarchy is social, it would cease to exist. Also, in the wake of World War Z, the few human beings left will fall into some sort of anarchy, so it is possible they will no longer need imbalanced power structures and will come together—despite old patriarchal and hierarchical frameworks—in the face of a common enemy. However, I have a feeling that both patriarchy and cockroaches will survive the apocalypse, at least as long as human beings live. I will demonstrate in this chapter how patriarchy will produce the kind of zombie community we will have, at least in the first waves of the attack, and how zombie confrontations will still be rooted in patriarchal ideas.

9

no doubt I'll write furiously on the subject, maybe even plan a protest or two, and thus probably get eaten early. Perhaps, though, my tangents have some practical import; feminism deals with very concrete problems, after all. That is, perhaps my interests will aid in coming up with preventative measures, for planning ahead to lessen the spread of the virus might just involve redressing injustices that are already happening. My intention here is to apply a feminist analysis to the impending zombie outbreak. I will outline the main points in feminist theory; then, with that theoretical lens, I will assess the makeup of the eventual undead community.

FEMINISM IN BRIEF

Feminism is a philosophical and political movement that has gained ground in response to discrimination against minority groups, most prominently—but not limited to—women. The reason for this discrimination can be found in patriarchy: social and ideological[2] organization that prioritizes and empowers men—usually non-disabled, wealthy, white men[3]—to the exclusion, and at the expense of, others. I am referring to the power structures we have built into our communities, power structures that affect politics, economics, law and social interaction. Patriarchy informs how we interact with one another and who has control over whom.

Feminists of the 1960s and 1970s had concrete strategies for challenging patriarchy and pushing for social justice. Their

---

2 When I use the term "ideology," I refer to our doctrine of beliefs or the collection of values and assumptions we draw from to make sense of and participate in a community. When our ideology is patriarchal, we operate within a system of assumptions about who deserves to be in control: the men, the wealthy, the non-disabled.

3 Not all men necessarily have authority. bell hooks has even argued in *Feminist Theory: From Margin to Center* that men are disempowered under patriarchy because they have to cut out parts of themselves—that is, they cannot identify with things that have been designated feminine—to live successful lives. This means they must play the part, must be "manly" and even "normal," to do well in a patriarchal community.

agendas involved achieving equality for women in the household, education, the workplace, the political and legal spheres, and so forth. These feminists made significant strides without having to burn a single bra (though, yes, I suppose you could say some did threaten to do so[4]).

In recent years, while still taking on these political objectives, feminists have become more theoretical, attacking patriarchal ideology that still dominates and controls women despite more reproductive freedom in the medical sphere and voting rights in political arenas. The latest feminists hold that femininity is a social construct, entirely the product of social conditions. They mean there is nothing essential to what is traditionally understood as feminine, nothing biological (thereby debunking all theories seeking to make sense of women's supposedly poor driving skills and sense of direction).

When we assume that anything beyond anatomy is essential to being a woman, we are constraining women, locking them into expectations: women must have great empathetic and interpersonal skills, their maternal instincts must kick in when they are around children, they must wear bras and high heels to be sexy (if these are criteria for being a good woman, then unfortunately I fail miserably on all counts). Their very bodies are monitored and controlled, expected to look and operate a specific way during single life, pregnancy, motherhood. Under patriarchy, women are largely not in control of themselves, for the discrimination launched against them is so pervasive, so taken for granted as true, that women internalize and perform being womanly: they serve as caregivers because someone has to do it; they want babies because their biological clocks are ticking away; they wear makeup because they don't want to be ugly. We're thus stuck being women, our womanliness made

---

4 At a 1968 demonstration, feminists filled a trash can with bras and other items thought to render women sexual objects (think of the clothing, shoes and makeup women are expected to wear and the kind of attention these things draw). A fire was never lit, though, because they could not obtain a permit. Journalists reported bra burning as a joke, in reference to the draft card burning taking place at the time. So much for the urban legend.

manifest in very narrow roles: the virgin, the damsel in distress, the matron, the temptress, the bitch.

These later feminists preoccupied with ideological control do not deal only with women. Instead, they acknowledge that we cannot make sense of women's identities without noting how gender intersects with other characteristics that have been marginalized, such as disability, class and race. In seeking to combat the ways in which they have been oppressed, feminists have related their stories, and identified not only as women, but also as black, Hispanic, poor, gay, transgendered, blind, deaf and so on. They cannot make sense of their narratives without also talking about other parts of themselves that mix in with their gender when they encounter oppressive treatment. Correcting sexist inequality therefore entails correcting other kinds of inequality. All of these characteristics are also understood under patriarchy as inadequate, less than ideal, and they are compared with a concept of what is normal or ideal, often embodied by the non-disabled, rich, white man. In this spirit, I will characterize how different kinds of inequality will affect the spread of the zombie infection; I will also account for how the normal and the ideal, as well as the atypical, will have roles to play even during the zombie apocalypse.

THE MAKEUP OF THE ZOMBIE HORDE

I hold that patriarchy will have bearing on the spread of the infection and the constitution of the undead, so I will chart the course of the eventual epidemic and make sense of it in reference to the feminist theory I have related above. People will be rendered zombies from what is suspected will be a kind of disease: highly contagious and spread virally via blood transmission. The infection will likely be created in a medical laboratory sponsored by a government or corporation. Symptoms will include rotting flesh as though the body were a corpse, the loss of intelligence and identity, and an insatiable appetite for human flesh (some say brains specifically, but I have never understood why creatures that make little use of their own minds would consider such a body part a delicacy).

The first to be infected, or at least eaten, on the road to our eventual zombieland will be anyone whose body falls short of the athletic ideal (the first rule of survival, after all, is cardio conditioning). More specifically, anyone whose body is physically impaired will be susceptible to the outbreak: wheelchair users who cannot run away, fat people who cannot run fast, visually impaired persons who cannot see an attack coming, and so on. Paralympics aside, being athletic entails having a certain kind of body. Ideas about athleticism are thus bound up with what we consider to be the "norm." Normal embodiments are envisioned to be fully and optimally functioning, and variations from the norm are considered limitations, inadequacies, impairments. With ideas about what is normal built into our ideologies, we assume it is better to be able to walk, to see, to run without getting winded. It's a strange, almost fictitious, concept considering that so few people can be or stay normal: I require eyeglasses in order to see, my father in his old age uses a cane to get around, a colleague has chronic pain and so forth.

We build societies around what we consider normal rather than account for different bodies; as examples, there are not enough ramps and too many auditory fire alarms, respectively leaving wheelchair users stranded outside buildings and deaf people potentially unaware of danger when the alarms go off. Perhaps people with bodies vastly different from the norm will be the first targets in World War Z not because their bodies are disadvantaged but because they will have to escape attacks in settings built for "normal" bodies, essentially obstacle courses for atypical bodies.

Location is bound to play into how the virus spreads, so we should pay attention to where people with disabilities can be found. Aged populations who deal with a range of impairments and are found in highly concentrated areas (nursing homes, hospitals, Florida RV parks) will be easy targets. Institutions for people with intellectual disabilities and mental health problems have yet to be shut down completely, and these highly populated buildings, built to lock people in, will be likely grounds for the infection to spread quickly.[5] Inmates

---

5 People with mental health problems and intellectual disabilities have struggled to shut down institutions across North America. They often argue that disabled persons belong in the community and that

of institutions will come to constitute a marvellous zombie buffet: some bound to their beds, others too heavily medicated to react appropriately to a threat, all behind bolted doors with no means of escape. Along the same lines, since disability is largely treated as something medical, many people with disabilities can be found in hospitals receiving medical or rehabilitative treatment. This is unfortunate, since hospitals will be epicentres for zombie outbreaks, likely leaving many victims wishing they had pursued that alternative health option at the spa in some secluded woods. It is safe to assume, then, that a significant number of disabled persons will become living-impaired during the initial waves of the infection.

Since low-income neighbourhoods will also be ideal breeding grounds, there will be a class component to the undead population. Illnesses and injuries tend to be caused by poor living conditions, unclean and labour-intensive employment positions, and high-stress environments. People who cannot afford to move away from chemical plants, lack employment benefits that include comprehensive drug plans, lack the means to purchase dietary options and gym memberships that tend to produce the idealized embodiment, and so on, are far more prone to infections and outbreaks already.

Granted, the living dead take up a different vocation upon crossing over, and when one's flesh is rotting away it is difficult to determine whether, in a previous life, that body was subject to either pricey health regimens or working-class strains. Hence, class representation will not be as readily apparent as disability, for fat zombies or wheelchair-using zombies will be easier to spot than zombies originally from low-income housing. Nonetheless, I've been to zombie walks, and though I might have last gone as a prissy, well-to-do, undead prom queen I have seen my more blue-collared brethren carrying with them their old identities via props and shreds of clothing. Indeed, the infected will leave their previous walks of life abruptly, whether they were strippers, car mechanics, or diner waitresses; however ridiculous this motley crew looks, it will take to

being locked away in asylums is no different from the imprisonment of criminals.

the streets in uniform: residual markers of their old identities. In this way, class representation will be apparent in the zombie community.

Race will also be represented since members of racial minority groups often find themselves in lower-income brackets due to oppressive conditions. Canada, for example, already routinely fails to address the health concerns of indigenous people on reserves (illnesses such as the H1N1 virus spread faster due to poor living conditions; alcohol consumption and mental health problems are exacerbated by inadequate support services), when these health problems are largely the result of colonialism. In light of these conditions, reserves will no doubt serve as ground zeroes in Canada during the zombie apocalypse.

When World War Z reaches global proportions, countries with high population rates and low GDPs—often the results of years of being colonized and exploited by Western powers, and now struggling with debts and interest payments still imposed by these powers—will likely be easy breeding grounds for the virus. The global community has done little to address epidemics in the past, such as the spread of HIV/AIDS in Africa; it is doubtful that, should the zombie epidemic reach developing countries, countries that enjoy more privilege will implement any collaborative defence strategies. Even if the infection is the result of expensive, government-funded research or shady activities at some umbrella corporation, laboratories will likely be outsourced and located near populations that historically have been dismissed and discriminated against, an already common practice for dangerous scientific and industrial work (Bhopal is an awful and telling example[6]).

Arguably, aside from *Resident Evil*'s Alice,[7] women will strug-

6 In 1984, there was a large chemical explosion at the Union Carbide plant in Bhopal, India, poisoning half a million people to the point of death or disability.

7 In the case of *Resident Evil*, though, Alice eventually has that advantageous, genetically engineered body. Therefore, even she does not contradict patriarchy since medical control and manipulation of female bodies are common patriarchal practices.

gle because, like disabled persons, they too might lack the swiftness to escape or the strength to fight. I would argue that women do not typically lack these qualities because of biological limitations. Rather, I submit that our current culture promotes an ideal feminine body that is dainty, delicate and slight, and occupies very little space.[8] If many women are not prepared for the outbreak, then it will be because their bodies have been subjected to surveillance and control within the confines of patriarchy.

That said, women might stand better chances of survival than the other minority groups represented in the undead community as long as masculine, paternalistic ideology includes ideas about the protection and rescue of women. The most important lesson I took away from *Evil Dead* was: don't leave your women alone, for they are most vulnerable to zombie attacks and even tree-related assaults. According to this logic, the only skills a woman would need during World War Z are batting her eyelashes and playing the damsel in distress effectively. In other words, under patriarchy, the best chance a woman stands of surviving a zombie apocalypse—since patriarchy otherwise disables and disempowers women—would entail capitalizing on just how sexualized she is and latching onto some man who can take care of her. However, this defence strategy—depending on others—is dangerous during a holocaust when people can easily be infected after zombie engagement and, as the horror movies attest, rarely share with the group that they have been infected.

This is not to say that the living dead will lack any white, non-disabled, upper-class, male representation. What I have described is the possible first wave of the virus whereby certain population demographics are more likely to be attacked based upon their proximity to sites of outbreaks and/or their inability to escape or fight off attacks. Those who embody the norm in a patriarchal culture will still be prone to infection, but

8 Proper ladies take up less space when sitting cross-legged, for instance. Even their bodies must be compact in order to fill up as little space as possible; eating disorders are all the rage these days as they ensure women are neither fat nor muscular.

usually not as victims. Rather, this segment of the population will become infected more typically through the act of engaging zombies in combat.

Those who engage the undead will typically be in police and military professions, which are still largely gendered even in modern Western culture. Therefore, while class and race representations are disputable in this example,[9] these professions will still typically employ non-disabled men. The qualities thought to be conducive to taking on these careers—aggression, leadership—are considered part of the concept of masculinity, which, like femininity, is socially produced and sold as the ideal in a patriarchal culture. Men, too, are pushed into the roles associated with their gender: "real men" protect their women, bring home the bread, settle disputes with their fists and shoot every zombie in their paths, all without shedding a single tear. Although there will be high risks associated with the masculine jobs that will constitute humanity's defence against the zombie horde, the people launching attacks will have the skills and equipment required to survive World War Z, and will thus have better, arguably the best, chances. Also, these embodiments of the norm cease to be so normal or ideal once infected and turn into something entirely other.[10]

WHAT THE ZOMBIE SIGNIFIES

Once infected, these reanimated corpses will come to represent monstrosities, no matter what their bodies represented

9 The military actually targets and recruits people from lower-income households who lack the financial resources to access educational and employment opportunities with lower risks. I would even suggest that lower classes and racial minorities will be overwhelmingly represented in the military personnel who will combat zombies precisely because people from these demographics will have had few options available to them pre-World War Z thanks to social inequality.

10 I am using the term "other" deliberately because it is found in philosophical literature. The other, everything that is alien to us, in a postmodern sense, represents that which we fight against, that which we consider so different from ourselves that it has to be our enemy. Zombies are our other. Women, disabled people, lower classes and racial minorities are also already other to the patriarchal ideal.

while used by the living. There might be rare examples of heroes making bodily defacements look cool, with the help of chain saws and machine guns as prosthetics, but the main spectacle of this show will always be the undead. Limbs torn off, skin decaying, uneven gait, their bodies will come to be seen as broken, evil, monstrous. These bodies will be striking in their variance from the norm; the norm being white, fit, attractive, wealthy, intelligent, able bodied, male and, in this case, living.

As I have tried to demonstrate, we already have segments of our population whose identities are designated atypical and therefore less valuable relative to what is considered normal. These identities are made manifest on the body, for instance, by skin colour and disability. Class representation is worn on the body too: the worker's calloused hands and dirty fingernails, the hand-me-down and Bi-Way clothing someone with a low income can afford. Women's bodies historically have been understood as sites of contagion, pollution and messiness, which women try to hide by appearing delicate and wearing pretty things. In any of these cases, there might be no issue with eyeballs popping out of sockets and faces being half eaten off, but these minority groups nevertheless have bodies that have been read, judged and long regarded with disgust.

In a sense, zombies represent minority groups we already cast aside, seek to control, fight and eliminate. Those infected first and most intensely will be those who, as I have tried to make clear, are at risk as a result of inequality and discrimination. Those most at risk have already been segregated, marginalized, disempowered, controlled. Therefore, even as humanity unites against the living dead, even amid anarchy, patriarchal ideology will still persist since the supposed best of humanity, those capable of survival, will be the ones pitted against the monsters, the old monsters of our supposedly civilized culture.

There is practical value, even urgency, as the threat of apocalypse looms, in ensuring equality and ending oppression: we might at least limit and lessen the most likely sites of the impending outbreak. My call to action has nothing to do with stocking up on food and guns; I prefer instead to consider how we might shake up patriarchy, how we might address power imbalances that will carry over into the postapocalyptic world if they are not dealt with now. Our current social injustices will only serve to fill the ranks of this impending army of darkness. These ranks do not have to consist of those whom we have already been fighting pre-World War Z, not if feminists have their way and we work harder at thinking through and addressing how minority groups are politically and ideologically controlled and disempowered.

REFERENCES

Anderson, Paul W.S., dir. 2010. *Resident Evil: Afterlife.* Screen Gems, USA, 97 minutes.

hooks, bell. 1984. *Feminist Theory: From Margin to Center.* Cambridge, MA: South End Press.

Raimi, Sam, dir. 1981. *Evil Dead.* New Line Cinema, USA, 85 minutes.

THE ZOMBIE THREAT TO DEMOCRACY

ADAM SMITH

For those committed to the defence of liberty in its democratic forms, it is crucial to have a clear picture of democracy's enemies so that, when the conflict arises, we are prepared for victory. It is our job as political scientists to supply this picture, to explain it to the citizenry and, if need be, to take up arms ourselves against those villains most likely to effect the destruction of free societies.

There is now a broad consensus that democracy's greatest enemy is the zombie horde. Although strong arguments exist for assigning this role to the traditional evil mastermind, the distinctions between them are finally to the advantage of the undead. The empirical evidence alone is overwhelming; even a cursory survey of the literature reveals that diabolical plots are nearly always unravelled, whereas zombie attacks have an alarmingly high rate of success. For example, according to *Wikipedia*, James Bond villains have been defeated in one hundred percent of recorded cases. In contrast, in all of the more than sixty zombie attacks listed by Max Brooks (2009) in the definitive *Zombie Survival Guide,* humans always lose.[1] Or, as Omnicomic's Jonathan Pilley (2009) makes bluntly clear, "zombies always win."

Additional reflection on the categorical dissimilarities between mastermind and zombie might suggest reasons for this disparity. Consider that masterminds are defined by broad intelligence and prefer to hold their power in solitude. Consider also that the mastermind, normally blessed with genius, wealth and a well-equipped lair, not to mention suave manners and an exotic accent, will be attractive even to his detractors. Dr. No has his island, Lex Luther is a billionaire and Professor Moriarty in *The Final Problem* is a "man of good birth and excellent education, endowed by nature with a phenomenal mathematical faculty" (Conan Doyle 1893).

The undead possess no such qualities. They move in herds without individual personalities. Their physique is unattractive, to say the least, and their mental powers in no way compensate for these deficiencies. One has only to watch a few minutes of footage from *Night of the Living Dead* (Romero 1968) to see that zombies lack a certain sense of panache. One does not respect, envy, understand, or feel compassion for them (though victims are sometimes traumatized by encounters with recently zombified companions, who might briefly invite sympathy before their new appetites become manifest).

Suffice it to say that the mastermind, being evil, also has the virtue of being interesting. He or she is often a tragic figure with a complex personality and a Shakespearean back story. The undead, however, cannot actually be evil because they are, first and foremost, boring. It is now generally agreed that this is why their attacks are so successful, why they are doubtless the most urgent of many threats to the democratic order, and why we in the ivory tower must publish diligently against them or perish in the attempt.

---

1 To be sure, humans sometimes "win," but only after nearly all of them are killed or zombified. In these cases, "winning" means little more than "surviving."

THE NATURE OF ZOMBIES

In the popular imagination, zombies are completely "mind-less." To us, they seem more akin to animals or even viruses than to the human beings they used to be. Zombie mindlessness is of a particular kind, however, and when we describe the undead as "boring" we are really referring to their mindlessness. This is central to the nature of the zombie.

When we say in common parlance that zombies are mindless, we must mean that in a certain sense they are "irrational" since, of course, they are not literally without minds (their brains having been altered, but not removed).[2] Of course, this prompts the question of how rationality should be defined. Some suppose that to be rational is to choose logically those means that will accomplish a given end, but under this definition there are few more fully rational creatures than the undead. Their goal is to consume brains and, as I have already noted, their chosen means have proven highly effective. Others will suggest that the ends themselves must be included in the calculus so that goals can be called rational or irrational. This is a more satisfying position, but it leaves unanswered the question of how to determine which ends are which. Even among human cultures, there are incompatible answers and no clear way of negotiating (rationally) among them. How, then, do we presume to declare zombie goals irrational?

For our purposes, I suggest we bypass this complex debate and use the word *rational* to mean nothing more complicated than the ability to alter our perceptions or adjust our behaviours in accordance with the dictates of circumstances. In other words, rationality is simply the capacity to change your mind. Used in this way, the term "rational" describes some important contrasts between humans and zombies.

Among other factors, the zombie is distinguished from the human by the fact that it cares only and forever about one thing: eating brains. A zombie never changes its mind about this. It is perfectly single-minded and so by our definition it is irrational.

2　I will bracket for the time being the question of mind-brain equivalency.

There is an interesting confluence of terminology here. We call zombies mindless, but only in a figurative sense since they still have their brains. By mindless, then, we apparently mean irrational, and irrational means "unable to change one's mind." Therefore, it seems that, for zombies, mindless actually means "single-minded."

This single-mindedness is exactly what I described earlier as boring. Whether they are good or evil, living human beings are "interesting" (i.e., rational) to the extent that they care about many different things. Even the aforementioned mastermind, whose dream is to take over the world, also cares for things not wholly subordinated to that dream, such as Siamese cats or sharks with "frikin" laser beams. In fact, the most interesting mastermind is always able to change his or her mind, moving from Plan A to Plan B when confronted with the unwelcome interventions of the hero.

The nature of the zombie, then, is to be boring, but *boring* is now a significant word. To be boring is to be irrational, and to be irrational is to be single-minded. Conversely, to be interesting is to be rational, and to be rational is to be able to change one's mind in the sense of moving from one thought to another as necessary. Zombies are boring and irrational because they are stuck on eating brains. Humans are interesting and rational to the extent that they don't get stuck on any one thing. One might even say that, in contrast to zombie nature, this is human nature.

THE NATURE OF DEMOCRACY

The first thing to say about democracy is that it is a system of government designed for human beings, not zombies. That is, democracy is supposed to help human beings stay human. This implies that it is possible for human beings to become more or less human, and the existence of zombies—former humans—is clear proof that this is so.

Most of us are familiar with the basics of democracy: elections, majority rule, limited jurisdictions, the division of powers and the rule of law are all crucial to democratic life. These are mechanisms designed to let humans be rational. Democracy allows us to change our minds as the situation demands. On this account, democracy can be understood as a way to keep things interesting.

"Interesting," however, is not the same thing as "exciting," and this is an important distinction. The difference between interesting and exciting is more or less the difference between an argument and a fistfight. It is also the difference between an argument and, for example, the Spanish Inquisition (which nobody expects).

This rational mean between the neighbourhood brawl and the imperial boot is the democratic sweet spot, where people have a plurality of conflicting goals sufficient to provoke an interesting debate, but insufficient to provoke an exciting resolution by anarchic violence or official oppression.

Democratic rationality requires for its sustenance both a system of laws and a culture of habits, but in light of the zombie threat it is the culture that requires our focus. Specifically, democracy requires that habit of thought called "tolerance," a virtue as peculiar as it is indispensable. In recent times, tolerance has become associated with the more egregious forms of "political correctness," in which (for example) teachers "tolerate" a student's insistence that two and two make five so as not to hurt his or her feelings.

Yet, in its original formulation, the term was considerably more robust and more strictly addressed to less petty concerns. John Locke (1689) wrote his seminal *Letter Concerning Toleration* in the wake of the devastating Wars of Religion and was motivated by the fact that intolerance had led not to hurt feelings, but to mass murders. Arguments among denominations had degenerated into brawls, then into burnings, and then into destruction of the continent by rampaging armies of Protestants or Catholics. The arguments had been interesting. The resulting war had not. Tolerance was devised to keep arguments from becoming wars.

This, by the way, is very different from the politically correct version of the term. In our time, tolerance is taken to mean the absence of argument, which incidentally is a goal shared by those intolerant bores who incited the wars. Let us be clear that this is not what tolerance means. Tolerance is about how we respond to disagreement, not about how we avoid it.

For the sake of keeping things interesting, then, democracy requires vigorous disagreement about as many things as possible and an equally vigorous agreement to tolerate those with whom we disagree. Tolerance is therefore indispensable. But in what sense is tolerance also peculiar?

It is peculiar because, while democracy cannot survive in its absence, tolerance can also spell democracy's doom. This is the so-called paradox of tolerance and it becomes especially important in the face of the zombie threat. As the noted zombologist Karl Popper put it, "Unlimited tolerance must lead to the disappearance of tolerance. If we extend unlimited tolerance even to those who are intolerant, if we are not prepared to defend a tolerant society against the onslaught of the intolerant, then the tolerant will be destroyed, and tolerance with them" (1971, 265n4).

A zombie, to put it crassly, will always eat your brain before you can use your brain to form arguments against brain consumption. The only way for tolerant humans to defeat intolerant zombies is to be intolerant of them. If we tolerate them, then we die or become zombies ourselves. The paradox of tolerance is therefore at the heart of the zombie threat to democracy.

Earlier I claimed that the zombie horde is the most urgent of many threats to democracy. It bears emphasizing that "most urgent" is not hyperbole, but precision, because zombies by nature are those creatures best equipped to turn our greatest strength—our brains—into our greatest weakness. The history of efforts to turn back the horde is one of almost total failure, unless the survival of some lucky remnant upon the smoking ruins of civilization is to be called success. We must see the threat more clearly if we are to oppose future attacks more creatively and, one hopes, with less "exciting" results.

THE NATURE OF THE ZOMBIE THREAT

To repeat: a zombie will always eat your brain before you can use your brain to form arguments against brain consumption. One might reasonably insist that this is hardly a paradox, since only a brainless idiot would try "arguing" with a zombie. It is generally understood that, when zombies attack, brains should be used to secure the safehouse and to locate weapons, prefer-ably napalm and shotguns, though chainsaws are favoured by some for their ability to lighten the mood. Perhaps this is just one more case of academics overcomplicating the obvious?

Again, when the undead are at the windows, paradox-es might be of small use. Their purpose here is to prepare us for that fight, not to fight it for us, and in that respect the ob-vious could not be much more complicated. Confined to that purpose, the definition of the threat in terms of the paradox of tolerance should have as its intended result the formation of more competent zombieslayers, which is quite difficult, not the actual slaying of zombies, which is fairly simple.

The effect on democratic character of understanding the sense in which a zombie cannot be tolerated (which is to say a zombie cannot be argued with) is to deepen our commitment to tolerance (which is to say our ability to argue without shoot-ing people). Since tolerance is a paradox, we can be tolerant only to the extent that we can negotiate that paradox, and to negotiate that paradox is first of all to make good judgments about who is and who is not to be tolerated. Since we can be-gin with the self-evident premise that zombies are of the lat-ter class, their nature—particularly their nature as irrational beings—can teach us a lot about how to make these good judgments.

So we confront the paradox of tolerance, and commence our defence of democracy, by appealing to the previously outlined suggestion that "rational" means "interesting" and that "inter-esting" means "interested in more than one thing." The con-tention therefore is that the most important reason for us as democratic citizens to be intolerant of zombies is not the fact that they want to eat our brains (though that is also a good rea-son), but the fact that eating our brains is the only thing they want to do.

This suggests that, whatever else might distinguish them, those whom we do not tolerate will have in common a rather zombie-like single-mindedness. They will demonstrate at first an unwillingness, and later an inability, to see more than one star in the sky. They will despise conversation, unless it is cen-tred strictly on their "one thing." They will, in short, be boring.

(This condition, however, will not by itself justify intolerance on our part. We might use force only to oppose them when their "one thing" happens also to be our destruction. Plenty of people are obsessed with working out or writing philosophy, but these characters pose no danger such as the paradox of tolerance identifies.)

Negotiating the paradox and defending democracy therefore require that we be as quick to recognize zombie irrationality as we are to mock the excesses of the politically correct. Our defence is so far a rather scientific affair, involving careful observation and the straightforward application of knowledge. This alone is enough to improve our chances considerably in the struggle against the zombie threat. It will, for example, increase our ability to distinguish bloodied and hysterical fellow humans from the recently infected and soon-to-be zombified.

Yet, as I suggested above, zombies' irrationality is the most important reason for us to be intolerant as democratic citizens, not simply as human beings. I say this because the other side of the paradox of tolerance is that, while we might have correctly determined which creatures cannot warrant toleration, in the process of defeating them we might finally have become something far from democratic: a character close in nature to the enemy whom we destroyed. In other words, we ourselves become boring, not because we are obsessed with eating brains, but because we are obsessed with killing the braineaters. Just as critical as the science, therefore, is the art of fighting zombies. To negotiate the paradox of tolerance, and to defend democracy, are as much about how we meet the threat as they are about accurately identifying the enemy. In other words, it is crucial to be intolerant in a certain way.

And here again we might be instructed by the nature of zombie irrationality. It is clear from the literature that zombie attitudes are just as boring as zombie objectives. With few exceptions, the undead are invariably grim. Their power derives directly from their humourless clarity of purpose, which, depending on their class, provides either unlimited endurance (that is, the classical Romero type) or explosive power (as in the English strain created by the so-called Rage virus in *28 Days*

Later). These hitherto overwhelming advantages of the zombie persist not in spite of their irrationality, but because of it.

Democratic citizens have no legitimate recourse to this kind of empowering certainty because it is not at all democratic. This strategy is employed by people whose character is no longer democratic. One might then question whether they are not already infected and do not themselves require the timely intervention of a well-oiled chainsaw.

So it is with considerable frustration that I note the depressing consistency with which zombie tactics have been used by well-meaning humans, inevitably resulting in either the consumption or the zombification of their brains, which for a true lover of liberty amounts to the same thing. Frustration, I say, but not judgment, for who, in the face of the slavering undead, does not feel within himself or herself the focusing power of fear, or the obsessive lure of revenge, or the temptation to sacrifice even a close friend for the sake of sweet escape?

The art of the zombieslayer, the perfection of which is in the interest of all true defenders of democracy, is to form characters such that, even when trapped in a burning farmhouse with no more shells for our sawn-off shotguns, we will be able to remember that acting like zombies only makes us into zombies and that, instead of matching grim with grim, we must take the time to laugh.

To be sure, this is a particular sort of laughter, not to be confused with the "evil laugh" of masterminds such as Emperor Palpatine in *Star Wars* or with the gurgling snort of the undead. Rather, democratic laughter is of the "ironic" kind. Irony is about keeping room in our brains for more than one thing and finding the contradictions amusing instead of disconcerting. The ironic zombieslayer will consider the hopeless pickle that is the burning farmhouse and, upon finding herself entertained by the fact that death can follow so closely the plot of so many formulaic horror films, will proceed to make some heroically dry quip that inspires in her comrades some brilliant, nick-of-time strategy—which of course would not have happened had she been so obsessed with impending death that she forgot to tell her joke.

The question of how to be effectively intolerant of zombies—in other words, of how to actually defend democracy as opposed to just "killing zombies"—is answered, then, by our working assumption that rationality (and democracy) are distinguished by being interesting. One might conclude from this that the best way to fight the zombie threat to democracy is simply to have as much fun as possible while doing so.

Many have fallen not for want of weapons, but for lack of style. It is not the gauge of our sawn-off shotguns, but the manner in which we wield them. Do we draw back with a plucky grin, pleased with the weight of the double barrel, hands a-tremble with very human fear, to remark on the sheer absurdity of it all? Or do we give over our minds to one thing—desperation, anger, fear, or whatever—and trust in its power to deliver us, forgetting all else, zombies in spirit already?

Let it not be said that those charged with the defence of our liberties left home without their wry smiles. Let not grim determination be seen crowding nostalgia or hope for the future from the faces of those whom we send to fight. Let us fight zombies like human beings! Let us be intolerant as only the tolerant can be. Let us win the day by being ourselves.

REFERENCES

Brooks, Max. 2009. *The Zombie Survival Guide: Recorded Attacks.* New York: Three Rivers Press.

Conan Doyle, Sir Arthur. 1893. *The Final Problem.* Classic Literature Library. http://sherlock-holmes.classic-literature.co.uk/the-final-problem/.

"List of James Bond Villains." 2011. *Wikipedia.* http://en.wikipedia. org/wiki/List_of_James_Bond_villains#References.

Locke, John. 1689. *Letter Concerning Toleration.*

Pilley, Jonathan. 2009. "Why Zombies Always Win." *Omnicomic.* http://www.omnicomic.com/2009/02/why-zombies-always-win. html.

Popper, Karl. 1971. *The Open Society and Its Enemies.* Vol. 1. Princeton: Princeton University Press.

Romero, George A., dir. 1968. *Night of the Living Dead.* Walter Reade Organization, USA, 96 minutes.

CLASSIFICATION AND CAUSATION OF ZOMBIFICATION, AND GUIDELINES FOR RISK REDUCTION AND MANAGEMENT

TONY CONTENTO

This chapter provides a system of classification of zombie infection, with a discussion of modes of causation, along with updated recommendations for prevention and control of zombie
infections associated with both the reanimated dead and the infected living in North America. The chapter does not supercede
previous safety and prevention reports, the safety manual *The
Zombie Survival Guide* (Brooks 2003), and the training film *Zombieland* (Fleischer 2009), but it is intended to expand on previous suggestions for control, eradication and removal, along
with additional suggestions for detection, testing, vaccination
and treatment. These recommendations are based on the possibilities for multiple modes of infection coupled with appropriate principles of infection control and accumulating evidence
based on the fact that most infections will result from direct
physical contact with infected humans. Indirect infections from
other sources will be discussed briefly where appropriate. The
recommendations contain updated specific measures for limiting exposure to zombies, methods of eliminating zombie infes-
tations and new possibilities for outbreak control.

BACKGROUND

In 1968, in *Night of the Living Dead,* filmmaker George A. Romero introduced the American public to an epidemic of reanimation of recent human corpses in rural Pennsylvania. Prior to release of this film, public perception of the animated dead was limited to folktales, mythology and superstition. Romero's portrayal of these individuals and their potential for harm was filmed with a fair, realistic, documentary honesty. Since then, other filmmakers, authors and electronic entertainment designers have decided to direct their attention to education on and prevention of what was previously an unknown group of diseases. I have defined four types of *non-mortuus contagio* (Smith? 2009) or zombies (with two subtypes), based on the common traits of reanimation of the recently deceased and/ or behavioural modifications that lead to bite attacks and/or cannibalism. I offer recommendations for risk reduction and management of zombie outbreaks and suggest directions for researchers and health officials to expand our knowledge of each zombie type. These recommendations are based on current understandings of the prevalence and epidemiology of zombie outbreaks in North America.

CHEMICAL VERSUS BIOLOGICAL AGENTS

Anecdotal evidence of victims of zombification dates back to prehistory and antiquity (Brooks 2003, 2006, 2009; Davis 1988), but these accounts are sporadic and sparse. Mixed in with these accounts of the reanimated dead are accounts of victims of applications of pharmaceuticals, torture and respondent conditioning. These individuals are commonly referred to among practitioners of the Caribbean and West African tradition of Vodou as *zonbi* or zombies (Davis 1988; Halperin 1932; Schrader 1994). Victims of this ritual are exposed to a mix of animal and herbal extracts yielding the potent neurotoxin tetrodotoxin (Davis 1985; Kuriaki 1957; Suzuki 2005) and possibly the hallucinogenic compounds found in datura (Littlewood and Douyon 1997; Steenkamp et al. 2004). These chemicals cause complete muscle paralysis and vivid hallucinations, respectively. Combined with ritualistic burial, they typically lead to hypoxia and brain damage; psychological programming produces a near-catatonic state. This leaves the victims of this ritual as compliant servitors who are effectively lobotomized, called the *zombi cadaver* (Littlewood and Douyon 1997). However, these individuals do not display cannibalistic behaviour, nor have they experienced "brain death." Even though they are the basis for the etymology of the term "zombie," they are not the focus of this chapter.

The *non-mortuus contagio,* or the flesh-eating zombies, share the common traits of physical deterioration and/or behavioural modifications that lead to bite attacks and possibly cannibalism, all caused by a transmissible agent. These individuals might be the infected living or the reanimated cadavers of the recently deceased. There is much variation in their accessory symptoms due to the variety of causative agents involved in transmission. I have divided the various types of zombies into four categories, classified by causative agent (Table 5.1). I have described each agent, the mode of transmission and the effects on the affected for each type. I have also listed the descriptions for Vodou zombies for completeness.

The first zombie type that I describe is that depicted in *Night of the Living Dead,* which I call the Romero type (Figure 5.1). The Romero zombie is a reanimated corpse. The victim must have died within forty-eight hours. The causative agent for this type is an airborne chemical that might be radioactive. Romero offers clues in his film about the possibility of the agent coming to Earth via a crashed satellite contaminated with a radioactive compound, but the true source of this agent is unclear or classified. The compound is capable of reanimating a large number of corpses at low prevalence. The bodies affected by this agent are slow moving and driven to attack unaffected humans and consume their flesh. These corpses lack most higher-brain functions, but are capable of some cognitive ability (Romero 1978, 1985). Romero-type zombies can operate simple machines (doorknobs, stairs, etc.) and recognize familiar places and people. It has been suggested by other filmmakers and authors that these zombies are potentially trainable and might still serve some role in our society if managed properly (Currie 2006; Lowder 2001; Romero 2009; Wright 2004). For example, in the film *Fido,* zombies are trained through classical

Table 5.1. Defined Types of Zombies. Each type has been categorized by agent, route of transmission, physical and behavioural modifications of the victims, and examples in the literature. The Vodou zonbi is included for completeness.

Type	Vodou Zonbi	Romero Zombie
Agent	Chemical: combination of tetrodotoxin and possibly datura (Davis 1985; Kuriaki 1957).	Potent, airborne chemical agent. Potentially radioactive or extraterrestrial.
Route of Infection/ Introduction	Direct contact with eyes and mucous nasal membranes.	Presence of the chemical.
Agent Properties	Fast-acting neurotoxin, causing muscle paralysis (Kuriaki 1957). No known antidote.	Reanimation of recently deceased victims, a day or two after demise.
Victim Physical Characteristics	Complete muscle paralysis. Possible brain damage if buried alive due to hypoxia. Typically slow moving and clumsy after recovery.	Slow moving and clumsy.
Victim Behavioural Characteristics	If combined with datura, paralysis will be accompanied by vivid hallucinations. This combined with the hypoxia of the burial leaves most victims complacent and obedient.	Victims display an insatiable hunger to consume living, human flesh. Victims retain some cognition and can occasionally be trained to perform simple tasks.
Examples	*White Zombie* (Halperin 1932); *The Serpent and the Rainbow* (Davis 1985, 1988); *Witch Hunt* (Schrader 1994).	*Night of the Living Dead* (Romero 1968); *Shaun of the Dead* (Wright 2004); *Fido* (Currie 2006).

Fast Zombie	Solanum Zombie	Columbus Zombie
Recombinant neurotrophic virus.	Solanum agent, originally suggested to be viral (Brooks 2003); possibly fungal.	Prion.
Fluid contact with mucous membranes or bloodstream.	Blood-fluid contact with the host bloodstream.	Primary victims: oral ingestion of tainted meat; secondary victims: blood-fluid contact with the host bloodstream.
Virus capable of infecting the limbic system and present in most bodily fluids.	Cold-resistant virus capable of reanimating corpses and/or affecting victim's limbic system.	Slow-acting mode of infection and disease progression. Heat and cold resistant. Acid resistant. Protease resistant.
Ubiquitous hemorrhaging; increased speed, endurance and strength to human maximum due to adrenal gland overactivity.	Slow moving and clumsy, capable of anaerobic respiration.	Ubiquitous hemorrhaging; some necrosis of skin and other tissues. Normal human speed, endurance and strength.
Victims display very aggressive, violent behaviour, along with the desire to infect and/or harm uninfected individuals. Victims will attack uninfected humans, typically with bite attacks, possibly to increase rate of infection.	Victims display an insatiable hunger to consume living, human flesh as well as several instinctive modifications (moaning, swarming, reliance on bite attack) (Brooks 2003, 2006, 2009).	Victims display an insatiable hunger to consume living, human flesh, possibly to replenish lost tissue or energy reserves. Victims display very aggressive, violent behaviour, along with desire to harm uninfected individuals.
28 Days/Weeks Later (Boyle 2002; *Fresnadillo* 2007); *Resident Evil/ Biohazard* series (Hosoko 2001); *Book of All Flesh* (Lowder 2001).	*Zombie Survival Guide* and subsequent attack record compilations (Brooks 2003, 2006, 2009).	*Zombieland* (Fleischer 2009).

Figure 5.1. A Reanimated Human Corpse of the Romero Type. This image was taken by a trail camera equipped with night vision and a motion detector in Washington State outside Seattle. This victim is a newly deceased corpse activated by the Romero agent. Due to the condition of her skin, she has probably been deceased and reanimated for less than forty-eight hours. She displays the cannibalistic behaviour common to this zombie type.

conditions to act as gardeners, cleaning staff and adult companions. The action of the Romero agent is a reactivation of the nervous and musculoskeletal system. The consumption of human flesh is most likely to maintain cellular respiration for the production of biological energy, but it is not known if these victims have a functional digestive system. All other organ systems are thought to be non-functional.

Figure 5.2. A Living Infected Human Victim of the Rage Virus. This image was taken at a federal quarantine facility in Washington State outside Seattle. The victim was recently infected with the agent, the photograph having been taken less than thirty minutes after exposure. Note the hemorrhaging of the eyes and oral cavity and the obvious aggressive behaviour.

The second zombie type I have called the "fast" zombie. These zombies are not reanimated corpses and are in fact humans infected with a recombinant virus (Boyle 2002; Fresnadillo 2007; Hosoko and Mikami 1996). The virus itself is of human origin, optimized for fast infection and maximum transmission. One example of this type of virus is the Rage virus (Boyle 2002; Figure 5.2): a neurotrophic virus capable of near-immediate modifications to a victim's behaviour and hemorrhaging of the skin and mucous membranes. The fast action (Fresnadillo 2007) of this virus suggests that a number of compounds are present in the envelope or capsid surrounding the virus specifically designed to increase the rate of infection. The point of entry for this virus is the bloodstream, but it is possible that the mucous membranes of the sinuses, as well as the external nasal nerve, serve some important purpose both as a reservoir for a new virus and as an entry point to the central nervous system (CNS). Carriers of the Rage virus transmit it, but do not display any of the symptoms common to the infected. Carriers also display heterochromia, or differences in individual eye colour, that could be due to a neural crest defect, similar to the defects common to type 1 Waardenburg syndrome (Read and Newton

1997). Waardenburg syndrome typically causes changes in cranial architecture and can block or remove the point of entry for infection of the CNS, hence the absence of symptoms in carriers despite the presence of the virus. Victims of the Rage virus suffer from ubiquitous aggressive behaviour due to modifications of the limbic system and overstimulation of the adrenal gland. These modifications lead to extremely aggressive and violent behaviour. These behavioural changes also cause the victim to seek out uninfected humans and attack them until they are infected or dead. Humans infected with the progenitor virus and its derivatives, a similar recombinant fast zombie virus created by the Umbrella Corporation as part of its biological weapons division, display behavioural modifications similar to those of victims of the Rage virus (Hosoko and Mikami 1996). However, the progenitor virus is mutagenic, causing severe genetic and morphological changes in all organ systems of its victims.

The third type of zombie is caused by infection with the Solanum agent (Brooks 2003). Solanum was originally described as a naturally occurring virus in the works of famed journalist and zombiographer Max Brooks (2003, 2006, 2009). In his books, Brooks describes Solanum as a viral agent capable of modifying the human nervous system into a new organ system, self-sufficient and separate from the other organ systems. The rest of the organ systems cease to function, brain death occurs, and the new brain organ is reactivated after three to four hours. This new brain organ is capable of anaerobic respiration (production of energy in the absence of oxygen) and no longer requires introduction of new cellular materials via the digestive tract. The brain organ is modified to produce complex behavioural patterns in the victim, including pack/swarm patterning, simple but novel communication ("the moan") and a predilection for biting non-infected humans. This biting behaviour will most likely increase the rate of infection, as the digestive tract of the victim is no longer functional. These higher behaviours lead me to suggest that perhaps the viral component of the Solanum agent is not the true or sole cause of this disease. I hypothesize that a fungal agent is a more likely candidate, causing morphological and behavioural changes that lead to a maximum spread of the pathogen. Although some viruses can cause changes in behaviour—the aggression and hydrophobia associated with rabies being the most obvious example (Bingham and van der Merwe 2002)—the behavioural patterns combined with the reorganization of the nervous tissue into a new morphology suggest that a more complex agent is the cause of this disease.

Homologous examples can be easily found in the insect world. Fungal pathogens such as *Ophiocordyceps unilateralis* (Andersen et al. 2009) in ants and *Entomophthora muscae* in flies (Moller 1993), as well as the nematomorph *Spinochordodes tellinii* in grasshoppers (Biron et al. 2005; Biron et al. 2006), all cause widespread behavioural and morphological changes in the host organisms: searching for the highest point in the canopy just prior to death, displaying sexual behaviour to lure mates for new infection via copulation (before or after death), or swimming in a non-amphibious/non-aquatic species (leading to death by drowning), respectively. These behavioural changes reduce fitness by preventing reproductive success and turn these insects into "zombies," leading to maximum dispersal of the agent and infection of new hosts. Like these fungal pathogens, Solanum is specific to one species, causing death without reanimation in any other animal in which it is introduced. I suggest that antiviral therapies were unsuccessful in treating Solanum (Brooks 2006) because a eukaryotic pathogen was the cause. Due to this hypothesis, I divide recommendations for the Solanum agent into two possible sub-types in further discussion: both a viral agent and a possible fungal agent.

The final type of zombie is caused by what I call the Columbus agent (Figure 5.3), first introduced in the zombie survival training film *Zombieland* (Fleischer 2009). The Columbus agent, named after the narrator of the film, is a prion. Prions are infectious proteins capable of catalysis and aggregation with homologous host proteins (Hadlow et al. 1980). Host proteins are usually membrane bound and found in nervous tissues. Catalysis by the infectious form of the protein converts the membrane-bound protein into a free, more soluble form. Once removed from the cell membrane, free prions are able to either remove more host proteins through further catalysis or

Figure 5.3. A Living Infected Human Victim of the Columbus Type. This image was taken by urban photographer Megan McQuinn near Kansas City, Kansas. This victim has undergone complete, widespread infection of the nervous system by the Columbus prion, as can be observed from the modification of her eyes and the presence of hemorrhaging. It was reported that the victim was already displaying aggressive behavioural changes and had just finished feeding on a human rib bone.

aggregate into insoluble amyloid-like plaques. It is the formation of these plaques that causes neurological cell death and tissue necrosis, thus causing the spongiform brain damage disease. Diseases such as bovine spongiform encephalopathy (BSE, or mad-cow disease), kuru and Creutzfeldt–Jakob disease are all caused by prion agents. The difference between the host protein and the infectious protein is only structural. Due to the nature of the amyloid fold found in the infectious prion protein, it is extremely stable. This stability makes it resistant to denaturation by heat, proteases, radiation and most chemical treatments. This means that an infectious prion in the food supply will not be deactivated by cooking or digestion. The Columbus agent was first released in contaminated beef (Fleischer 2009). Due to the slow progression of most prion disorders, the Columbus agent was not detected until the symptoms finally manifested. These symptoms include hemorrhaging, necrosis of the skin, aggressive behaviour and cannibalism. Because of the sporadic nature of symptom presentation within the infected population, a large number of victims were able to attack and infect the uninfected around them. Due to the prevalence of food-borne illnesses throughout the past decade due to self- and deregulation of the US beef industry (Heyvaert 2009), as well as the standard practice of mixing meat from dozens of carcasses to produce ground beef (*Sofos* 2007), the Columbus agent was able to infect a majority of the population of North America through consumption or secondary infections. It is not known if the Columbus zombie is merely an infected human or a reanimated corpse; nor is it known if its cannibalistic behaviour is for consumption or merely a mode of infection. However, it is more likely that these victims are the infected living.

TREATMENT OPTIONS

Treatment options only truly exist for the infected living types of zombies. In the case of the Romero agent, the victims are already deceased. Still-living victims of bite wounds should be given broad-spectrum antibiotic treatment for the likely infection and sepsis, because the combination of the toxins and micro-organisms associated with decomposition in human corpses will most certainly kill the victim within a few days. The bite itself is not known to cause death, but it can carry the Romero agent into the victim if it is not already present. Treatment is also ineffective for Solanum victims who have been infected for more than twenty-four hours. Antiviral therapy for Solanum has proven ineffective, but, if Solanum is indeed associated with a yet-unidentified fungal agent, immediate antifungal therapy might prevent tissue reorganization and death (Sable, Strohmaier and Chodakewitz 2008). Further study is required before specific suggestions for a treatment regimen can be made. Due to the rapid onset of symptoms after infection with the Rage virus in fast-type zombies, therapy is possible but success unlikely. Aggression and hemorrhaging become evident within less than one minute after exposure (Fresnadillo 2007). The virus itself must release a cascade of compounds that causes these symptoms immediately upon contact with the cells of mucous membranes. These compounds must be hormone-like in nature in order to produce such a widespread reaction in such a short time. Hormones are freely diffusible in the bloodstream, so a hormone-like compound would most likely affect the tissues of the endocrine system to produce a secondary release of other native hormones, probably tapping into the fight-or-flight response associated with the adrenal gland. Immediate sedation and antiviral therapy might prevent the spread of the Rage virus to the CNS, but treatment must be administered quickly before the victims suffer fatal damage to their kidneys and endocrine systems. Prophylactic antiviral therapy and beta-blockers (to reduce the effects of the adrenaline surge) might be suggested for health-care workers and security personnel working in Rage virus hot zones to prevent the aggressive first response to infection. There is a strong possibility for treatment of infection with the Columbus agent, because this agent is a prion. Prion diseases are characterized by their slow progression, so the asymptomatic infected are good candidates for treatment with several available anti-prion and anti-beta-amyloid therapies (Ghaemmaghami et al. 2009; Sakaguchi 2009a, 2009b; Sakaguchi, Ishibashi and Matsuda 2009). However, treatment of the Columbus infection would require the design of accurate identification and detection of the infectious agent.

MOLECULAR DETECTION METHODS

Detection of the Romero agent would be the most difficult and least useful (Table 5.3). Although it would be possible to detect the radioactive Romero agent in water and soil samples (Dragovic and Onjia 2007; Forte et al. 2007), it is likely widespread and present in most areas near the supposed satellite crash site (Disandro 2008). Some of the isotope is probably transferred to bite victims, but the prevalence of the isotope in many regions suggests that almost all people have at least a low-level presence of the agent in their bodies. Still, testing might reveal regions with little to no contamination for possible resettlement. Regions of high concentration of the isotope should be banned for settlement, water use and agriculture.

There are several standard methods for detection of viruses in blood and other tissues (Bingham and van der Merwe 2002; Fooks et al. 2009). For fast zombie and Solanum viral agents, direct fluorescence assays (dFA), reverse-transcriptase polymerase chain reaction analysis (RT-PCR) and enzyme-linked immunosorbent assays (ELISA) can all be designed to allow for laboratory and field testing. The dFA and ELISA tests use antibodies created in laboratory animals to detect the presence of proteins or other molecules found in a virus. The RT-PCR test can be used to detect gene transcripts created by the virus. Antibodies to antigens present on the virus must be isolated for the dFA and ELISA tests, while viral RNA transcripts or native marker gene transcripts must be identified to produce qualitative RT-PCR testing. These procedures are well understood, so a working test could be produced in a short period of time.

If the Solanum agent does indeed have a fungal or eukaryotic component, this agent must first be identified through histological or pathological analysis from cell culture and tissue

Table 5.3. Detection Methods for Zombification Agents. This table reviews the suggested detection methods for blood/fluid samples from victims of zombification. The Vodou *zonbi* is included for completeness.

Type	Agent	Detection Method
Vodou	Toxin	GC/MS analysis for TTX (Suzuki 2002, 2005), HPLC-photodiode array/mass spectrometry test for Datura (Steenkamp 2004).
Romero	Chemical/Radiation	Analysis by ultra-low-level scintillation counter-equipped with an alpha–beta discrimination device for water samples (Forte 2007); analysis by gamma ray spectrometry and pattern recognition for soil samples (Dragovic 2007).
Fast	Virus	Direct fluorescence antibody test (dFA), ELISA test, RT-PCR (Bingham 2002; Fooks 2009).
Solanum	Virus	Direct fluorescence antibody test (dFA), ELISA test, RT-PCR (Bingham, 2002; Fooks, 2009).
Solanum	Fungus	PCR testing, ELISA analysis, Metabolite assay, histological/pathological analysis (Stevens 2002).
Columbus	Prion	Protein misfolding cyclic amplification (PMCA) technology and histological/pathological analysis (Castillo 2005; Saá 2006).

samples of the victims. Considering the virulence of the Solanum agent, it should be easily located and identified. Afterward, PCR analysis for genomic DNA sequences, ELISA analysis and metabolite assays (which detect compounds produced by metabolism unique to fungi or compounds released by the fungus or host organism during infection) (Stevens 2002) are all common methods used to determine the presence of fungi. The Columbus agent might be more difficult to identify because it is a prion. Prions are not easily analyzed by common proteomic techniques. However, pathological samples of amyloid plaques should yield enough protein sequence data to identify the native protein using MS/MS analysis and proteomic database searches (Bendheim et al. 1982; Wadsworth et al. 2008). Tandem mass spectroscopy is a technique that breaks compounds down into smaller, charged fragments. These fragments can be identified by their charge-to-mass ratio and will produce a specific pattern. Computer databases of known patterns can be used to identify protein sequence and identity. Once the native and infectious proteins have been identified, protein misfolding cyclic amplification (PMCA) technology can be used to detect the presence of infectious prions in a blood or tissue sample (Castilla, Saá and Soto 2005; Saá, Castilla and Soto 2006). This technology uses a sample from the brain tissue of an infected patient to detect the presence of an infectious prion. If the patient's sample can convert a sample of healthy recombinant prion proteins into infectious prions, then the test is positive. This test is quick and accurate. Once an infection has been identified, anti-prion treatment can begin to slow or halt the progression of the disease (Sakaguchi 2009a; Sakaguchi, Ishibashi and Matsuda 2009). The test can also be employed to survey the meat supply to prevent future outbreaks.

VACCINATION

Vaccination (Table 5.4) for both the Rage and Solanum viruses is possible, but there are many obstacles to production of these vaccines. Use of attenuated viruses, or non-infectious viruses, is not suggested. In the case of the Rage virus, responses to the non-nucleic acid components of the virus might be more than sufficient to cause the symptoms of aggression and hemorrhaging. An antigen must be chosen to produce a vaccine that stimulates a sufficient immune response to prevent widespread infection, but does not cause any other reaction in the victim. Even then, this vaccine might only prevent infection and not the initial symptoms. A vaccine for the Solanum virus would pose similar problems. Vaccination initiates humoral immunity through the activation of antibody-producing B cells. However, antibodies cannot cross the blood-brain barrier. The Solanum agent, however, appears to bypass the blood-brain barrier easily and cause rapid modifications to brain tissues within twenty-four hours. Humoral immunity would only clear a virus that is in the bloodstream outside the brain. The virulence of the Solanum agent might be too much for vaccination to offer protection. Vaccination against fungal agents might be possible for any fungal component of the Solanum agent. Antibody-based vaccines or prophylactic immune-boosting treatments might offer some protection from this agent (Cassone 2008), but again the virulence of this agent might be too much to prevent infection via vaccination. Much progress has been made in prion vaccine research (Sakaguchi 2009b), which gives hope for a vaccine against the Columbus agent. However, any potential application of this research is still many years away.

PREVENTION AND MANAGEMENT
Prevention of future outbreaks typically requires removal or isolation of all infected individuals. Although removal and disposal of the reanimated dead might seem to have fewer ethical concerns, many victims of the Romero and Solanum agents might still appear to most individuals as human beings. It should be stressed to individuals involved with zombie control planning that these victims have experienced brain death. Bait-and-incapacitation tactics might be the only effective way of removing these long-lasting zombies from the environment. Although the cold logic of the Redeker Plan and the methods employed at the Battle of Hope (Brooks 2006) seem to make sense, only careful preparation will deal with the emotional and psychological stress expected in those involved in removal missions. Some have suggested that Romero zombies maintain enough cognition to be trained for manual labour (Currie 2006; Lowder 2001; Romero 2009; Wright 2004). There is some logic to the employment of these victims in simple positions in industry or in high-risk occupations. However, they still represent a population of infected individuals. Regardless of the training and control systems employed, contact with the uninfected could eventually lead to a new outbreak.

Controlling the Rage virus is much less proactive. Victims of this virus typically starve to death after a few weeks, as they cease to eat shortly after infection (Fresnadillo 2007),

Table 5.4. Zombie Treatment, Prevention and Management. This table reviews the current and possible treatment and vaccine options for each defined zombie type, along with management and disposal recommendations. The Vodou *zonbi* is included for completeness.

Type	Treatment Options	Vaccine Possible
Vodou	Counselling, psychological and psychiatric therapy to repair emotional damage.	No.
Romero	None for deceased victims. Strong antibiotic therapy for victims of bite attacks.	No.
Fast	Antiviral therapy might be possible to prevent onset of the disease, but only if it is delivered immediately after infection.	Yes.
Solanum (Viral)	Antiviral therapy might be able to prevent death/reanimation.	Yes.
Solanum (Fungal)	Antifungal therapy might prevent death/reanimation.	Antibody-based vaccines or immune-boosting treatments might offer some protection against reanimation.
Columbus	Antibody therapy has proven effective in halting or slowing the progression of other prion disorders, as long as it is administered early.	Yes.

Quarantine/Removal Suggestions	Remains Disposal Suggestions
Due to the compliant nature of these victims, a sanatorium-type setting would be a viable option.	Typical burial practices.
The possibility of luring deceased victims to a holding facility might exist. It has been suggested that the least-aggressive victims can be trained to perform simple manual labour (Currie 2006; Romero 2009).	Because of the high likelihood of reanimation post-demise, immediately after confirmed brain death the spines of all deceased should be severed and separated, between the C7 and T1 vertebrae (see Figure 5.4). Cremation of the remains should be completed within twenty-four hours.
Due to the aggressive nature of the infected, quarantine or containment might be impossible. Isolation of the uninfected might be a better course of action, followed by testing of all survivors for presence of the virus.	Due to the highly infectious nature of the virus, all waste associated with the victims, including the victims themselves, should be incinerated following disposal methods similar for viral hemorrhagic fevers (Lloyd 1998).
Although there are ethical problems with the Redeker plan, isolation of the uninfected and removal of the reanimated as they become less active are the only other courses of action.	Similar cervical dislocation performed to prevent Romero reanimation. All solid waste associated with the victims, including the victims themselves, should be bagged and incinerated. Liquid waste should be treated with bleach or a phenolic disinfectant.
See above.	See above.
Management similar to that of the reanimated dead affected by the Romero compound.	Solid waste should be incinerated or autoclaved and then buried. Liquid waste and surfaces/tools should be treated using these recently published guidelines (Rutala 2010).

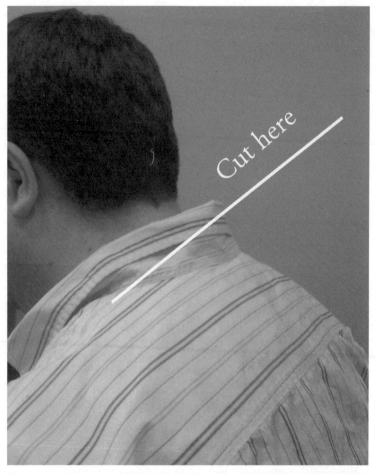

Figure 5.4. Suggested Cervical Dislocation Site. This is the recommended cleavage site for cervical dislocation of Romero- and Solanum-type zombies. The spine should be completely severed, taking care to use complete barrier protection to avoid contamination. A non-conductive shunt should be inserted into the cut site to ensure that no connection exists between the brain and the rest of the CNS.

so quarantine and isolation are the most effective policies. Although it might be possible eventually to treat those infected with the Columbus prion, efficacy of the treatment is questionable for victims with advanced symptoms. I suggest that a policy of sedation, treatment and possible euthanasia for victims at early stages of the disease might be effective, similar to a methodology employed with later-stage victims, as is suggested for the Romero and Solanum zombies.

In regions with the presence of the radioactive Romero agent, special preparation of human remains should be ensured. A cervical dislocation and separation technique should be performed on all human remains immediately after confirmation of brain death. A cleavage of between C7 and T1 vertebrae should be performed, and a non-conductive shunt should be inserted to ensure separation (Figure 5.4). Also, cremation of the remains should be undertaken within twenty-four hours of demise. Similar treatment of remains is suggested for the Solanum agent, with additional incineration of all solid waste associated with the victims, collection of liquid waste and treatment with bleach or a phenolic disinfectant. Due to the highly virulent and potentially toxic nature of the Rage virus, I suggest that the same guidelines used for viral hemorrhagic fevers (Lloyd and Perry 1998) be employed when handling remains and waste associated with fast zombies. Updated guidelines for dealing with the remains of patients with other prion diseases should be effective for the management of remains of Columbus zombies (Rutala and Weber 2010).

APPLICATION AND UPDATES
The recommendations in this chapter represent global measures to minimize the likelihood of human exposure to infected zombie victims in North America. Although different geographical areas might have variations in the composition of their zombie populations, the measures should be effective in all areas. These recommendations might be modified in the future as new data or advances in technology become available. These recommendations and additional information concerning the various types of zombification agents can be obtained by contacting the author via email at tonycontento@gmail.com.

ACKNOWLEDGEMENTS
This update is based on recommendations from Robert Smith?, who provided assistance with preparation of the manuscript; Patrick J. Moore, who provided technical assistance, carefully reviewed the

manuscript for content and offered field photography of several types of contemporary zombies; Megan McQuinn, another zombie field photographer who provided an early outbreak photograph of a Columbus-type zombie; and W.P. Montague, who suggested that a fungal agent might be present in Solanum infections.

REFERENCES

Andersen, S., S. Gerritsma, K. Yusah, D. Mayntz, N. Hywel-Jones, J. Billen, J. Boomsma and D. Hughes. 2009. "The Life of a Dead Ant: The Expression of an Adaptive Extended Phenotype." *American Naturalist* 174: 424–33.

Bendheim, P., R. Barry, S. DeArmond, D. Stites and S. Prusiner. 1982. "Antibodies to a Scrapie Prion Protein." *Nature* 310: 418–21.

Bingham, J. and M. van der Merwe. 2002. "Distribution of Rabies Antigen in Infected Brain Material: Determining the Reliability of Different Regions of the Brain for the Rabies Fluorescent Antibody Test." *Journal of Virological Methods* 101: 85–94.

Biron, D.G., F. Ponton, L. Marche, N. Galeotti, L. Renault, E. Demey-Thomas, J. Poncet, S.P. Brown, P. Jouin and F. Thomas. 2006. "'Suicide' of Crickets Harbouring Hairworms: A Proteomics Investigation." *Insect Molecular Biology* 15: 731–42.

Biron, D.G., F. Ponton, C. Joly, A. Menigoz, B. Hanelt and F. Thomas. 2005. "Water-Seeking Behavior in Insects Harboring Hairworms: Should the Host Collaborate?" *Behavioral Ecology* 16: 656–60.

Boyle, D., dir. 2002. *28 Days Later.* Fox Searchlight Pictures, USA, 113 minutes.

Brooks, M. 2003. *The Zombie Survival Guide: Complete Protection from the Living Dead.* New York: Three Rivers Press.

———. 2006. *World War Z: An Oral History of the Zombie War.* New York: Three Rivers Press.

———. 2009. *The Zombie Survival Guide: Recorded Attacks.* New York: Three Rivers Press.

Cassone, A. 2008. "Fungal Vaccines: Real Progress from Real Challenges." *Lancet Infectious Diseases* 8: 114–24.

Castilla J., P. Saá and C. Soto. 2005. "Detection of Prions in Blood." *Nature Medicine* 11: 982–85.

Currie, A., dir. 2006. *Fido.* Lionsgate, Canada, 93 minutes.

Davis, W. 1985. *The Serpent and the Rainbow: A Harvard Scientist's Astonishing Journey into the Secret Societies of Haitian Voodoo, Zombis, and Magic.* New York: Simon and Schuster.

————. 1988. *Passage of Darkness: The Ethnobiology of the Haitian Zombie.* New York: Simon and Schuster.

Disandro, J. 2008. "Zombie Mythology: George A. Romero's Effect on Modern Cinema." *Horror Films.* Suite101.com, http://horrorfilms.suite101.com/article.cfm/zombie_mythology.

Dragovic, S. and A. Onjia. 2007. "Classification of Soil Samples According to Geographic Origin Using Gamma-Ray Spectrometry and Pattern Recognition Methods." *Applied Radiation and Isotopes* 65: 218–24.

Fleischer, R., dir. 2009. *Zombieland.* Columbia Pictures, USA, 88 minutes.

Fooks, A., N. Johnson, C. Freuling, P. Wakeley, A. Banyard, L. McElhinney, D. Marston, A. Dastjerdi, E. Wright, R. Weiss and T. Müller. 2009. "Emerging Technologies for the Detection of Rabies Virus: Challenges and Hopes in the 21st Century." *PLoS Neglected Tropical Diseases* 3: e530.

Forte, M., R. Rusconi, M.T. Cazzaniga and G. Sgorbati. 2007. "The Measurement of Radioactivity in Italian Drinking Waters." *Microchemical Journal* 85: 98–102.

Fresnadillo, J.C., dir. 2007. *28 Weeks Later.* Fox Atomic, USA, 99 minutes.

Ghaemmaghami, S., B. May, A. Renslo and S. Prusiner. 2009. "Discovery of 2-Aminothiazoles as Potent Antiprion Compounds." *Journal of Virology* 84: 3408–12.

Hadlow, W., S. Prusiner, R. Kennedy and R. Race. 1980. "Brain Tissue from Persons Dying of Creutzfeldt-Jakob Disease Causes Scrapie-Like Encephalopathy in Goats." *Annals of Neurology* 8: 628–32.

Halperin, V., dir. 1932. *White Zombie.* United Artists, USA, 69 minutes.

Heyvaert, V. 2009. "Globalizing Regulation: Reaching beyond the Borders of Chemical Safety." *Journal of Law and Society* 36: 110–28.

Hosoko, M. and S. Mikami, dirs. 1996. *Biohazard/Resident Evil.* Capcom Entertainment, Japan.

Kuriaki, K. and I. Wada. 1957. "Effect of Tetrodotoxin on the Mammalian Neuro-Muscular System." *Japanese Journal of Pharmacology* 7: 35—37.

Littlewood, R. and C. Douyon. 1997. "Clinical Findings in Three Cases of Zombification." *Lancet* 350: 1094–96.

Lloyd, E. and H. Perry. 1998. *Infection Control for Viral Haemorrhagic Fevers in the African Health Care Setting.* Edited by CDC/WHO [online manual]. Atlanta: Centers for Disease Control and Prevention.

Lowder, J. 2001. *The Book of All Flesh.* Albany: Eden Studios.

Moller, A.P. 1993. "A Fungus Infecting Domestic Flies Manipulates Sexual Behaviour of Its Host." *Behavioral Ecology and Sociobiology* 33: 403–07.

"Problems with Realism in Zombie Fiction." 2011. In *Zombiepedia: The Zombie Survival Wiki.* http://zombie.wikia.com/wiki/ Problems_with_Realism_in_Zombie_Fiction.

Read, A. and V. Newton. 1997. "Waardenburg Syndrome." *Journal of Medical Genetics* 34: 656–65.

Romero, G.A., dir. 1968. *Night of the Living Dead.* Walter Reade Organization, USA, 96 minutes.

———. 1978. *Dawn of the Dead.* United Film Distribution Company, USA, 126 minutes.

———. 1985. *Day of the Dead.* United Film Distribution Company, USA, 102 minutes.

———. 2009. *Survival of the Dead.* United Film Distribution Company, USA, 90 minutes.

Rutala, W. and D. Weber. 2010. "Guideline for Disinfection and Sterilization of Prion-Contaminated Medical Instruments." *Infection Control and Hospital Epidemiology* 31: 107–17.

Saá, P., J. Castilla and C. Soto. 2006. "Ultra-Efficient Replication of Infectious Prions by Automated Protein Misfolding Cyclic Amplification." *Journal of Biological Chemistry* 281: 35245–52.

Sable, C., K. Strohmaier and J. Chodakewitz. 2008. "Advances in Antifungal Therapy." *Annual Review of Medicine* 59: 361–79.

Sakaguchi, S. 2009a. "Systematic Review of the Therapeutics for Prion Diseases." *Brain Nerve* 61: 929–38.

———. 2009b. "Prospects for Preventative Vaccines against Prion Diseases." *Protein and Peptide Letters* 16: 260–70.

Sakaguchi, S., D. Ishibashi and H. Matsuda. 2009. "Antibody-Based Immunotherapeutic Attempts in Experimental Animal Models of Prion Diseases." *Expert Opinion on Therapeutic Patients* 19: 907–17.

Schrader, P., dir. 1994. *Witch Hunt.* Home Box Office, USA, 100 minutes.

Smith?, R.J. 2009. "A Report on the Zombie Outbreak of 2009: How Mathematics Can Save Us (No Really)." *Canadian Medical Association Journal* 181: E297–E300.

Sofos, J. 2007. "Challenges to Meat Safety in the 21st Century." *Meat Science* 78: 3–13.

Steenkamp, P., N. Harding, F. van Heerden and B. van Wyk. 2004. "Fatal

Datura Poisoning: Identification of Atropine and Scopolamine by High Performance Liquid Chromatography/Photodiode Array/Mass Spectrometry." *Forensic Science International* 145: 31–39.

Stevens, D. 2002. "Diagnosis of Fungal Infections: Current Status." *Journal of Antimicrobial Chemotherapy* 49 Supplement 1: 11–19.

Suzuki, O. and K. Watanabe. 2005. *Drugs and Poisons: A Handbook of Practical Analysis.* 2nd ed. Berlin: Springer.

Wadsworth, J., C. Powell, J. Beck, S. Joiner, J. Linehan, S. Brandner, S. Mead and J. Collinge. 2008. "Molecular Diagnosis of Human Prion Disease." *Methods in Molecular Biology* 459: 197–227.

Wright, E., dir. 2004. *Shaun of the Dead.* Focus Features, UK, 99 minutes.

ZOMBIE INSTRUCTORS: A CAREER MADE FLESH

KATE SMALL AND ROBERT SMITH?

Have you ever wanted to teach a class where your students couldn't talk back? Ever wanted a room full of trainees who didn't spend their entire time text messaging, surfing the internet or loudly gossiping about you? Haven't you spent your whole career just waiting for students who cared only about brains? Then we have the career for you!

Zombies are the previously deceased who have returned to life in the form of the undead. Which can be handy when your great-uncle forgot to tell you where he stashed his fortune before casting off his mortal coil. Clinical symptoms include a discolouration around the eyes, open wounds and rotting flesh, with organs and bodily functions operating at minimal levels. So not a whole lot of difference for your great-uncle, who really wasn't at his best at the end there, was he?

It was originally thought that the best option was to arm yourself to the teeth, hit the zombies hard and then hit them harder the next time. For some reason, Americans were quite happy with this solution and adopted it enthusiastically. They did so before they actually had any zombies, but that's by the by.

Fortunately, zombies were eventually integrated into society. So now the only thing we have to fear is all those over-enthusiastic Americans. And they've been able to learn basic skills (the zombies, that is, not the Americans). But who can teach them? Zombie instructors, that's who!

Creating training programs to develop zombie instructors is complex, with almost conflicting knowledge, skills and behaviours. A zombie instructor isn't a friend or a parent or a manager. Instead, a zombie instructor has to ignore the special perfume of decaying flesh and be badass enough to play executioner if the zombie student is failing the course. Are you tough enough to handle it? (Applicants with experience with fifth graders may jump straight to the submission stage.)

HOW DO I KNOW IF I'M A ZOMBIE?
Zombies are humans who have died, therefore ceasing their human identity and human rights associated with life. A zombie gains a new identity with its own code of rights.

HOW CAN ZOMBIES MAKE A CONTRIBUTION?
Zombies in the workforce can only perform roles that

- provide limited face-to-face human contact;
- do not include any food or primary production or any manufacturing where there is the potential risk of human infection; and
- are not in health care or health-related fields.

Accepted zombie industries include

- infrastructure (roads, sewers, etc.);
- mining;
- waste disposal; and
- manufacturing.

Zombie law enforcement allows for the destruction of any zombies who

- pose a threat to human contamination;
- pose a threat to human life;

- no longer meet the physical requirements needed to perform work tasks; or
- no longer meet the cognitive requirements needed to perform work tasks.

UNCLE Z WANTS YOU!

Zombie law enforcement must be performed by certified zombie instructors. They must be registered and certified and must comply with zombie laws.

Zombie cognitive ability allows zombies to understand basic instructions. There are no emotions, no cognizance of consequences and limited reasoning skills, depending on the length of time since infection.

In terms of zombie physical ability, due to the body being dead, there is no regeneration or healing of injuries. Loss of functionality occurs over time. Zombies must be at a certain level of physical ability to be able to work. This must be assessed on a monthly basis.

Zombies must wear full-body "wetsuits" that allow their rotting flesh to be covered from head to toe. This resolves issues regarding "walking dead body smell," body parts falling off and animals dining on the zombie's body. It would not do to have a zombie doing a garbage run being snacked on by dogs and feral cats looking for a nice meal.

Zombie rights allow only adult zombies to work. Zombie youth must register in zombie schools.

Considering these key assumptions, zombie instructors would have multiple roles:

- law enforcement and potential execution;
- trainer of the work/role; and
- assessor of the cognitive and physical abilities of the zombie as well as the competency in the work role.

KEY SKILLS, KNOWLEDGE AND BEHAVIOURS REQUIRED OF A ZOMBIE INSTRUCTOR

Looking for a calm, fulfilling career path in education? Don't even consider being a zombie instructor.

A career in zombie instruction could be one of the most dangerous careers an individual can have. There is a specific set of skills, knowledge and behaviours a zombie instructor must exhibit to be able to safely and effectively train and assess zombies for the workplace.

A zombie instructor must possess the following skills:

- familiarity with zombie-terminating weaponry, including but not limited to flame-throwers, shotguns, cricket bats and Dire Straits records;
- the ability to identify dangerous situations and react according to zombie enforcement and zombie/human rights laws;
- the ability to identify and evaluate zombie cognitive and physical capabilities according to zombie rights and role-specific requirements; and
- the ability to train zombies in the relevant work role assigned according to current zombie educational practices.

Knowledge a zombie instructor must possess includes:

- understanding of zombie physiology, characteristics, key behaviours and capabilities;
- zombie rights laws;
- zombie enforcement laws;
- Occupational Health and Safety for working with zombies;
- zombie educational practices;
- zombie public contamination procedures; and
- zombie instructor certification and registration requirements.

AVAILABLE ZOMBIE COURSES

Zombie Basics	Introduction to zombies. Dispels myths, urban legends, pop-culture beliefs; focuses on providing the facts regarding zombie history, physiology and characteristics.
Zombies and the Law	Covers zombie rights and zombie enforcement laws.

Zombie Educational Theory	Theory and practice regarding the education of zombies.
Zombie OH&S	Occupational Health and Safety for working with zombies. Includes methods for reducing the risk of public contamination as well as processes for dealing with public contamination incidents.
Weapons Handling	Use of weapons for the safe termination of zombies according to zombie rights and zombie enforcement laws.
Zombie Certifications	Contains assessments for weapons handling; zombie rights; zombie educational theory and practice; and zombie OH&S.

So why not sign up today? You'll be entering a dynamic field, full of interesting people (and non-people), with many opportunities for career advancement. Your students might moan a lot, but that's no different from any other educational field. And if one misbehaves in class, nobody will think worse of you if you behead him or her in a burst of righteous fury, which will make you the envy of regular teachers everywhere! So come out and do your bit for the undead: they need all the brains they can get....

ACKNOWLEDGEMENTS
Robert Smith? is supported by an NSERC Discovery Grant, an Early Researcher Award and funding from MITACS. So, naturally, truckloads of taxpayer money were spent on research that involved setting traps and capturing zombies. Then we ran detailed experiments on them, often killing many of our students as a control to see if they would reanimate. Finally, we took enormously expensive trips to foreign lands so we could observe zombies in the wild, on the taxpayer's dime, from the comfort of luxurious armoured cars. Thanks for asking.

AIM FOR THE HEAD! THE ZOMBIE AS AN INTELLECTUAL MONSTER

ARNOLD T. BLUMBERG

It's one of those scenes that all zombie movie fans know well; in fact, they're usually way ahead of the characters on the screen when the big moment finally arrives. The zombies are shambling—or sprinting, let's be inclusive—toward our heroes, bullets are flying, blood is spraying, but nothing can stop "those things!" Then someone gets off that one lucky shot, nails one of the living dead right in the noggin, and down the ghoul goes like a sack of potatoes.

"Aim for the head!"

A weakness has been found and a strategy is born. But while the apocalyptic adventurers on screen reload and discover sharp-shooting skills they never knew they had, audiences pumped on pure adrenaline in the darkness of all those movie theatres aren't likely to think about the deeper meaning of that simple, battle-driven declaration. The zombie fighters might be firing at all those reanimated brains, but the zombie moviemakers have set their sights on a more intellectual target: our minds.

All forms of fantasy storytelling from grotesque horror to

star-faring science fiction have an allegorical aspect. The tales are told to entertain and provide an escape; however, whether crafted consciously to make a statement or merely meaningful as a by-product of the cultural mores of the society they're a product of, there is always a cathartic, multilayered element to the experience. Audiences witness real-world terrors reflected back at them through the cracked mirror of dark fantasy, and in doing so they might understand more about themselves and their culture or at least find some measure of release from their own worries when they emerge from the darkness of the local theatre and back out into the light of day.

The horror pantheon employs all manner of creatures that go bump in the night, from muck-encrusted swamp monsters and sea demons to sand-blasted mummies, hairy werewolves and shape changers, tentacled horrors from other dimensions, vampires both fetching and foul, and, of course, zombies. Although many horror icons serve as symbolic embodiments of our true-life terrors, arguably none of them is as direct and effective as the zombie in any of its many guises.

Put simply, zombies are us. They're your friends, your neighbours, your family members. When the monster comes from within—when your closest loved ones can forget everything they know and turn into mindless automatons ready to feed on your flesh, when even you yourself can lose your very identity and perhaps your soul, becoming an empty shell driven by the most primal of urges—that is true horror. More importantly, when the dead are brought back to life, or the living become enslaved and enraged by a mysterious mix of herbs and potions, a toxic spill, radiation or viral infection, you have the perfect recipe for allegorical commentary on the human condition.

The earliest zombie movies were fuelled by the Western world's xenophobic reaction to other cultures that shook Westerners to their Judeo-Christian core. Following the publication of William Seabrook's Haitian chronicle, *The Magic Island* (1929), folks were fascinated by the seemingly primitive adherents of "voodoo." The demonizing depiction of Voudoun seen in pop culture at the time was a horribly distorted look at a different spiritual tradition, but in those politically incorrect productions we can learn a great deal about the people who made them and the fear of anything foreign that consumed audiences of the era.

White Zombie (1932), still regarded as the first fully fledged zombie movie, followed one year after Universal's legendary *Dracula* (1931) and borrowed not only the same basic plot, but also its lead actor, Bela Lugosi. Set in the West Indies, *White Zombie* cast Lugosi in the role of the perverted voodoo priest Murder Legendre (subtle), eager to prey on the innocence of Madge Bellamy's Madeleine. Both films explored the sexual subtext of a sinful foreigner violating the purity of Western womanhood, but *White Zombie* is perhaps more potent, utilizing the then-still-fresh imagery of dark Haitian magic rather than the mouldy folklore of Eastern European vampires.

Val Lewton would revisit some of the same themes in *I Walked with a Zombie* (1943), while comedies such as *Zombies on Broadway* (1945, and more or less a humorous sequel to *I Walked with a Zombie*) played the same material for laughs, but in that first major era of zombie films the recurring use of voodoo and dark-skinned natives as icons of evil made the sentiments of the times clear. Decades later, the racial aspect of zombie horror would be given a new twist in *Black Demons* (1991), in which wronged slaves rise from their graves for revenge.

In the 1950s, horror and science fiction in general skewed toward more scientific scares. The advent of the atomic era coupled with the supposedly looming threat of insidious communist assimilation led to a horde of radiation-altered creatures from the ants of *Them* (1954) to the Cold-War-inspired alien pods of *Invasion of the Body Snatchers* (1956). During this time, zombies marched right in step and often emerged from atomic science gone awry or alien (read Communist) powers. *Invisible Invaders* (1959) and the infamous *Plan 9 from Outer Space* (1959) featured the dead reanimated by aliens in a bid to take over the Earth, while ten years later there were *The Astro-Zombies* (1968). The 1980s saw a resurgence in the Cold War and the accompanying fear of nuclear annihilation, which led to the radiation-spawned mutants of *Nightmare City* (1980) and *Night of the Comet* (1984).

Of course, one of the landmarks in the "zombie as metaphor"

movement came with the film that also forever redefined what the public thought of as a zombie in the first place. Only distant cousins of the enthralled, living slaves of sinister *houngans,* the flesh-eating, reanimated ghouls of George A. Romero's *Night of the Living Dead* (1968), brought with them not only a new way of portraying the zombie in cinema, but also countless opportunities for critics and academics to interpret this midnight monster mash as a high-minded exposé of race relations and social upheaval in America.

According to everyone involved, including Romero himself, no one making the movie had any intention of making a "message" picture. Their goal was a roller-coaster ride for the grindhouse, and their choice of an African American actor as their leading man was driven not by a desire to challenge racial boundaries or make a statement about the zombie as a symbol of disenfranchised Americans, but simply because dashing Duane Jones was a friend and the best man for the job.

Forty-plus years later, even Romero wavers on that point, saying that perhaps they did subconsciously weave in such intricate layers of social symbolism because they were just that clever; not a difficult thing to want to admit, when you think about it, and it helps when the weight of fandom over decades has convinced you that you were in fact that brilliant. To be fair, there is evidence that they were at least partly conscious of what they were doing: the use of grainy still shots in the movie's closing moments overtly and eerily paralleled newspaper coverage of the Watts riots. The film also offers a nice subversion within the genre itself in that the Black man, once a symbol of fear and danger in the early zombie movies, has now taken a heroic place at the opposite end of the spectrum in the struggle against the living dead.

And that's not all. You can match the cyclical resurgence of zombie films, and a recurring rise in popularity of horror cinema in general, to a corresponding catalytic occurrence of every major military/political action from World War II to 9/11. At such times, the effectiveness of zombie movies as allegories of fear, as well as cathartic escape valves, reaches epic proportions. Coming as it did during the height of the Vietnam era, when American families were exposed to the violent impacts of that controversial conflict as never before (in their own homes via their television sets), *Night of the Living Dead* features a number of undeniable visual and thematic parallels to that war. A few years later, a deeply disturbing variation on the classic "Monkey's Paw" tale called *Deathdream* (1974) pushed the connection between zombies and Vietnam further by directly addressing the disillusionment and detachment experienced by returning veterans.

Although Romero and his team might not have set out to make as much of a statement with *Night of the Living Dead* as some now believe, they can take credit for the fact that social commentary was very much a factor in the shaping of the follow-up, that tongue-in-cheek attack on mid-twentieth-century self-indulgent consumer culture, *Dawn of the Dead* (1978). Set largely in a shopping mall, soon to become a beloved setting for zombie fighting perpetuated in future films such as Japan's *Bio Zombie* (1998), the *Dawn of the Dead* remake (2004), and even the video games *Left 4 Dead 2* and *Dead Rising*, the original *Dawn of the Dead* makes no bones about its intentions. One crucial scene features our heroes musing about what has drawn so many reanimated corpses to the gleaming halls of the then new monument to the retail lifestyle:

> Francine: What are they doing? Why do they come here?
> Stephen: Some kind of instinct. Memory, of what they used to do. This was an important place in their lives.

Read that last line with dripping sarcasm and you'll have some idea of where Romero stood on the explosion of the new leisure economy. There's a problem with buying into your own hype, though, and his later efforts were too concerned with consciously maintaining his reputation as the premier maker of socially relevant zombie films at the expense of other considerations, such as plot, character and entertainment value. *Land of the Dead* (2005) took some half-hearted jabs at Bush-era America, especially the growing gulf between the haves and the have-nots. *Diary of the Dead* (2007) had no confidence in its ability to convey its message through its story and instead borrowed liberally from other horror hits, such as *The Blair*

Witch Project (1999), lifting dialogue and employing various characters to state the theme of emotionally detached voyeurism over and over until scenes of gore-soaked zombie carnage seemed subtle in comparison. Romero's latest effort, *Survival of the Dead* (2009), is another case of diminishing returns, with a look at zombie evolution picked up from *Land of the Dead* (a controversial subject with fans unless you're talking about the beloved Bub from Romero's 1985 entry, *Day of the Dead*) and a few pointed punches at the American healthcare system.

But let's get back to the mall. By the 1980s, American audiences had a reliable recurring enemy in pop culture. In the aftermath of Watergate and countless other political scandals, as well as Vietnam and interminable conflicts waged around the globe, movie monsters were often supplanted by the real threat: the government and the military. It's no surprise that, when the corpses awakened yet again, their undead condition was often the result of a government experiment gone awry or leftover toxins from bio-weapons or military projects. The dead might be munching on our brains, but they are just doing what comes naturally for them; the true figures of evil are the living representatives from the halls of power. Romero's aforementioned *Day of the Dead* is all about the military reaction to the zombie plague, but interestingly when pitted against our heroes—the scientists—it's the brash and bullying soldiers who seem to have the right idea. *Return of the Living Dead* (1985) and its sequels introduced the military secret known as Trioxin-245, a toxic sludge that not only brought the dead back to life, but also supposedly was the real cause of the events seen in *Night of the Living Dead*; the fact that the film was written by Romero's partner in the first film, John Russo, might have had something to do with that amusing little link. And have you noticed that once again science isn't coming off very well?

By the end of the twentieth century, afraid of everything around us (from our own leaders to the scientific advances we had made), zombies were positively overloaded with meaning that stretched back decades. The oft-repeated axiom "there are some things man was not meant to know" fuelled a lot of dark fantasy in any decade, but in postapocalyptic zombie films such as the *Resident Evil* series (2002–present) and all three adaptations of Richard Matheson's novel *I Am Legend*—*The Last Man on Earth* (1964), *The Omega Man* (1971) and (least inventively) *I Am Legend* (2007)—it's science once again that dooms mankind to a plague of the living dead. Matheson's original work was really about vampires, but its basic plot and imagery served the zombie genre well, and, together with *The Last Man on Earth,* directly inspired Romero to make *Night of the Living Dead* in the first place. Other films, such as *The Living Dead at Manchester Morgue* (1974), *The Evil Dead* (1981) and *Re-Animator* (1985) and its sequels (a Lovecraftian riff on the Frankenstein story and the ultra-low-budget *Meat Market* movies [2000–06]), all touched on the same important lesson: tamper with the delicate balance of nature at your own risk.

But there's more to it than just a fear of scientific progress. Many of these films also incorporate the fear that has spread like wildfire in the past twenty years. From AIDS to worldwide flu and other epidemics, the modern world is consumed with terror over tiny microbes. Whether it's a disease as yet undiscovered, an artificially engineered virus intended to cure cancer that instead mutates into a nightmarish corpse-reviving affliction, or a distillation of human rage carried in the blood, the living and living dead zombies of today are usually the walking, shambling or running symbols of suffering and sickness: a monstrous version of a global viral outbreak. Someone should really work out the mathematics of that kind of thing.

A Spanish variation on the classic, claustrophobic haunted house movie, *REC* (2007) was one of the most disturbing takes on the viral zombie metaphor, this time blending it very effectively with a religious element. Linking infection to demonic possession, *REC* was a one-two punch that used the zombie as both disease and spiritual corruption. The American remake, *Quarantine* (2008), had no additional insight into stateside fears of that nature but at least managed to respect the original source material even if it didn't really justify the need to remake it. A very inventive zombie-as-virus movie was the festival hit *Pontypool* (2008), which took the *28 Days Later* notion of a rage-like sickness but replaced blood as the means of transmission with the spoken word. Take that, defenders of literacy and language!

Zombie Honeymoon (2004) offered one of the most harrowing AIDS metaphors with its portrait of a newlywed struggling to keep her sanity while watching her husband transform before her eyes from the man she loved into a creature entirely alien to her. An interesting sub-genre is the zombie movie in which the AIDS/illness angle has been married to a look at how terminal patients try to manage their conditions while living in a world that has no further use for them. While not a brilliant example of cinema, *Shatter Dead* featured zombies that have no craving for flesh or brains and only want to rejoin society in their former roles, but their physical and spiritual deformities make that impossible. The results of their attempts to re-enter society prove as heartbreaking as they are gory and unsettling. The French film *Les Revenants* (*They Came Back*) (2004) also explored the idea of zombies (read undesirables) fighting for their right to exist alongside the living while relearning how to be human. The latter two films paralleled the struggles of coma patients, handicapped people or other medically disenfranchised individuals and eschewed thrills for thoughtfulness.

Speaking of French zombie movies, the 1978 tone poem *The Grapes of Death* might have been one of the most melancholy and quietly contemplative zombie movies ever made, touching on the same themes of viral infection, violence and alienation that informed so many of these 2000-vintage zombies. But if you want to explore one of the strangest, most insanely grotesque and deeply meaningful living-dead films ever made, you have to watch the Japanese reanimated schoolgirl epic *Stacy* (2001). If you want to know which themes are explored symbolically in its blood-and-guts-laden running time, you'll have to earn your degree in Japanese culture first; I'm still puzzling over it all.

The army of allegorical zombies marches on, sometimes in the unlikeliest directions. You might think a movie with a title as crude as *Zombie Strippers* (2008) and a lead actress, Jenna Jameson, whose career has largely been spent in hardcore pornography would be immune to the disease of social relevance. Perhaps surprisingly, its intellectual pedigree was established immediately when the filmmakers confirmed that the movie was inspired by Eugene Ionesco's allegorical attack on Communism and conformity, the play *Rhinoceros*. Not only are those familiar themes in the zombie genre, but also the movie's surprisingly fun, no-budget effects and the creepy undead Jameson balance its overt sociopolitical commentary on the Bush Administration and the dehumanization of adult entertainment.

Meanwhile, the mainstream comedy-adventure hit *Zombieland* (2009), starring Woody Harrelson as zombie hunter Tallahassee, features an on-the-nose climactic showdown featuring a band of survivors battling an undead horde in the middle of an amusement park. At a time when we are raising generations of children on first-person shooter video games, it's not hard to decode the symbolism when Tallahassee turns the place into his own human-sized shooting gallery. Since the film even uses on-screen text as part of an early running gag, it's almost surprising that final sequence doesn't feature an on-screen body counter and decreasing health and ammo bars.

Of course, this wasn't the first time the zombie genre shuffled into the comedy genre; remember *Zombies on Broadway*? The single greatest example of a brilliant cross-breeding of undead horror and situational comedy was 2004's *Shaun of the Dead*, which took the living-dead apocalypse seriously and found its laughs in the natural interactions of its characters while occasionally veering into seriously dark tragedy. The film also drew a parallel hinted at in previous films, such as the original *Dawn of the Dead*: that we are all living a zombie-like existence in a modern world filled with drudgery (work) and distractions (mass media). Unlike *Shaun of the Dead* and its more nuanced mix of funny and philosophical, *Zombieland* sometimes lapses into slapstick and derives humour from the zombies themselves rather than the characters and situations. But in both cases the blend of horror and humour serves another important purpose; as these shambling symbols of terror grow in number and chill us to our bones, we also need to laugh at—or with—them once in a while instead.

As we head further into the twenty-first century, the only thing we know for certain about the zombie as a reflection of our fears and concerns about the future is that it will almost certainly continue to rise again and again whenever we need to confront ourselves. Film holds up a mirror to society, and the zombie is our darkest and most accurate reflection. What forms these allegorical automatons will take we cannot predict, but perhaps the best advice for future zombie storytellers is to heed the lesson learned by all those who hunt the creatures down in an effort to end their unholy existence.

Aim for the head.

CULTURAL NARRATIVES OF BLOOD

MARINA LEVINA

Blood is liquid life. It is the most intimate liquid and a powerful medicine all of us can give and hope to receive. The idea of blood reaches deep into our consciousness. If you look at the history of blood, it is really the history of self-discovery of the human race. This series traces a long and bloody struggle to master the precious juice that flows inside us. Blood permeates all aspects of life, because blood is life. Blood has become a medical commodity and a miracle cure, but also a contaminated harbinger of death. For better or worse, if you control blood, you control life itself. (Red Gold: The Epic Story of Blood)

It started off as rioting. But right from the beginning you knew this was different, because it was happening in small villages, market towns ... and then it wasn't on TV anymore. It was on the street outside. It was coming through your windows. It was a virus, an infection. You didn't need a doctor to tell you that. It was the blood or something in the blood. By the time they tried to evacuate the cities, it was already too late. The infection was everywhere. The army blockades were overrun, and that's when the exodus started. The day before the TV stopped broadcasting, there were reports of infection in Paris and New York. You didn't hear anything more after that. (28 Days Later)

Zombies are everywhere. And we are trying to make sense of them. We create stories—fictional and not so fictional—to explain this yet-to-be-understood threat. To understand cultural narratives of zombie outbreaks, we must understand stories that we tell about blood itself. The dangers of zombies have been firmly connected in the public imagination with the fear of the "other" and possible contamination by their blood or essence. A zombie outbreak is firmly tied to the concept of tainted blood and illustrates the difficulty of containing an epidemic threat. Narratives of zombie outbreaks are tied to cultural fears that tainted or infected blood will contaminate our bodies and communities. In turn, fears of tainted blood are tied to a deep-seated, historical and cross-cultural understanding of blood as a source of our selves and our souls. Here, blood is life: a fluid that determines everything about our bodies and identities. Our humanity is seen as inextricably tied to blood and thus is unalterable, for blood penetrates every part of our body and cannot be easily replaced. Nelkin (1999, 275) identifies four repeated and related themes around which blood metaphors cluster: blood as the essence of personhood; blood exchange practices as a symbol of community solidarity; blood as a source of danger and risk; and, finally, "the concept of pure blood" as "extend[ing] well beyond the properties of a biological substance to include references to social relationships and moral as well as physical contamination." Zombie outbreaks are portrayed as a struggle to keep our bodies, and by extension our identities and communities, safe from contact with dangerous, or tainted, blood. The war on zombies is therefore a war on infected blood itself.

Blood was considered to be the seat of the soul and was viewed by many philosophers as the soul's principal tool (Camporesi 1995). The body could also be rejuvenated through various forms of consumption of young, and therefore innocent, blood. For example, Camporesi notes, the sixteenth century surgeon Jean Tagault observed that flesh can be renewed through consumption or transfusion of good blood, which is "vicious neither in quality nor in quantity" (19). According to Camporesi, around the same time

> physicians, apothecaries, charlatans, and great intellectuals [of the day] all agreed: the blood of a fresh, delicate man, one well-tempered in his humours, someone young, soft, and blooming with red, "bloody" fat—a fleshy man, of a "jovial" temperament and "cordial" character, preferably having red hair [associated with the colour of blood]—enjoyed the indisputable primacy when it came to the slowing of the aging process. (17)

The ancient Egyptians bathed in blood to regain youth and witches in the Middle Ages were thought to drink the blood of the young to keep their powers (Nelkin 1999). Nicolae Ceauşescu, the infamous and hypochondriacal Romanian dictator, was rumoured to keep little boys in his castle in order to draw blood from them periodically for his own rejuvenation (Nelkin 1999). Despite the detractors of such practices, obsession with the blood of the young illustrates the belief that, by consuming someone's blood, one would also consume the essence of that person. The cultural fears that came along with that belief sometimes resulted in the assignment of monstrous identities to anyone engaged in those practices. One of the more famous examples was Hungarian countess Elizabeth Bathory (1560–1614), who was thought to have killed hundreds of young women and, according to some accounts, bathed in their blood to retain her youth. In the modern day, she is referred to as the Blood Countess or Countess Dracula.

Zombie outbreaks are terrifying exactly because they tap into the cultural belief that through consumption of blood a person's essence is consumed as well. As zombies eat our flesh—and, incidentally, our blood—we are afraid that what will be lost is the very essence of humanity. Wald (2008), for example, argues that zombie narratives of the 1950s specifically referenced the loss of humanity at the hands of foreign invaders. She writes that Jack Finney's novel *The Body Snatchers* (1955) and the subsequent film, *The Invasion of the Body Snatchers* (1956), captured "the horror of a protagonist's dawning awareness that the humanity of his or her closest associates is being drained from them and the terrifying estrangement ... that results as they try to maintain their human connection" (160). Although these narratives exemplify cultural fears of Communist invasion, the connection between contamination of blood and loss of humanity is established throughout.

Of course, zombies are, first and foremost, consumers of flesh. In most zombie narratives, contamination of blood, and thus our essence, is a by-product of consumption; consumption becomes the goal in and of itself. However, these narratives emphasize the danger of blind consumption as a gateway to blood contamination. In fact, zombie hordes have only one goal in mind: consumption. As Paffenroth (2006) argues, zombies derive no nourishment from eating the living since they are mostly the same, even if they do not eat. And, because zombies are usually brain-dead, they do not actively think of elimination of the living. In these ways, zombies are exemplary consumers. The analogy between zombies and consumers is belaboured in George A. Romero's *Dawn of the Dead* (1978), in which zombie hordes attack the shopping mall, an image reminiscent of the Black Friday shopping day in the United States. In his analysis of zombie narratives, including the original *Night of the Living Dead* (1968), Wood (1985, 213), argues that the loss of human relationships in zombie films represents cannibalism as the "ultimate in possessiveness [or consumption], hence the logical end of human relations under capitalism." Elsewhere (Wood 2003), he argues that zombie consumption of flesh represents the symbolic destruction of social norms, human order and family structures.

These consumptions are viral in nature; they infect whomever is unfortunate enough to get in the way. Loudermilk (2003, 88) corroborates that "zombie desire is to consume/just consume/eternally/desire gone virally awry. So the post-modern zombie's desire to consume (flesh), thereby infecting all humankind, is not so different from the capitalist consumer's desire for more (goods, wealth, resources, status symbols) (exploiting peoples globally and polluting the planet)." A viral infection, to be effective, does not need to consume the entire body. This is why, Loudermilk argues, zombies rarely finish their meals. A mere taste and they move on to another fresh palette of blood and meat. Zombie outbreaks thus demonstrate the dangers of insatiable consumption without regard for moral or ethical consequences. Because of the connection between consumption and blood infections, zombie outbreaks demonstrate the dangers of turning blood into a commodity.

The dangers of blood commodification have, in fact, informed the social history of blood exchange. The Food and Drug Administration (FDA) has been responsible for regulating blood and blood products since 1973.[1] The "blood shield" poli-

---

1   FDA, Office of Regulatory Affairs, Sec. 230.120, Human Blood and Blood Products as Drugs (CPG 7134.02), http://www.fda.gov/ora/compliance_ref/cpg/cpgbio/cpg230-120.html.

BACKGROUND

The 31 January 1973 Federal Register (vol. 28, no. 20) announced the amendment and revision of 21 CFR, Part 273 (recodified as 21 CFR 600). The preamble to this announcement also directed attention to the classification of blood and blood products as drugs under the federal *Food, Drug, and Cosmetic Act* as well as biologics under the *Public Health Service Act*. Excerpts from the preamble responding to questions concerning the classification of blood as a drug follow.

> Section 201(g)(1) definition of drug in the Federal Food, Drug, and Cosmetic Act (21 U.S.C. 321), reveals that blood and related blood products fall clearly within that definition. That section states "The term 'drug' means (A) articles recognized in the official United States Pharmacopeia ... ; and (B) articles intended for use in the diagnosis, cure, mitigation, treatment, or prevention of disease in man or other animals."

Blood is covered by both parts of this definition. Human blood was first recognized in the United States Pharmacopeia (USP), 15th edition (15 December 1955), and has been included in each USP since that edition. Indications for use of blood products also fall directly within the broad therapeutic scope of the definition. Although it is true that blood is human living tissue, it is incorrect to assume that it must be either a living human tissue or a drug. That human blood and blood products can be characterized as living human tissue for some purposes, and as biologics for purposes of regulation under the *Public Health*

cy instituted in the 1970s insisted that volunteerism had to re-place whatever payment continued to exist for whole blood and to drive commercial blood from the market; among other measures, the FDA regulated that all whole blood and its components had to be labelled as derived from either "paid" or "volunteer" donors.[2] The very idea of paid donors came under political and social scrutiny largely due to the rising of post-transfusion infections and the publication, in 1971, of *The Gift Relationship*, a controversial book by Richard Titmuss, a professor of social administration at the London School of Economics, which passionately argued for the exclusive use of non-paid donors as a solution to the rising rates of infection.[3] Titmuss

Service Act (sec. 351, 58 Stat. 702, as amended; 42 U.S.C. 262), in no way alters the fact that blood is also a drug subject to regulation under applicable provisions of the federal *Food, Drug, and Cosmetic Act.*

POLICY
Human blood and blood products are characterized as biologics for purposes of regulation under the Public Health Service Act, as amended, and also as drugs subject to regulation under applicable provisions of the federal Food, Drug, and Cosmetic Act.
2   This blood policy did not extend to plasma and its derivatives presumably because plasma donors, as a rule, are financially compensated for their donations. The Red Cross and other regional blood banks are non-profit organizations that specialize in blood collection. Blood products, such as plasma and its derivatives (Factor VIII used for treatment of hemophilia, among other diseases), are collected and processed by for-profit pharmaceutical companies. Since the collection of blood for blood products is much more complicated and time consuming, the donors are almost always paid (Bayer 1999).
3   While critiqued for its condemnation of the commercial blood system in the United States and idealization of Britain's largely volunteer donor system (Hagen 1982), *The Gift Relationship* had an enormous impact on the future discussion of blood policy (e.g., Hagen 1982; Hough 1978; Johnson 1977). Richard Nixon's secretary of health, education and welfare put all blood donations under a system of federal control that labelled blood as either "volunteer donor" or "paid donor." In the 1970s, concerns about paid blood donation continued to grow, and in 1975 the 28th World Health Assembly of the World Health

argued that commodified blood was not safe; just as zombies driven by consumption spread infection, so too do paid donors driven by profit.

However, his criticism of paid blood was not based solely on the danger of paid donors. To Titmuss, volunteer blood donation exemplified the altruistic gift relationship that was the fabric of society: "The forms and functions of giving embody moral, social, psychological, religious, legal and aesthetic ideas. They may reflect, sustain, strengthen, or loosen the cultural bonds of the group, large or small" (1971, 71). For Titmuss, giving blood built and represented kinship, and he argued that most volunteer donors had moral reasons for donating blood. He defined morality as a desire to contribute to society and an identification with the "universal stranger," whom donors wanted to help (238). This reflected the role of blood as a socially binding fluid. He wrote, for example, that "blood as a living tissue may now constitute in Western societies one of the ultimate tests of where the 'social' begins and the 'economic' ends" (18). As a literal and metaphorical representation of life itself, contamination of blood—including zombie outbreaks—has been culturally constructed as contamination of life, and, with it, individuals, groups and nation-states.

Blood is therefore deeply connected to narratives of kinship in society. The claim "it's in the blood" is extended from individual to social bodies. In the eugenics movement, blood was a useful organizational tool because it embodied "the essence" of a person (racial, ethnic or otherwise) and therefore provided a totalizing account of that person's identity based on group membership. Adolf Hitler (1889–1945) infamously asserted that blood is unchangeable and eternal: "Classes vanish, classes alter themselves, the destinies of men undergo changes, but something always remains: the nation as such, as the substance of flesh and blood. To us [National Socialists] blood not only means something corporeal, but it is in a racial sense,

Organization passed a resolution calling for non-paid donor systems to be set up in all member countries. The resolution shared the assumption of Titmuss that paid blood, usually from the economically disadvantaged, was dangerous or impure (Glied 1999).

the soul, which has as its external field of expression the body" (cited in Linke 1999). Descent was defined in terms of blood; the definitional notion of race was based on blood, not on a person's skin colour or religious beliefs (Scales-Trent 2001). Jewishness was defined not according to religious practices but according to the "one drop of blood" rule. In March 1936, *Der Stürmer*—a German newspaper—wrote that "whoever has Jewish blood in his veins will sooner or later reveal the Jewish part of his character" (cited in Miller 1995). And the same beliefs about the nature of blood and bodies that informed Nazi policies also informed American racial policies of the time. The fears of "catching black," which permeated American culture at the time, were steeped in a belief in the essentialist properties of blood. For example, Saks (1988, 29–41) writes that

> race categories in America have long been based on ideas about "blood quanta." ... African Americans were identified by the "one drop of blood rule," which defined a person with even a drop of "black blood" as black.... [In the American South,] miscegenation laws used the metaphor of "black blood" to separate the legal concept of race from skin colour. The skin could lie, allowing a person to pass, but the blood represented "serological truth"; it defined and identified race.[4]

4 The use of race to manage, discipline and treat the body is illustrated by sickle cell anemia, which occurs predominantly in African American populations. As Tapper (1999, 3) argues, "sickling today is viewed as a black-related disease not simply because the majority of people suffering from the disease are blacks, but because various medical sciences in tandem with anthropology have represented it as a disease of 'black people' since the turn of the twentieth century." Until the 1940s, sickle cell anemia was viewed as a disease of "Negro blood" that can be passed on to the white population through interracial relationships (Wailoo 1997). As Wailoo points out, this was not a simple matter of "bad" or "prejudiced" science. The existence of racially identifiable blood was a real material experience for both physicians and patients. He writes, "for many physicians in the early 20th century, *Negro Blood* was a term with clear technological origins and with biological, social, and public health meanings. These physicians based their view on what was at that time hematological evidence and

Therefore, through the use of blood as a category of classi-fication, alliances are drawn, boundaries are established, and fellowships are declared. Franklin and McKinnon (2001, 15) write that, "as a classificatory technology, kinship can be mo-bilized to signify not only specific kinds of connection and in-clusion but also specific kinds of disconnection and exclusion." Much as a bite penetrates and breaks the boundary of the body, blood penetrates and affects the boundaries of group and na-tional identities. Therefore, a zombie viral outbreak repre-sents not just an infection that penetrates the boundary of the body but also, in a larger sense, an infection of the nation-state and our national identity. One of the things that makes a zom-bie outbreak terrifying is the loss of control that it represents. In other words, we struggle to control and preserve systems of classification and control over the borders of the nation-state in the face of an indiscriminate zombie attack.

This is especially evident in the chronicle of the last major zombie outbreak, *World War Z*.[5] Here the author, Max Brooks,

scientific understanding of ... the disorder" (137). Regardless of a pa-tient's symptoms or claims of racial whiteness, sickle cells and there-fore "Negro blood" were there, in the body, waiting to be found. Since mere visual evidence could not be trusted to identify "true" racial identities, bodies were once again classified according to genealogy or descent. But, as Tapper (1999) points out, even when black ancestry could be ruled out for three or five generations, doctors were still un-able to accept their subjects' claim to be "racially pure whites."

5   Here is a summary of the *World War Z* plot.

> *World War Z* consists of a series of interviews with men and women who survived the zombie war (*World War Z*). Each interview focuses on a spe-cific stage in the zombie war, and those interviewed vary radically in terms of diversity. The story is set not far in the future, when the global political situation is very nearly the same as it is today. Brooks chronicles the very first isolated outbreaks in China; the zombie disease (solanum) very quick-ly spreads to Africa, where it is thought to be a form of rabies. A major med-ical corporation, hoping to cash in on the scare African Rabies has caused, develops an entirely ineffective but well-selling drug called Phalanx to combat the unusual disease. Despite the media attention African Rabies re-ceives, many nations do not see the outbreaks as cause for major concern, and only Israel quarantines itself and prepares for the imminent disaster. A period towards the start of the war, known as the Great Panic, coincides

represents the outbreak not just in terms of infection, but also in terms of blood, descent and classification of racial categories. In this narrative, the zombie virus is racialized and localized; the story begins in China and highlights the Chinese government's unsuccessful efforts to contain the virus. The zombie virus reaches a wider global awareness only after an outbreak in Africa, referred to as "African Rabies." The virus spreads as illegal and often infected immigrants flood the boundaries of the Western nation-states. The only nations successful at preventing a major outbreak are Cuba and Israel. The former is helped by already-established policies of isolation and the latter by an early nationwide quarantine program. A narrative of racial fears, *World War Z* also establishes a parallel between blood infection and the insecurity of nation-state borders. The virus is finally contained through ethically problematic "safe zones." The lesson here is that a zombie outbreak can be prevented only through the re-establishment of a secure nation-state. Here an infected body and an infected nation are one and the same.

with the world's sudden realization that this disease is not something to be taken lightly. China, due to its large population and ineffective leadership, is very quickly over-run, and infected Chinese refugees help to spread the blight to the Americas and Europe. It's not long before the zombie population outnumbers the human population in both China and Africa. In many of the major cities in North America and Europe the disease also spreads quickly, and humanity suffers a crushing defeat in a New York suburb when the United States military attempts to face off against approximately 100,000 zombies in the streets. Air combat proves to be worthless against the zombie hordes because zombies do not rely on tactics or leaders: each zombie is, so to speak, a one-man army. Militaries the world over have to retrain themselves and break old habits, conventional warfare needs to be put to rest, and whole new strategies, tactics, and weapons need to be developed if the zombies are to be combated successfully. Eventually, it is realized that the armed forces are simply too few to protect everyone, and, following South Africa's lead, many nations opt to retreat and regroup within an easily defensible area [safe zones], clear the zombies out there, then push back into the zombie-controlled wastes and systematically wipe out the zombies, mile by mile, if need be. Part of the strategy, as cold as it is, is to use humans who could not be easily rescued as live bait, making it easier to clear out heavily infested areas. Everyone else who isn't actively fighting provides labour, making weapons and feeding the army.

Summary courtesy of Colin Kehm, www.allreaders.com.

It is in these and other ways that zombie outbreaks, blood infections and consumptions are mapped onto scientific, national and racial mechanisms of control. As blood becomes a site of power struggles, zombie outbreaks play an important role in the implementation and manifestation of mechanisms of power. Foucault (1978, 147) talks of a society of blood in which "power spoke through blood.... Blood was *a reality with a symbolic function.*" According to Foucault, blood owed its value to "its instrumental role (the ability to shed blood), to the way it functioned in the order of signs (to have a certain blood, to be of the same blood ...), and also to its precariousness (easily spilled ... too readily mixed)" (147). Because blood is precarious, meaningful and potentially dangerous, a breakdown in its control, especially evident in cases of infections, is often portrayed as a breakdown of the social order. In *28 Days Later* (2002), a film documenting a zombie-like outbreak in England, people become infected through not much more than a drop of blood; a fitting allegory of the "one drop of blood" rule. During the outbreak, people do not die to become zombies; instead, they are infected with the Rage virus.[6] They are consumed and subsumed by rage, their blood boiling, their eyeballs turning red. The infection has its origins in scientific laboratories where chimpanzees were exposed to hours of news coverage of bombings, shootings and protests; a commentary on the slow breakdown of our social fabric played along the narrative of blood infection. At the end, this particular blood infection destroys England. The country becomes a postapocalyptic wasteland where even the last keepers of the social order—the military—can no longer be trusted. This is a potent commentary on a deep connection between blood and society.

6 Although the infected did not die, they did behave throughout the film as super-fast zombies. There has been some debate about whether or not *28 Days Later* is a zombie film, but there is a general cultural agreement that classifies it as a zombie film, albeit one that reinvents the genre. The debate over generic purity is beyond the scope of this chapter, but I go with general classification and consider *28 Days Later* as a zombie narrative. For more on the debate, see http://blogs.cjonline.com/index.php?entry=3148 and http://horrorscififilms.suite101.com/article.cfm/28_days_later.

The subsequent zombie threats also illustrate how control over blood is often tied to regulation of social borders. However, in the age of globalization, border control is not easy to establish. Now the spillage of infected blood has global repercussions. In fact, most recent narratives of zombie outbreaks map social and cultural anxieties of the post-9/11 world. As Bishop (2009, 24) writes, "the primary metaphor in the post-9/11 zombie world is terrorism.... The transmission of the zombie infection is a symbolic form of radical brainwashing. Because anyone can become infected at any time, everyone is a potential threat; thus, paranoia becomes almost as important as survival." The paranoia over control is evident in the zombie apocalypse film *28 Weeks Later* (2007). A sequel to *28 Days Later,* it portrays London twenty-eight weeks after the Rage virus has turned a majority of the English population into the "infected." The virus is now effectively contained and eradicated, and the US-led military forces have reopened London for repopulation. Forming a "Green Zone" inside the city, which—like a "safe zone" in *World War Z*—is a heavily surveyed, guarded and regulated territory, the military allows limited numbers of refugees to return to their hometown. However, the virus reappears and efforts at contamination fail. In a desperate attempt to re-establish dominance, the military gives up on selective elimination of the "infected" and instead issues this command: "Abandon selective targeting. Shoot everything. Targets are now free.... We've lost control." The phrase "we've lost control" represents a discernible anxiety at the heart of efforts to contain and control blood infection in the post-9/11, global world. *28 Weeks Later* exemplifies the futility of modern warfare in viral conditions of terrorism and epidemics. Zombies are now indistinguishable from the general populace and hence we become the target of our design. *28 Weeks Later* illustrates the overarching problem of what it means to fight for control of a ubiquitous, self-sustaining, yet indefinable viral entity. The blood, once spilled, mixed and infected on the global scale, is hard to contain and even harder to control.

Cultural metaphors of blood have deeply informed our experience with zombie outbreaks. These metaphors symbolize the intertwining of bodies that can be resolved only through either physical or symbolic violence: elimination or contain-ment. It is through blood and bites that zombie outbreaks tran-scend a particular physiological function in the human body and become a signifier of matters of life and death. The dan-gers of zombies have been firmly connected in the public imag-ination with the fear of the "other" and possible contamination by their blood or essence. To understand a zombie outbreak as "an epidemic of signification" is therefore to study how the concept of tainted blood has been represented, constructed and understood as one of the metaphors of the disease (Tre-ichler 1999). The dichotomy between dangerous/exotic "oth-ers" and "innocent" victims frames the cultural experience of zombie invasions and becomes a powerful representation of zombie outbreaks. A zombie outbreak is portrayed as a war against blood, both individual blood and national blood. They are mapped onto the external struggle to keep our bodies, and by extension our communities, safe from any contact with dan-gerous blood. Zombie infection therefore carries with it a cul-tural assignment of fault. In the case of zombie outbreaks, the fault is directly related to metaphors of blood: a tainted es-sence affecting and infecting entire communities. Here, infect-ed blood is automatically "bad" or "evil," indistinguishable from personhood or the essence that it represents.

In the case of zombie outbreaks, tainted blood is associated with monstrosity and henceforth the loss of humanity. Meta-phors of tainted blood become metaphors of tainted communi-ties. With each zombie bite, blood is bound to ooze out. I have argued here that blood does not have the luxury of moral or so-cial neutrality. It is deeply connected to its sociocultural iden-tity as the liquid of life. Therefore, zombie stories tell us what it means to occupy a body that inevitably leaks blood. And, as in any compelling story, there are heroes and villains, danger and suspense, monsters and humans. The most important thing is to follow the blood trail where it leads us: to a deeper cultural meaning of what it means to be human.

REFERENCES

Bayer, R. 1999. "Blood and AIDS in America: Science, Politics, and the Making of an Iatrogenic Catastrophe." In *Blood Feuds: AIDS, Blood, and the Politics of Medical Disaster,* edited by E.A. Feldman and R. Bayer, 19-58. Oxford: Oxford University Press.

Bishop, K. 2009. "Dead Man Still Walking: Explaining the Zombie Renaissance." *Journal of Popular Film and Television* 37, 1: 16–25.

Boyle, D. and T. James, dirs. 2003. *28 Days Later.* 20th Century Fox, 113 minutes.

Brooks, M. 2007. *World War Z: An Oral History of the Zombie War.* New York: Three Rivers Press.

Camporesi, P. 1995. *Juice of Life: The Symbolic and Magic Significance of Blood.* Translated by R.R. Barr. New York: Continuum.

Foucault, M. 1978. *The History of Sexuality.* Vol. 1. Translated by A. Sheridan. New York: Vintage Books.

Franklin, S. and M. Susan, eds. 2001. *Relative Values: Reconfiguring Kinship Studies.* Durham: Duke University Press.

Fresnadillo, J.C., dir. 2007. *28 Weeks Later.* 20th Century Fox, 100 minutes.

Glied, S. 1999. "The Circulation of the Blood: AIDS, Blood, and the Economics of Information." In *Blood Feuds: AIDS, Blood, and the Politics of Medical Disaster,* edited by E. Feldman, 323–48. Oxford: Oxford University Press.

Hagen, P.J. 1982. *Blood: Gift or Merchandise: Towards an International Blood Policy.* New York: Alan R. Liss.

Hough, D.E. 1978. *The Market for Human Blood.* Lexington: Lexington Books.

Johnson, D.B. 1977. *Blood Policy: Issues and Alternatives.* Washington, DC: American Enterprise Institute for Public Policy Research.

Linke, U. 1999. *Blood and Nation: The European Aesthetics of Race.* Philadelphia: University of Pennsylvania Press.

Loudermilk, A. 2003. "Eating 'Dawn' in the Dark: Zombie Desire and Commodified Identity in George A. Romero's 'Dawn of the Dead.'" *Journal of Consumer Culture* 3, 1: 83–108.

Miller, L.R. 1995. *Nazi Justiz: Law of the Holocaust.* Westport, CT: Praeger.

Nelkin, D. 1999. "Cultural Perspectives on Blood." In *Blood Feuds: AIDS, Blood, and the Politics of Medical Disaster,* edited by E. Feldman and R. Bayer, 274–92. Oxford: Oxford University Press.

Paffenroth, K. 2006. *Gospel of the Living Dead: George Romero's Visions of Hell on Earth.* Waco, TX: Baylor University Press.

Saks, E. 1988. "Representing Miscegenation Law." *Raritan* 8, 2: 29–41.

Scales-Trent, J. 2001. "Racial Purity Laws in the United States and Nazi Germany: The Targeting Process." *Human Rights Quarterly* 23, 2: 259–307.

Tapper, M. 1999. *In the Blood: Sickle Cell Anemia and the Politics of Race.* Philadelphia: University of Pennsylvania Press.

Titmuss, R.M. 1971. *The Gift Relationship: From Human Blood to Social Policy.* New York: Pantheon Books.

Treichler, P. 1999. *How to Have Theory in an Epidemic: Cultural Chronicles of* AIDS. Durham: Duke University Press.

Wailoo, K. 1997. *Drawing Blood: Technology and Disease in Twentieth-Century America.* Baltimore: Johns Hopkins University Press.

Wald, P. 2008. *Contagious: Cultures, Carriers, and the Outbreak Narrative.* Durham: Duke University Press.

Weston, K. 2001. "Kinship, Controversy, and the Sharing of Substance: The Race/Class Politics of Blood Transfusions." In *Relative Values: Reconfiguring Kinship Studies,* edited by S. Franklin and S. McKinnon, 147–74. Durham: Duke University Press.

White, L. 1993. "Cars out of Place: Vampires, Technology, and Labor in Eastern and Central Africa." *Representations* summer 43: 27–50.

Wood, R. 1983. "An Introduction to the American Horror Film." In *Movies and Methods,* vol. 2, edited by B. Nichols, 195–219. Los Angeles: University of California Press.

———. 2003. *Hollywood from Vietnam to Reagan—and Beyond.* Rev. ed. New York: Columbia University Press.

MAINTAINING ACADEMIC LIBRARY SERVICES DURING THE ZOMBIE APOCALYPSE

SARAH MCHONE-CHASE AND LYNNE M. THOMAS

WHY DO WE NEED ACADEMIC LIBRARIES WHEN WE HAVE GOOGLE?
Although public, academic and special libraries have played important roles in managing information during wars and pandemics, we contend that reliance on academic libraries in particular for information needs during the zombie apocalypse, as opposed to reliance on Google searches or other publicly available internet resources alone, will significantly increase the chances of human survival. Chiefly, academic libraries have access to information resources that are not publicly available. These resources include, but are not limited to, large databases of up-to-date, peer-reviewed, scientific, engineering, technical and medical (STEM) journals, in addition to historical caches of paper versions of the same. "Grey" literature—such as commission reports, theses, dissertations, locally produced datasets, conference proceedings, technical specifications and standards, and other materials "produced on all levels of government, academics, business and industry in print and electronic formats, but which is not controlled by commercial publishers," as defined by the New York Academy of Medicine—also exists

primarily in academic libraries (New York Academy of Medicine Library 2009).

In addition to holding these non-public information caches, library professionals have knowledge of how to manage these resources, make them widely available and interpret them accurately, in multiple formats. As such, the resources and the librarians themselves combine to form a centralized information asset. This asset can be used to combat zombies on two fronts: first, in front-line battle; second, in providing information to researchers trying to combat the cause of zombification through medical/scientific research.

Libraries and librarians have a deep and abiding commitment to helping the public and making useful information available for the greater good as well as a reputation for being trustworthy sources of information. This commitment is best expressed through the Code of Ethics of the American Library Association, the first tenet of which is this: "We provide the highest level of service to all library users through appropriate and usefully organized resources; equitable service policies; equitable access; and accurate, unbiased, and courteous responses to all requests" (American Library Association 2008). In other words, librarians are willing to share what they know and to guarantee that their information is correct. However, one should not be so naive as to expect that all of humanity will react in a similar manner. Crucially, libraries in the zombie apocalypse can combat misinformation that will inevitably be spread on the public web, by media outlets, organizations or individuals who have less than altruistic intentions.

Given these numerous information types and sources and our commitment to the ethical provision of good information to the public, academic libraries and librarians are uniquely qualified to accommodate and mitigate a wider variety of doomsday zombie scenarios than members of the general public using freely available information on the Web, as we demonstrate below in our history of previous library responses to wars and pandemics, and in our specific response scenarios for future zombie outbreaks.

This chapter takes its understanding of zombie infection and pathology from Munz et al.'s (2009) model of a zombie epidemic. In particular, library responses are predicated on the most likely scenario posited by the authors of the article for survival, the "impulsive eradication" model, which specifically calls for swift, escalating physical attacks to reduce the zombie population while simultaneously searching for a way to provide immunity or treatment for the unaffected population. This model for zombie infection functions as a cross between an epidemic and a war for library disaster-planning purposes. Given the swiftly moving nature of a zombie epidemic, we also assume that any outbreaks will be national or international in nature, not merely localized, which will directly affect planning and response mechanisms by academic libraries.

PREVIOUS LIBRARY RESPONSES TO EPIDEMICS AND WARS

Academic libraries have a long history of public response to epidemics and wars, as evidenced in the literature through articles that recognize user needs in such situations and document previous responses after the fact. For example, Ferguson (2003) and Robertson (2006), both responding to the recent SARS epidemic, emphasize the need for libraries to incorporate epidemics into their disaster plans (plans for continuing library services after a disaster, such as a flood, fire or tornado, have occurred). Robertson in particular emphasizes aspects of pandemics that otherwise might be overlooked by library disaster plans, such as the creation of "clean teams" (i.e., uninfected, quarantined workers) and the provision of remote services (either in person from an off-site location or electronically) during quarantine. Quinlan (2007) documents the history of library responses to the 1918 influenza epidemic and reminds us of the toll such events take on library staff in addition to the community at large.

In times of war, the library community has also provided essential support to service personnel on the frontlines via the provision of reading and reference materials, both fiction and non-fiction, through, for example, the Library War Service in World War I, the Victory Book Campaign and the Joint Committee on Library Research (1940) Facilities for National Emergency in World War II and the Books for Troops program during Operation Iraqi Freedom (Souers 2004). Lacy (1953) notes the central function of academic collections as repositories of knowledge related to enemies and allies, in terms of both providing information to those responsible for planning and execution of the war, and documenting propaganda, public information and eventual outcomes for both world wars.

In 2008, Featherstone, Lyon and Ruffin published an article about an oral history project through the National Library of Medicine that documented a wide variety of roles for libraries responding to different kinds of disasters, including epidemics, weather/nature events and campus violence. As expected, libraries met traditional expectations of providing leisure reading for displaced users of all ages, soldiers and frontline responders, and salvaging physical collections that would be crucial in rebuilding the Gulf Coast area after Hurricane Katrina. Libraries also functioned as community centres, aided displaced patrons with filing applications for federal assistance, finding new accommodations for those patrons and their pets, and contacting and tracking loved ones as they were found.

Libraries also partnered with state and federal agencies, public health departments, local police and fire departments to coordinate hotlines and call centres to aid responders, volunteers and those in need of assistance on the Gulf Coast. Librarian volunteers at shelters gathered reference materials, such as heavily used medical guides, for local medical personnel, providing accurate information as victims were being treated. A librarian built a database that identified the victims of the 9/11 attacks, and a librarian compiled and furnished information binders to Toronto Public Health locations during the SARS epidemic (Featherstone, Lyon and Ruffin 2008). In short, libraries functioned as the servers for disseminating accurate, timely information during major emergencies that allowed first responders to concentrate on doing their own jobs.

ACADEMIC LIBRARY RESPONSES TO THE ZOMBIE APOCALYPSE

Academic library responses to a zombie event must, as in any disaster, be predicated on the infrastructure available during or after the event. As technology levels are potentially rolled back through infrastructure destruction, historical materials on engineering, building methods, agriculture, manufacturing, transportation and communications, most of which are only held in academic research libraries, will quickly become directly relevant to user communities. This chapter posits three possible infrastructure scenarios for which libraries can provide services, assuming that the library has a current disaster plan. In all three scenarios, further infection must be controlled through quarantine enforcement and the designation of "clean teams." These essential, uninfected library staff, cross-trained in different library functions and kept separate from users and other staff, provide continuing services remotely while preventing exposure. These scenarios also assume some access to the library building and/or its resources (either in person or remotely), even if it is limited.

The first scenario assumes that the basic current infrastructure remains relatively intact: the internet is available and working; telephones, fax machines and other communication methods are also in use; or, at worst, the internet is reliable when phone and fax lines are not. The second scenario assumes that some sort of zombie infiltration has brought down the majority of internet servers in a particular region and that telephone (or possibly fax) is the only method of communication reliably available. This could occur through the loss of electrical power in a region, breaks in phone or cable lines that connect regional hubs, regional hubs going down through other zombie-related chaos, or server congestion on key sites. The third scenario posits that all telecommunications and computing infrastructure is down, and that we must rely solely on paper-based resources and local knowledge. Given the track record of cell phone network overloads during times of emergency, we do not think they are reliable enough to include in any emergency scenario, particularly during the immediate aftermath of an event.

Each scenario has some commonalities. As we anticipate that a zombie infestation will be national or international in nature, it is likely that university libraries in rural areas not near population centres will fare the best in terms of safety and ability to maintain services (Universities of Montana and South Dakota, you're in good shape). These university libraries are likely to be overwhelmed with information requests due to the collapse of libraries in populous areas (the East Coast, for example, will be toast) and therefore should plan for additional staff hours during the zombie apocalypse to handle increased demand.

Library buildings should be adequately prepared for a lockdown through the stockpiling of non-perishable food and clean water and the acquisition of multi-use tools that can also serve as anti-zombie weapons (e.g., inexpensive garden shovels, which can also be used in the event of a partial building collapse or dire gardening event). Radios, walkie-talkies and other short-distance communication tools will help to keep library staff in touch with other campus units to monitor zombie movements. If we can keep our networks running and the building secure and sanitary for its inhabitants, then the library can easily maintain services until the immediate danger is past. All staff, but especially those on zombie combat duty, will need adequate rest periods and spaces to rest. Since the most likely immediate scenario is that library staff will be locked down on campus rather than working remotely from home, libraries are strongly advised to add a garden shovel or two to their disaster kits in preparation for the zombie apocalypse. Heavy reference tomes, of course, will also work in a pinch; however, we know from personal experience that elephant folios are unwieldy in close-combat situations.

Lockdown situations require active coordination between security services and library staff to protect people within the affected building. Remaining calm despite the presence of slavering zombie hordes is key. Those present in the building should turn off the lights, stay away from windows and doors, and remain as quiet as possible until evacuation is deemed safe in order to avoid attracting additional zombie attention.

With adequate supplies, the likelihood of surviving a physical zombie attack within a library building is high. Inhabitants of the building should be encouraged to move to an upper floor, with elevators turned off and stairwell access locked, to provide additional barriers between uninfected people and zombies trying to enter the building at the ground floor level. Once everyone is accounted for, the designated "clean team" members of uninfected library staff should set up their work spaces in a secure area to maintain continuity of library services.

Zombies identified within the building by designated library or security staff with anti-zombie training must be dispatched immediately to avoid further infection. Patrons or staff within the building reasonably suspected of zombie infection through visible, credible evidence of bites must be isolated from the rest of the library's inhabitants, in a secure area (e.g., a lockable storeroom with no windows and a single door), preferably on a different floor from uninfected building inhabitants. Since zombies are generally unintelligent, a speedy decoy might be sufficient bait to lure them into a lockable closet.

If evacuation is not possible, then the next step is to solicit volunteers willing to wield garden shovels in the defence of other users and staff from potential zombie onslaught. Experienced *Left 4 Dead* and *Resident Evil* players, and horror fans among library staff will be well suited for such a task. (To improve the number of anti-zombie trained staff, libraries are strongly encouraged to assign *World War Z* or *The Zombie Survival Guide* for professional development brown bags.) Anti-zombie fortification should be particularly easy for universities with library buildings constructed between 1965 and 1980, since numerous campus protests across the country led architects to design easily locked-down public buildings with limited entry opportunities to defend against student uprisings. The main entrance in most libraries is far more visible than employee entrances and fire exits, and should be the most heavily (and easily) defended, since a single point of entry will likely create a zombie bottleneck that will prevent a small team of defenders from being overrun.

SCENARIO 1

Clearly, in terms of ability to communicate and provide services, retaining internet access, with or without phone or fax, is the best possible scenario, and is the most likely if the "impulsive eradication" option for fighting zombies is used. Institutions have the option of either shutting down the library and sending all staff to their respective homes, where they can provide services from mobile devices or home computers, or placing the library in lockdown, keeping those already in the building within the library. We prefer the lockdown option; sending people home makes personal safety and continuity of library services more vulnerable. In either case, the bulk of frontline library information services (reference questions, interlibrary loans) can continue to be provided remotely, through telephone and fax if available, in addition to texting, chat software, email, blogs, collaborative and social networking software, and use of the library's website and databases. Staff who acquire and catalogue materials (particularly electronically) can make just-in-time additions to the catalogue and library databases as information continues to flow from state and national agencies, as well as campus response units, in response to the emergency.

Since misinformation in an emergency is particularly rampant, it behooves libraries to combat bad information with good information. Libraries should post emergency response websites as soon as possible, gathering relevant links for users that include reliable information from the Red Cross, the Centers for Disease Control and other national agencies. Consistent linking to reliable websites by libraries across the country will raise their relevance rankings so that they come up at the top of Google searches, beating out unreliable websites.

SCENARIO 2

In this scenario, information sharing between libraries and their users (or other libraries) can happen only if staff are physically present in the library buildings. Access to library resources in a situation where internet access is deeply unreliable forces us to rely on our phones and fax machines (think Katherine Hepburn in *Desk Set,* but with terrorizing zombies and access to a fax machine). Reference and interlibrary loan requests can be filled relatively easily through teamwork. Knowledge of how materials within the library are organized and indexed will allow librarians to locate information quickly even without access to the online catalogue. Required materials can be accessed in paper copies, photocopied and faxed, or even read aloud over the phone if necessary. At this stage, paper copies of journals, indexes and reference books, as well as government documents, will be central to the provision of services. Librarians who specialize in these areas should cross-train colleagues in preparation for the zombie apocalypse.

SCENARIO 3

This is the worst-case scenario, likely due to a massive zombie infestation in central technical control areas, such as the National Security Administration or the headquarters and server farms of major telecommunications and web companies (Verizon, Comcast, Google, etc.), coupled with destruction of or disconnection from satellites controlled by those entities. Assuming that television and national radio are no longer broadcasting, short-wave, HAM and CB radios might be reasonably viable methods of communication. Frankly, the likelihood of many reference questions at this point is slim, so libraries should emphasize survival of staff as well as document the fall of civilization as thoroughly as possible.

AFTERMATH: WIN (OR LOSE)

Academic libraries are in a unique position to help rebuild society after the zombie menace has been defeated. Technical specifications for rebuilding vital infrastructure, documentation of destroyed architecture and geographical information for the optimal placement of new structures are all housed in academic libraries. The ability to reconstruct destroyed buildings is predicated on the ability to maintain and service machinery used to do so; academic libraries often house the necessary technical and engineering specifications. Theses and dissertations on green technologies might lead to leaps forward in infrastructure sustainability.

Community members will also need access to academic libraries to begin rebuilding their lives and campus culture. The library, often a focal point on university campuses, can function as a *de facto* heart of the university as campus groups from different disciplines work together to rebuild what was lost. Documentation in the university's archives of local culture and campus traditions can lead to revivals of traditions that otherwise would be destroyed. Social services and psychological help can be provided through the library as a distribution point for referrals. Academic libraries also house resources for psychological and social work professionals who need to retrain outside their original areas of expertise to provide services to the local community after a disaster.

If society is to leverage hard-won knowledge for the next zombie apocalypse, then it needs to know how the current infestation was beaten (or not). Academic libraries are where that documentation will be. Librarians not only collect just-in-time information from the CDC and the NIH to distribute to the community, but they also hold on to it, create a record of it, organize it to be found again, and make sure that the pattern of actions taken can be reconstructed, learned from and critiqued. Academic libraries will document the whole academic zombie experience as part of their mission. If society does not survive the zombie apocalypse, then academic libraries will have documented the downfall of civilization for future discovery and reconstruction.

However, our money is on survival of the human race by leveraging academic library resources and personnel in the fight. After all, the best way to fight zombies is to leverage what academic libraries have and zombies lack: information and the ability to use it.

REFERENCES

American Library Association. 2008. Code of Ethics. http://www.ala.org/ala/aboutala/offices/oif/statementspols/codeofethics/codeethics.cfm.

Featherstone, R.M., B.J. Lyon and A.B. Ruffin. 2008. "Library Roles in Disaster Response: An Oral History Project by the National Library of Medicine." *Journal of the Medical Library Association* 96, 4: 343–50.

Ferguson, A.W. 2003. "Back Talk—Does Your Library Preparedness Plan Have a Section on Epidemics?" *Against the Grain* 15, 3: 109–10.

Joint Committee on Library Research. 1940. *Guide to Library Facilities for National Defense.* Preliminary ed. Edited by C. Cannon. Chicago: American Library Association.

Lacy, D. 1953. "War Measures: Past and Future." *Library Quarterly* 23, 3: 238–51.

Munz, P., I. Hudea, J. Imad and R.J. Smith? 2009. "When Zombies Attack! Mathematical Modelling of an Outbreak of Zombie Infection." In *Infectious Disease Modelling Research Progress*, edited by J.M. Tchuenche and C. Chiyaka, 133–50. Hauppauge, NY: Nova Science Publishers.

New York Academy of Medicine Library. [2009]. *What Is Grey Literature?* http://www.nyam.org/library/online-resources/grey-literature-report/what-is-grey-literature.html.

Quinlan, N.J. 2007. "In Flew Enza: What We Can Learn from the Way American Libraries Responded to the 1918 Influenza Pandemic." *American Libraries* 38, 11: 50–53.

Robertson, G. 2006. "Pandemic Perspective: How an Outbreak Could Affect Libraries." *Feliciter* 3: 111–13.

Souers, K.L. 2004. "The Library and the Community It Serves in Times of War: Everything Old Is New Again." *Florida Libraries* 47, 2: 16–19.

ZOMBIES ON BROADWAY

ANTHONY WILSON

The entire history of humanity is littered with the results of the two instinctive reactions any individual takes to any change in his or her situation: fight or flight. Survival by violence or survival by discretion as the better part of valour. By the beginning of the twenty-first century, Western civilization as a whole had re-created these responses at a societal level. To any major change or threat, Westernized humanity now had two reactions: we destroy it, or we make it famous. Or both, in either order.

We can see this in many of the pivotal events of the early part of the century. Within two or three years of the destruction of the World Trade Center in New York, two nations were being destroyed by disproportionate force given their original involvement, and films were made so that the populace could munch on popcorn while sharing the vicarious thrill of being a firefighter on the forty-ninth floor. Alternatively, one could consider the fall of the vampire movie by 2014 with the advent of the fourth *Twilight* film. After nearly a century of entertainment, this movie was so irredeemably hated by everyone that the entire genre came to the point of collapse.

Indeed, again and again throughout recent history, the combination of idolizing and then subsequently or simultaneously destroying rears its head, but in few places has the combination been so starkly drawn and vivid as in the zombie crisis of the past twenty-five years.

Indeed, a quarter of a century further down the line, it is difficult to put ourselves into the mindsets of those who were there when it began. It is almost laughable, given what came later, that, upon discovery of the first cases of zombification, the general reaction of the press and the governments of the world was a kind of amused cynicism: zombies were entertainment, so far as everyone knew, and the "real" kind—for those who even believed that it was anything more than a publicity stunt to start with—were treated as entertainment even then. As we all know—and as many learned to their cost—it quickly became far less funny.

We're not here to dwell on the decisions made and the extreme and arguably knee-jerk reactions taken by some of the governments of the day. We are certainly familiar enough with those stories; everyone has a story to tell and, of course, what remains of Pittsburgh will forever be a reminder that, when the chips are down, humanity's most obvious principle is to hit the problem with large bombs until it goes away.

Of course, we were saved by the stratagem of inoculation, and the world was saved by scientists. The team of geneticists, viral biologists and mathematicians who led this research were, of course, famous for their allotted fifteen minutes but, being scientists, were swiftly forgotten. Very few in the general public, even now at this slim distance, can name all four— Vanderdeken, Vaughan, Chen and Smith? (yes, even with the trademark question mark in her name)—and in this they are not dissimilar to J. Robert Oppenheimer, whom very few people can name as the inventor of the nuclear bomb.

Having avoided extinction—or, at the least, total zombie conversion—humanity now had a major shake-up, perhaps the most dramatic and drastic since the extinction of the Neanderthals, and we treated it as perhaps we should have come to expect. The initial panic reaction gradually subsided and, although we had stood on the brink, the general consensus was that it probably couldn't have been as bad as everyone said it was going to be, for the simple reason that we had all survived. There was even a reaction suggesting that total zombification had been the scaremongering of scientists, and possibly zombieism itself had even been designed by them to make money for themselves. There are, of course, conspiracy theorists everywhere.

But the success of the containment of zombieism, and the absolute halting of the spread of the disease through both the inoculation stratagem and a massive—and very expensive—series of awareness campaigns, unfortunately did nothing for those who had succumbed already. Although we are able to suppress their urge to kill, scientists were then, and continue to be, unable to find a method of reversing the process of zombification. So, instantly and spectacularly, humanity was presented with an ethical dilemma, as people whom once we knew as living, breathing beings, entirely on an equal footing to us, suddenly became, to all intents and purposes, human-shaped vegetables.

It was hardly a new situation. Since the advances in medical science in the latter half of the twentieth century that allowed a body to continue when the mind had gone, families, parents and partners had gone through the agony of deciding what to do with their child/parent/spouse who had been involved in a horrendous accident. Behind this vacant shell on a bed, wired up and bleeping through machines, that awful sucking sound as oxygen is forced into the lungs, lay memories of someone who walked, talked, laughed and filled our memories. The same with the families of those who suffered from Alzheimer's, or Parkinson's, or Huntington's. How do you help the woman who bore you and raised you, but now can't even recognize your face?

But never before had such a problem been encountered on such an all-encompassing scale. Nowadays, it is shocking to think that almost all world governments gave permission, even though the zombies were no longer infectious or determined to kill, for families to allow the termination of infected relatives. It is a testament, perhaps, to humanity's capacity to hope—and this in spite of the debates about euthanasia of the elderly and terminally ill that had been going on worldwide around that time—that almost no terminations were reported. Defying official expectation, this created a new problem. The governments of the world had assumed that soon there would be pyres of zombie flesh everywhere, but no one wanted that, and to go ahead with it anyway would fly suicidally in the face of public opinion. But it was obvious that there was no way that the zombies could be kept in any central facility; there were simply too many of them. Given that they were now safe, and that the disease would spread no further, there was simply only one thing to do: the zombies were sent home.

What followed surprised most people. Against all expectations, within weeks of returning home, reports began to come in that the zombies were making an improvement. The medical and scientific worlds were initially cynical, but, once they saw the evidence, it was difficult to refute it. What surprised everyone was that zombies began to respond to stimuli: in simple ball games, they made the effort to catch the ball and bring it back; they recognized certain rituals, such as going to bed (even though they don't sleep) and sitting down as a family to watch TV. They even watched *Desperate Housewives* and appeared to understand something of what was happening, although it was not always easy to question them on Bree's motives afterward.

And one girl, Tracey, even reported that her older sister, Helena, who had learned ballet as a young teenager, was now starting to copy her tap dance moves when Tracey was practising at home.

There was a huge amount of disagreement in the scientific world. There was simply no way to test whether the reactions of the zombies in the home were a result of direct, deliberate decision-making in the brain—self-initiated activity—or a kind of mimicry or auto-suggestion, like Pavlov's dog. Even an EEG scan didn't help as one of the side-effects of zombieism appeared to be that the brain generated a consistent and all-encompassing electrical charge that masked which part of the brain, if any, an impulse came from.

What the scientific community thought, of course, didn't matter a whit. Whether these zombies were Pavlovian or Descartian, the families and loved ones quickly claimed that they could see flashes of the old personalities coming back. Even though the zombies were always amenable to suggestion and did anything somebody wanted them to do on cue, those close to them were certain that it really was Kelly, or Bruce, or Amjad, or Miley in there. Indeed, some of the parents of teenagers who had been zombified actually expressed a preference for the zombie versions, stating that their behaviour had dramatically improved and that the family was much happier now. The same was true of absent fathers, who were now always at home. For a minority, albeit a small one, this loss of willpower was almost seen as a boon.

And because families were starting to see their loved ones still deep beneath their zombie facades, the public perception began to twist toward the idea that this was a massive human tragedy. Which, of course, it was. And the best way humanity deals with a tragedy is to televise it, tug at the public heartstrings, and raise some money. Barack Obama believed that zombies should be able to "take their place in this great concept we call human society," and the way to achieve that, it turned out, was with ZombieAid.

Despite the lack of imagination inherent in the name, ZombieAid was both a truly international event and a resounding success. Cheryl Cole, whose husband was one of the first to be infected, brought literally hundreds of pop stars, some of them famous, to rerecord her best-selling single "Fight For This Love" as a charity fundraiser, while concerts by other well-meaning celebrities, comedy shows, and other such live and faux-live performances raised millions toward giving zombies the chance to have a better life, even though it wasn't entirely clear how money was necessarily going to help creatures that had no desires and practically no needs.

Tracey, of course, appeared on ZombieAid. Worldwide, this smiling twelve-year-old girl hugged her lumbering, shambling older sister, she declared her deep and undying love for her, and together they demonstrated a few dance moves that Helena had learned by watching. Their mother, dabbing tears from her eyes, declared to the world that she was so proud of both of her daughters; their father announced that he would do everything in his power to help her and that he was already planning a sponsored hike in the Himalayas because that would earn lots of money for her, and besides, he'd always wanted to go there. The two-minute segment ended with Tracey smiling at the camera and Helena sitting next to her, gazing into space and reminding the more cynical among the audience of the eponymous Bigfoot in *Bigfoot and the Hendersons*.

It was widely believed that Tracey's smiling face added fifteen percent to the total amount raised on the night of ZombieAid, while Helena became the unlikely pin-up girl for Zombie-kind everywhere.

When thinking about how zombies could "take their place in a functioning society," it was to Helena and her dance moves that the general consensus of popular thought kept returning. Because dance is a sequence of repetitive moves, albeit very complex at a professional level, and because zombies, it turned out, were able to learn very complex sequences of repetitive moves, the two were suddenly entwined in the public perception as closely as the names Torville and Dean or Jekyll and Hyde.

It turned out that this was exactly the right thing to do. Although there were a few false starts, and some zombies took to dance more readily than others (although, strangely, there was no correlation between those who had been good at dance before zombification and those who were good afterward), many zombies turned out to be passingly good at picking up a routine and staying in rhythm.

The first semi-professional zombie dance troupe appeared on BBC children's TV flagship current affairs program *Blue Peter*. In many ways, it was the first fundamental breaking down of barriers between zombie and mainstream humankind, as the dance troupe—called Not Lying Down—performed to a high level and in a modern style. Their choreographer, who had formerly worked with Michael Jackson, was nearly in tears at the end of the performance. He said—and he clearly believed it fervently—that his zombie charges had raised their game for the live performance. That, if nothing else, he said, clearly proved that zombies understood what was happening to them and the context of their actions. Obviously, no one could have been certain whether or not he was right, but more and more people were convinced.

It was at this point that Simon Cowell got involved.

Cowell was known the world over for the type of reality show that allegedly brought talented but ordinary people into the public eye. Along the way, such programs garnered huge audiences—notably by showcasing the frightening number of people who much-mistakenly believed they were talented—and, almost incidentally, garnered Cowell huge quantities of money. The new show, *Zombies Got Talent* (Cowell eschewed the grammatically correct alternative), was immediately slammed by the usual suspects as being in very poor taste and a prurient way of entertaining the paying masses at the expense of those who are less fortunate and those who are incapable of defending themselves. This was totally true, of course, but—and this will surprise none of us—the show was a resounding success. Every effort was made to make it seem as humane as possible. All of the zombies who were paraded in front of the paying public were supported by members of their families and their former friends, and the acts were, surprisingly once again, of genuinely high quality. The zombies had certainly proven themselves to be more than capable of learning the routines, and some had reached levels of speed and delicacy of which many "normals" would be and were quite envious.

It was also Cowell, almost accidentally, who brought in this new terminology. Suddenly, the human race was neatly divided into zombies and "normals." Since he was using the word *normal* in a derogatory way, and praising the zombies on screen, no one really spotted that, as it entered the lexicon, it was dividing the species by value judgment. It is an insidious term that has been impossible to stamp out, one that leaves the absolute implication of "abnormality" as a negative, no matter how nicely it was initially couched. We have Cowell to blame, or to thank, for that as well.

After the initial outcry over zombie rights, the show settled down. Some commentators began to speculate that, in many ways, *Zombies Got Talent* was kinder than its "normal" counterpart since the zombies didn't really understand the nature of the disappointment—only their families understood it—so the crushing destruction of self-confidence, for which Cowell's previous shows had been infamous, was no longer an issue. Others, perhaps harsher, pointed out that, since there was no satisfaction for the zombies involved in actually winning, the whole style of entertainment was more akin to a dog show than a reality talent show.

The top prize for *Zombies Got Talent* was full training and a week in the chorus of the West End production of *Fame!* Since zombies didn't breathe beyond their need to produce grunting noises when hunting (which seems evolutionarily odd in many ways), as singers they couldn't be remarkably good, but as dancers they were, and it was no longer a surprise. The winner of the first series, a slender zombie formerly known as Daniel, surprised many not just by performing expertly in his weeks' run on stage (the best attended of the entire show, it turned out), but also by being promptly hired as a full-time dancer immediately thereafter. In fact, given that zombies had the additional advantages that they didn't throw temper tantrums and didn't get sick, many of the final ten contenders in the show were soon snapped up by *Fame!* or other West End dance-based shows.

And that opened the floodgates. It soon became obvious what a boon zombies were to everyone when it came to performance. Not only were they not prone to actually having personalities, often a disadvantage in chorus work on stage, but also their exactitude in performance—simply because the only way they could learn was by precise rote—was often more impressive than that of the "normals." And they wouldn't get bored after a six-month run, didn't have "issues" with their girlfriends or boyfriends that resulted in sub-par performances, and didn't get ill. Above and beyond all other considerations, of course, they simply cost less. As a result, and possibly to reduce a groundswell of negativity when zombies became a regular part of theatregoers' lives, ticket prices, which had been exorbitantly and often prohibitively expensive, came down. About six months after Daniel had first trodden the boards, most West End and many Broadway shows had at least one, and often many more, zombies as part of the chorus, initially at cheaper rates than before the zombie invasion, and somehow everyone was happy with that. The ticket prices soon went back up, but people felt better than might have been expected, and the main reason given was the introduction of the Zombie Performers' Benevolent Fund surcharge, which provided money for the families of the zombies to help look after them, at least at first.

Before the arrival of zombies, it had been an open secret that professional shows employed two types of performers for the cast: singers who could kind of dance and dancers who could kind of sing. Anyone attending any professional show could see that one group of the chorus were put at the back, given simple moves to do and belted their hearts out on ramped-up microphones, while another group were placed at the front of the stage, given far more complex moves and sang into microphones that were barely switched on. Of course, with the advent of zombies, you could go the whole hog. The zombies were taught to mouth the lyrics, even though they couldn't sing, while a group of professional singers were put backstage on microphones and no longer had to pretend to dance. The lead actors continued to be "normal," and the whole thing came together like a dream. It was artifice, of course, but then so much of theatre always has been, so audiences bought into it.

And still the bubble refused to burst. It was the dream of a lifetime (for Tracey at least) when she took the role of Christine in *The Phantom of the Opera* and her sister danced in it. In the famous sequence when Christine looks into the mirror and her reflection moves independently of her, it was, naturally, Helena who played the reflection. There wasn't one performance where the sisters failed to get a standing ovation, even though everyone agreed that, actually, Tracey's voice wasn't the best there had ever been by a long way and that, in fact, Helena reacted with as much love toward Tracey's understudy (who was much more vocally talented) as she did toward her own sister. It was, in fact, fairly widely acknowledged that Tracey would never have been successful had her older sister not been a famous face with a difficult background. Comparisons were drawn to winners of other reality TV shows who had their entire fame resting on their emotional insecurity, an illness or, in a fascinating piece of circular logic, an inability to deal with the fact of their fame.

Just as not every talented "normal" dancer or singer can or will end up on the professional stage, so too with zombies. Unfortunately, while there are other options for the fully human dancers among us—teaching, choreography, dance criticism, physiotherapy, *et cetera*, not to mention a full career change— practically all those options require a certain amount of creativity and original thought, the very things the zombie part of the population so conspicuously lacked. This left them with only the activities that people in the past would turn to if they were desperate.

Not so long ago, in developing countries, where poverty was not simply a statistic but a terrifyingly real way of life, people would take any job, quite simply do anything, to provide for their families. These jobs, often under horrendous conditions and with minimal rest, now became the preserve of the zombified part of the population. Instead of working sixteen-hour days to sew blouses and shirts that would be exported to the Western world at a several thousand percentage markup, families in some places now sold off their zombie children to large corporations for a tiny percentage of the profit from what they had created. Even in what would have been utterly inhuman working conditions—twenty-four-hour working days with practically no light—it was difficult to get people to become outraged over this. It had become even cheaper to create the clothes, and that was a priority. And—so the tract went—it was repetitive work, and zombies liked repetitive work, and it was their families' faults because they had sold them in the first place. And if the working conditions were inhuman, well, it was laughed, that hardly mattered.

News of some parents in the poorer nations of the world withholding the booster inoculations from their younger children, to allow zombies to infect them so that they too could be sold, resulted in zombie charities appearing in earnest. The Zombie Liberation Front ("zombies are people too!") and the Christian-based Human-Zombie Alliance ("God made human and zombie alike") were at the more liberal end of the spectrum, trying to raise awareness but finding, against all probability, that they had come too late. ZombieAid had made everyone mentally tick the "I have helped zombies" box in their heads, while zombies such as Helena and Daniel, and all the others in the visible world of performance, had lulled people into the sense that zombies were doing okay. And no amount of shock tactics or true information seemed to shock the vast majority of the world out of their complacency.

Even the news of zombie prostitution failed to shock people. It was the ideal situation, of course, for the kind of people who enjoy making money at the expense of others. Practically all sexually transmitted diseases, and certainly the serious ones, require both bloodflow and a homeostatic temperature level in the body to survive. Zombies had neither, their body temperature being several degrees lower than that of a "normal" human; assuming you were inoculated—and, if not, that was entirely your fault—there was no fear of transmission of disease. With no need for condoms, this was simply the safest and most efficient way to get sex. Although it took a long time to become public knowledge, this had been happening almost from the moment that the inoculation stratagem had proven effective. Zombies couldn't complain, they could be trained to react in appropriate ways, and their bodies could be warmed to a level that people found comfortable. It was quickly possible to fly to any number of islands as a zombie sex tourist. Zombie children as young as nine years old, both boys and girls, were purchased from desperate families who had no real understanding of what was happening. There was no proof that zombies were aging (we now know that they do, but much more slowly), so these abused children would be children for a long time to come.

And still the Western world seemed not to care; they were only zombies, not "normals," after all. Zombies were so much a part of our lives, so widespread and so instinctively accepted by now, that, barring the occasional angry editorial in a newspaper, what should have been considered atrocious quickly became old news. Perhaps the most damning indictment of all came in the defence, uttered often and seemingly without irony, that the world hadn't been that much different before the zombie virus struck.

Of course, the biggest problem was that these stories were impersonal. The numbers of zombies working in sweatshops (not that zombies sweat) and the numbers of zombie sex workers were just that: numbers, statistics. People didn't have faces and names to latch on to, and, to make something famous, a face and a name are necessary. But even they might not be enough.

Tracey and Helena worked well together for a few years, appearing in a variety of shows, and eventually starring in one that was, literally, written for them. Called *Another Life,* it told the world's first "real-life" zombie love story, even though everyone knew that zombies didn't fall in love, not really. Three weeks into the run, Tracey, whose lifestyle had been squeaky-clean up to that point, was found dead in a stranger's bathtub, with positively scary amounts of cocaine running through her system. To this day, no one is certain whether or not it was an accident or deliberate suicide, though conspiracy theorists note that Helena was getting much more applause and kudos in *Another Life* than Tracey was receiving.

You might like to hope that Helena showed some reaction when told about Tracey's death, but you would be disappointed. Helena spent the rest of the day as she normally did, sitting and staring into nothing, perhaps lost in a place that no one else could get to, perhaps just literally switched off. That evening she performed as normal and seemed not to register that it wasn't Tracey whom she was playing opposite. When people cannot communicate, not with words, not with looks, not with body language (unless they are trained to mimic it), it remains impossible to gauge even vaguely what they are thinking. The mood off stage that night was palpably tense, but, looking at the zombies performing, everything seemed to be perfectly normal.

Six weeks later Helena disappeared. No one knows why. It remains possible that she was taken home by her parents, though they always denied it, but, if so, perhaps they had tired of people watching their daughter as if she were a performing monkey. Helena might have been kidnapped and put to work doing unspeakable things, with no one except her patrons ever finding out (though one imagines, with that sort of person, they were proud of this particular notch on the bedpost, her being famous and all). It is unlikely, but not impossible, that she is working making clothes for affluent teenagers in the United Kingdom. She might simply have forgotten what she was doing and wandered off.

In the wake of her disappearance, there was a massive manhunt, fuelled by publicity and carried by the internet. Many people claimed to have seen Helena, in places as varied as Aberdeen and Alice Springs, Wyoming and Zanzibar, but there has never been any positive identification. Helena was never seen again.

Nowadays, all these years later, Helena is simply a curiosity, a might-have-been, a myth as strong and as elusive as Elvis. No one is able to comment accurately on where she is and what she is thinking. But then no one was ever able to do that.

Perhaps Helena was tired of being used, of other people getting paid for what she was doing. Perhaps she simply couldn't cope with the celebrity lifestyle any more than her sister—perhaps—had been able to. Or, in the end, she might just have been trying to do something different and find another life, perhaps to get over her pining for a sister whom she had lost so many years ago, and—in the same way as Tracey—never quite got back again.

RECLAIMING PUBLIC SPACES THROUGH PERFORMANCE OF THE ZOMBIE WALK

SASHA COCARLA

With the stench of rotting flesh, the guttural, animalistic groans and the haunting noise of their dragging limbs, zombies have managed to remain a frightful mythical monster in popular culture. Zombies are bodies without emotions, acting on primal instincts alone. They speak to everything that we as humans are not supposed to be. Their predisposition toward brains, flesh, blood and gore creates an uncomfortable fascination for horror fans. However, I would argue that the popularity of zombies in North America is also largely attributable to the fact that their very existence counters many dominant norms that circulate within our society, specifically calling us to question ideas surrounding beautiful bodies, life and death, structured spaces, and mass consumption.

In a capitalist economy fuelled by the pathological need for continual growth, it becomes clear that the zombie of modern film and television often acts as a stand-in for the true cultural dupes of mass consumption: us (Dendle 2007, 51). They also symbolize apocalyptic events, when humans and all their daily spaces and practices are slowly taken over by the undead:

animated corpses. In popular zombie films, the undead are almost always portrayed in public spaces, walking—or dragging—themselves from place to place, consuming in the most literal of ways (i.e., eating human flesh). As they move slowly through public spaces, invoking fear in the humans around them, they take on a familiar appearance: us, just going through the motions. The commentary here is clear: we, too, can be zombies, even if our hearts are still beating.

The popularity of zombies is found not only in the abundance of zombie films created over the years (*Night of the Living Dead, Army of Darkness, 28 Days Later* and *Shaun of the Dead,* to name but a few), but also in the ways that zombies have infiltrated our daily lives. The flesh and gore associated with zombies have managed to creep their way into nearly every facet of popular culture—works of fiction and comic books (*The Zombie Survival Guide, Pride and Prejudice and Zombies, The Walking Dead, Blackest Night*); video games (*Left 4 Dead, Resident Evil, Dead Rising*); board games (Zombies!!!, Last Night on Earth); music ("Walk like a Zombie" by the HorrorPops, Rob Zombie, Zombie Girl); and even zombie pinups and porn (ZombiePinups.com, *Porn of the Dead*). One of the most interesting examples of zombies in everyday culture is the zombie walk, in which mass groups of the "living dead" congregate in large cities all over North America and Western Europe, and march in the streets. This is a relatively recent phenomenon, with the first documented, non-commercial zombie walk taking place in Toronto, Ontario, in 2003 (Dalgetty 2007). These walks are comprised of individuals, primarily teenagers and young adults, dressed and made up as zombies, walking, shuffling and dragging themselves slowly through urban spaces. As the zombies shuffle and drag themselves along, they cause a spectacle: they halt traffic, stop pedestrians from shopping "normally," disturb onlookers and raise questions. Because our urban spaces are highly ordered and regulated places, the purposeful disruption of the zombie walk—the performance of the living dead in public areas—affords the opportunity to reclaim urban spaces and disrupt dominant ideologies, even if only momentarily.

Very few monsters have managed to embed themselves within the popular imagination as successfully as zombies.

Although most monsters originate in folklore, then move to literature and finally enter mainstream cinema, the zombie is one of the few monsters that has moved directly from folklore to the popular imagination (McIntosh 2008, 2). McIntosh notes that our fascination with zombies seems to trace back to Haitian folklore via the ethnographies of ethnobiologist Wade Davis. According to his reports, there are two types of literal zombies: the spirit zombies (*zombie jardin*) and the type that has made its way into popular culture: the body raised from the dead (*zombie corps cadavre*) (2). The zombies—or victims—are put into a near-death state by means of a poisonous mixture made in part from the toxins of a blowfish and then later revived through the use of another mixture (3). Through this process, the victims end up losing many of their mental faculties, functioning at a much slower pace than normal, allowing them to be easily controlled by the individual who poisoned them.

Although such descriptions can be found in a few travelogues dating back to the late eighteenth century, it was not until the US military occupation of Haiti from 1915 to 1934 that Haitian folklore began to make its way out of Haiti and into American news reports and cultural imaginaries (McIntosh 2008, 4). As with many cultural exports, accuracy was not of most importance in disseminating this new information. Instead, a sensationalized and magical image of Haitian voodoo began to be promoted. It was specifically the image of a slow-moving individual in a trance-like state that became the model for the horror monsters we see today.

Entering the scene in 1932, with Kenneth Webb's stage production of *Zombie,* and later that year with the first zombie film, *White Zombie* (Halperin brothers), the majority of the content of these films dealt with female possession for men's sexual pleasure and/or black-white racial issues (McIntosh 2008, 5). The zombies in these films generally stayed the same, with only a simple change of scenery to suit the era's political climate. For the most part, they were simply slow versions of humans, with less tidy clothing. McIntosh notes that this all changed— and would forever change the face of zombie films thereafter— with George A. Romero's 1968 *Night of the Living Dead* (8). Both that film and Romero's following two films, *Dawn of the Dead* and *Day of the Dead,* deal with issues pertinent to North American culture. They provide a visual commentary for the horrific aspects of our culture that we normally do not question.

Night of the Living Dead predominantly takes place in a family's farmhouse and depicts the characters fighting for their lives against a horde of zombies that threaten to infiltrate from the outside. "Much of the narrative attention," Dendle contends, "is thus devoted not to attacks or human-zombie conflicts, but to re-examining the middle-class household of heartland America" (2007, 50). The movement from urban spaces into gated communities allowed individuals to better defend their modern homes, values and ideals against the monstrous "other" that lurked outside the door. This apocalyptic sense is also evident in *Dawn of the Dead,* "a social commentary on American mass consumer society as zombies overtake survivors barricaded in a shopping mall, and *Day of the Dead,* when the world is apparently almost completely overrun by zombies and there are only a few survivors left" (McIntosh 2008, 9). Romero's films are important for the simple reason that they forever changed public perception of the zombie and allow for an intriguing, easily accessible creature that has quickly become the monster of choice for many performances.

To properly situate the zombie walk as a performance of subversion and reclamation, the construction of our current city spaces needs to be discussed. How do these spaces limit the possibility for subversion and social upheaval? Also, the zombie walk is a particular type of performance that draws heavily from the Situationist International's theory of *détournement:* the reclaiming of already existing objects/spaces/ideas found in society and then using them for alternative purposes. Finally, the performance of the undead, though tinged with political curiosity, is a site of extreme playfulness. It is within the space of performance and play that the zombie walk is able to momentarily subvert dominant social norms and replace them with the utterly grotesque.

STRUCTURED SPACES

Traditionally, city spaces have been seen as the pinnacle of modernity: spaces where industry, technology and capitalism converge. "Modernization was always economically driven by capitalism and, as Marx observed, capitalism, by its very nature, is driven by the constant need to transform and revolutionize the means of production" (Morley 1996, 52). It was within this new space of production, where prior ties found between the producer and the product became obsolete, that mass consumerism was able to emerge and flourish. The push in modern cities was to produce new objects—commodities—that allowed capitalism to grow. But simple production of products would not be sufficient in adding to the economy of the modern city. People needed to buy these things; they needed to consume the products at almost the same speed as they were being created. The reason behind the purchases did not really matter. All that truly mattered was that money was being spent.

In a space defined by its continuous chaos and constant movement toward unattainable ideals of perfection, the art of consuming then became one way for an individual to attempt to make sense of the topsy-turvy, modern world. Although our current cities might not replicate the sites of mass production that signified the modern city during the period of industrialization, they still function to produce areas that specifically promote a very modernist social reality: capitalism, individuality, consumerism, rationality and the quest for continuous progress. This space, based upon modernity but flourishing in the postmodern world, now needs to compensate for what is no longer: the city based on industry. Instead, our urban centres are created to portray all the positive aspects of the city, but without ever actually being the city. This fragmentation, play and constant struggle over creating new realities, while not becoming real (because the "real" is what is left behind in the first place), lies at the heart of postmodern thinking.

In this regard, "postmodernism" stands in to remind us that everything we take for granted as "natural" occurrences of modernity—once again, capitalism, individuality, the "rational" subject—is not natural, but a fabrication or cultural creation of our society (Hutcheon 2002, 2). For the purposes of this chapter, the zombie stands in as a postmodern figure in that it disrupts many of our notions of what a rational, modern individual looks like. At its most basic level, the zombie is not alive,

117

yet it walks, talks and consumes like a rational, human subject does. The zombie walk then becomes a postmodern act in that it is comprised of a postmodern subject (the zombie) that causes disruption in modernist spaces (shopping malls and city streets). Our postmodern spaces are not entirely dismantling the realities of our past; instead, they are realizing, verbalizing, and critiquing all that is wrong with modernity. Although the main institutions of modernity have not necessarily changed (we continue to spend and consume), the convergence of the postmodern and the modern creates a temporary, topsy-turvy upheaval in which we can question and view our surroundings in new ways.

The conflicts and contradictions previously found at the centres of modern cities can now be seen more clearly at the edges of our urban centres. In this context, space is structured in a very particular way, making our lives increasingly more organized and monitored. Space itself can come into existence only by what it is surrounded by. A key example is how the space that is our modern city exists only because of the boundaries that surround it—what separates it from suburbs and rural areas. The suburbs that mark the boundaries of our current urban spaces speak to changes in social and cultural values that often have been overlooked in the analysis of city centres (Low 2003, 387). Low notes that the major thrust of suburbanization began in the 1950s and 1960s with middle- to upper-class, white, North American families moving out of urban centres and away from densely populated and racially and ethnically diverse areas (390). The move was into a space deemed safer and more monitored than the inner city, where violent upheavals were supposedly taking place. This new space was created with the intention of keeping all the "positive" features of the modern city without bringing along the "riffraff" that seemed to be limiting progress. Within this space, people would be able to continue to work toward the rational, clean, regulated, consumer-based ideals that pervaded the modern city without having to witness the mass inequalities that resulted from fast-paced modernization.

In fact, within these new suburban environments, the average middle-class family would never have to encounter anything that would suggest an alternative to their current lifestyles. The suburban space became a defended space not only where people who were inside would be kept safe from urban horrors, but also where the key qualities of modernity would not be questioned. The fear instilled in suburban inhabitants was matched by the visual landscape of their environment (Low 2003, 403). Walls, gates and guards became the material boundaries that matched the tenants' ideological basis for the creation of suburbia. This obvious and literal boundary between the urban city and the suburban area then becomes the basis for what the urban centre must be.

Along with suburban spaces being key examples of what is and what is not an urban space—or what is and what is not allowed in such spaces—Joshua Nichols (2008) discusses the schizophrenia that our modern city is created from by primarily removing all that is unwanted. If our modern city (and subsequently suburbia) are based upon all that is rational, then the only way to ensure its stability is to expel all that is deemed irrational. In such modern spaces, "the author as architect constructs this ideal city by selectively amplifying particular social structures that he or she views as essential and eliminating or at the very least containing the structures and elements that he or she deems inessential or irrational" (460). The qualities deemed abject are removed to the outer sides of the city, thereby making the city itself unimaginable without the abject. It is schizophrenic because the city cannot come into existence without recognizing the very qualities it wishes to disregard.

One such site of wretchedness is the cemetery, built upon our very desire to avoid death—the most dismal quality of being human. Nichols draws the reader's attention to the tensions that surface as a result of having such spaces (e.g., the cemetery) structure our entire existence within the city. He argues that, while the boundaries of the cemetery are clearly demarcated, it is not as clearly contained as we would like to believe (2008, 468). Although it might be relatively out of sight, the sign of the grave (along with its constant reminder of impending death, pathogenic diseases and rotting corpses) cannot be removed from our minds.

SITUATIONIST INTERNATIONAL
One of the most prevalent qualities of modernity still permeat-

ing our current city spaces is the constant regulation that we and our spaces must subscribe to. Within these spaces, everything is monitored to the point where even play and leisure—commonly believed to be based upon "freedom"—are strictly scrutinized and specifically defined. In urban spaces that have immense diversity (through both the populations and their actions), social boundaries can be disregarded and transgressed (Stevens 2007, 16). By recognizing the conventions that exist, one is periodically able to undo the tight regulations that regularly uphold the urban city and loosen the space to allow for subversion.

Although for the most part our cities strictly define what is and what is not acceptable for us to be or do, at times people pursue activities that were not originally intended for specific spaces. It is not the space or the activity that necessarily makes a moment more open, however. "For a site to become loose, people themselves must recognize the possibilities inherent in it and make use of those possibilities for their own ends, facing the potential risks of doing so" (Franck and Stevens 2007, 2). By recognizing the potential for play, the actors—or "zombies"—are able to self-express and entertain themselves and others temporarily in a changed space removed from the rigidity that normally comprises the city. As Franck and Stevens indicate, the outcomes of these events are numerous; they can create fear in those around them since they seem unfamiliar and disruptive, or they can be regarded as regular occurrences (3). Above all, however, the activities within these spaces, performed by key individuals, can completely subvert (if only momentarily) the dominant ideologies upon which our modern city is based.

If there is potential for movement and freedom within these "loose" spaces, how does one go about finding or creating it when our current conditions speak to the opposite? The Situationist International was one group that championed creative subversive actions in order to reclaim our cities. "The Situationist International (SI) was established in 1957 and published twelve issues of a journal, *Internationale Situationniste,* until 1969" (Plant 1992, 1). Although tied specifically to the political and artistic happenings during that time (including Dadaism,

Surrealism and the political upheavals of the 1960s), many key sɪ ideas can still be found in the reclaiming-of-space performances done today (including the zombie walk).

Drawing heavily from Karl Marx, the Situationists viewed our modern capitalist society as an accumulation of spectacles (Plant 1992, 1). To draw capital into the economy, people needed to consume, and the reasons for their consumption were of little or no importance. The alienation evident between the producer and the object being produced, as well as that between the consumer and the object being consumed, soon found its way into every facet of our lives: our experiences, emotions, creativities and desires. In this respect, Plant suggests, citizens of these cities became spectators of their own lives, viewing everything from the outside and experiencing their lives once-removed (1). Under the guise of a plethora of choices, happiness was considered to be found only through the acts of consumerism and consumption. Within this space of fabricated freedoms and choices, we no longer question the spectacle that we are in because we have become the spectacle itself. This space "induces passivity rather than action, contemplation rather than thinking, and a degradation of life into materialism" (Marcus 2002, 8).

From the viewpoint that subversion can occur only through that which is to be subverted, the main basis for the sɪ theory was that the ingredients for a new society would be found within the spectacle itself (Plant 1992, 31). The main goal of this movement was to create *situations* in everyday spaces that would momentarily destabilize the modernist assumptions we took for granted or read as "natural." Instead of having performances occur only in theatre settings, the Situationists sought to disrupt the familiar in spaces that were read as "comfortable" (Raunig 2007, 173). Emphasis was on causing spectacle in intentional and artificial ways, and spectacle depended on interaction between the "actors" and the "observers." In such spaces, for the status quo to be flipped, there needed to be interaction with the audience watching. As will become more evident below, by having bystanders interact in the zombie walk (even if through the simple act of turning away in fear of the zombie horde), the audience is implicated in the spectacle and there is the momentary potential to call "natural" beliefs into question. It was believed that, through recognizing the false freedoms we supposedly have and utilizing all the components that create our modern spectacle in creative and imaginative ways, a new society can emerge that will replace the inequalities modernity imposed on us.

Given that the SI movement was both an artistic movement and a theoretical critique of the constructedness of everyday life, it seemed only fitting that the means through which subversion could occur would be through creative attempts induced with political commentary. One such act was the *dérive,* where people would experience their cities in ways that had previously been obsolete or at least made to appear as such. To *dérive* is to walk about a city with the only goal being to use and recognize that space in a new way, picking up on the moods and nuances evident within it. We are so preoccupied with getting from point A to point B in our everyday lives that we fail to experience the city as it exists, and instead we live it as we are told to: sticking specifically to the pre-established paths, streets and buildings that outline the areas we can and cannot walk. The Situationists would map out the city's substructure, and shift in and out of public spaces, all the while documenting odours and tonalities that created a particular cityscape (Marrifield 2005, 31). The ultimate goal was to reacquaint inhabitants with their city, filling in the gaps that left them detached from their lived environments. By uniting the city with its inhabitants, Marrifield argues, the Situationists wanted to create a site that was ultimately disruptive to the mechanized motions of this urban space (48). However, the process had to be playful to remove itself from the serious rationality that lingered over the city.

The second SI concept that speaks to the playful tactics involved in the subversion of space is the use of *détournement.* This is a way to reclaim the lost meanings of many objects, acts and institutions that fill our cities' spaces. It is a process of almost flipping around the original intentions of a given artifact to uncover its truthful, invisible meanings. It is plagiaristic because the materials used are those that already appear and have a purpose within our cities and within the spectacle (Plant

1992, 86). It is subversive because we use creative means to un-do the original intentions that these objects had and, by exten-sion, reclaim the objects and utilize them for our own purposes in dismantling the capitalist city. Through *détournement,* one can "force people to think and rethink what they once thought; often [one would] not know whether to laugh or cry. Either way, *détournement* couldn't be ignored: it was an instrument of propaganda, an arousal or indignation, action that stimulated more action" (Merrifield 2005, 50).

The Situationists' use of *détournement* has been the prima-ry influence on many current subversive acts. Specifically, the act of "culture jamming" heavily evokes the spirit of using al-ready existing objects in society to point out their hidden (and sometimes not-so-hidden) capitalist ideologies. The very act of culture jamming is subversive. "It is about playing with fa-miliar forms of communication and interaction (posters, bill-boards, official language, protocol, spaces) and imagery (logos, ad spreads, official documents) and turning them back against the culture that created them" (Liacas 2005, 62). If our culture is made up of signs, and if capitalist intentions are delivered through these signs, then it only seems fitting that subversion occurs through the reclamation, destruction and re-creation of these signs. However, Tom Liacas brings up important ques-tions that modern culture jammers face and that the Situation-ists did not seem to tackle. "Can something that grows out of the mainstream possibly serve to change it?" (65). Although the Situationists argued for the importance of using the items of the spectacle to dismantle the spectacle itself, these subver-sive acts can get caught up within the momentum of capitalism needed to claim (and then sell) everything.

Within the growing trend of culture jamming, there appears to be two outcomes: either the growth in popularity will result in a complete upheaval of our current culture, dismantling the dominant powers in the process, or culture jamming and oth-er subversive acts will become subsumed by the capitalist jug-gernaut to remain viable. Although this prediction is daunting, Liacas goes on to state that this playful reclamation of main-stream symbols is most meaningful and subversive through the individual culture jammer: "By appropriating and manipulating mainstream symbols, the culture jammer cuts the monolithic authority of consumer culture down to size, and gains a certain sense of personal control over it" (2005, 66). Even if that space of subversion exists only for a short time, it still exists.

PERFORMING PLAYFULNESS

As is evident in the arguments of the SI theories, performance and play are two integral parts of dismantling dominant powers that circulate within our cities. Although definition of the word *performance* is as fluid as the performance acts themselves, I use the word to refer to "all the activity of an individual which occurs during a period marked by his continuous presence before a particular set of observers and which has some influence on the observer" (Goffman 1959, 22). To situate the zombie walk in this discussion of performance and play, it is important to touch on the theories of Victor Turner, Arnold van Gennep, Richard Schechner and Roger Caillois, and how they best interact with our understanding of the "living dead." All four theorists have been influential in moving the acts of performance out of the theatre and into the realm of the social, speaking to the ways in which our everyday acts represent some form of performativity that can transport us from one area of existence to another.

Victor Turner was a cultural anthropologist best known for his work with the Ndembu people on rituals and rites of passage. Drawing heavily on ethnographer Arnold van Gennep, Turner developed a model for analyzing the social dramas he witnessed during the rites of passage among the Ndembu and argued for its use in explaining our daily acts of performance. Through rites of passage, an individual would transition from one role in his or her society into a completely new position (e.g., from childhood to adulthood). Turner, drawing on this notion of rites of passage, found more interest in the "in-betweenness" evident in this transitional performance as opposed to van Gennep's emphasis on the "set-apartness" of performance (Carlson 2004, 16). Both Turner and van Gennep argued that, to transition from one role in a given society into another, one must enter three distinct spaces. First, there must be some separation from or a breach in an accepted norm.

Second, there must be a crisis that forms, followed by employment of resolution tactics: the space of transition (Carlson 2004, 17). And third, there must be reintegration into the original cultural situation, where the one transitioning has moved into his or her new role. By existing in the space in between— the second stage of transition—and through performing the required acts of that given situation, one changes the final outcome of his or her identity. In that middle space, one has no fixed identity; she is not what she once was, but not yet what she will become. It is only through performing that one emerges and then transitions into a new space of existence.

This liminal space—in between two concretely defined spaces—provides one with room that is removed from daily activities and social prescriptions. Performance within this space "may invert the established order, but never subverts it. On the contrary, it normally suggests that a frightening chaos is the alternative to the established order" (Carlson 2004, 19). It is this "frightening chaos" that holds the potential to momentarily undo dominant ideologies at play in our society. Realizing that the concept of liminality might not match the greater degree of autonomy displayed by individuals in postindustrial societies, Turner modified the concept to create the notion "liminoid." This idea represented liminal-like moments when agents experienced social dramas in more individualized ways, often entering into these spaces more freely, out of choice over obligation (Alexander and Mast 2006, 11). Although the liminal speaks to an aspect of society, the liminoid refers to a break from society, a momentary space for play. There are definitive changes in the roles that one has within traditional liminal spaces (e.g., the wedding ceremony signifies the change from single to married), but the liminoid represent brief fissures in time and space where subversion can occur in the moment, but where no concrete changes in roles occur in the end.

In our cultural imaginary, zombies stand in as "liminal-like" characters; they are not alive, yet they are not entirely dead. The "living dead" occupy a space that is in between, disrupting many of the commonly held ideas surrounding life after death and the containment of bodies. No longer relegated to the cemeteries that line the peripheries of our cities, the "dead" become reanimated and slowly creep their way back into spaces that remind them of yesterday. The fact that zombies exist (imaginary or otherwise) calls us to question how previously held ideals and beliefs are not always what they seem. By performing the living dead, the "zombies" in the zombie walk beg bystanders to recognize that they are neither alive nor dead and playfully disrupt (momentarily) the popular imaginary.

Richard Schechner has been, arguably, the key theorist who has taken the concept of performance out of the confines of the theatre structure and into the open social arena. For Schechner, performative acts allow for liminality to enter into our social contexts. Within this space, one can destabilize the normative structures, inspire criticism, and propel the actor and audience toward re-enchantment with their social circumstances (Alexander and Mast 2006, 12). The zombie walk marks a space where upheaval-via-performance is purposefully placed in the foreground of where many of our everyday actions occur: shopping malls and city streets. By bringing the living dead into spaces occupied by the living, the zombie walk participants can create questions about who is allowed to occupy which spaces and when "others" are permitted in these zones. They also use the space for means other than what it was originally designated for. Instead of shopping and simply going through the motions of everyday life, the "zombies" march with no purpose other than to create fear and confusion; they are disorderly in both their movements and their use of the spaces around them. By moving performance into the mainstream, individuals are provided with a space where they are free to question the dominant ideologies that permeate their culture, under the guise of play. Play allows one to momentarily step outside the boundaries that regularly seek to confine him and move into a space that is not recognizably real, under the guise that it will not actually do any long-term harm.

Finally, as stated by the Situationists, the only way for a performance to hold some element of subversive potential is for it to be playful. If the act is not based within the realm of leisure and freedom, it becomes seen as another necessity on the already long-running list of social obligations. French theorist Roger Caillois described the four types of games, some of which are beneficial to understanding the political potential that performative acts carry. As stated in his "The Classification of Games," play can be created by four specific means: *agôn* (games based on reason), *alea* (chance games), *ilinx* (pure pleasure) and *mimicry*. The latter two are both helpful in understanding the performance of the zombie walk. Mimicry is a form of play that can "consist not only of deploying actions or submitting to one's fate in an imaginary milieu, but of becoming an illusory character oneself, and of so behaving" (Caillois 1961, 19). Within the performance, one's "original" persona is temporarily abandoned for an alter-ego, in this case a zombie. This new persona that is taken on—that is mimicked—allows the actor to utilize that liminal/liminoid space to promote ideas that might not be allowed while in her "natural" state. Although mimicry calls for continuous invention and creativity, the goal is simple (in theory), according to Caillois: to fascinate the spectator "while avoiding an error that might lead the spectator to break the spell. The spectator must lend himself to the illusion without first challenging the décor, mask or artifice which for a given time he is asked to believe in as more real than reality itself" (23). The participants in the zombie walk mimic the monsters they see in their favourite horror movies. This performance temporarily provides them with a space to be deviant, not only by the presence of their costumes, but also by forcing onlookers to recognize the abject state they have chosen to perform.

Ilinx, or vertigo (which it is often associated with), refers to play without any purpose: pure pleasure. This type of play is subversive because it seeks to destroy the stability of everyday life, turning lucidity into panic through the awareness of the body as set free from the normal structures of control (Carlson 2004, 22). Participants in this performance display *ilinx* through the fact that their enactment of the walking dead destroys the stable and rational notion of the city as a space for the living and the cemetery as the controlled environment for the deceased. As the zombies are let loose upon the city, they display catastrophic panic through the very presence of their animated corpses. Through their play, they symbolize the ending of the rational world and the beginning of immorality.

THE ZOMBIE CITY

The zombie walk is a unique phenomenon in both the ways that it is performed and the means by which it comes to fruition. Central to the zombie walk performance are the spaces that the actors occupy. Created primarily underground, through word of mouth, and by online message boards and communities, the zombie walk does not use mass forms of communication, ensuring that the walk will remain as surprising as possible. During the walk itself, participants often make their way around city streets and in spaces that the zombies of horror films usually occupy: shopping malls. The whole performance is done entirely in character, mimicking their every move and moan, limp and lurch. In 2007, the Toronto crowd of zombies numbered over 1,000, the largest on record (Dalgetty 2007). The magnitude of this presence, taking over the streets of Toronto, shuffling slowly among the masses of humans, speaks to the uncomfortable nature exuded by this performance. These horrors—the walking dead—created fear and discomfort in the onlookers, Dalgetty notes, resulting in some shop owners in Toronto chasing away the zombies in order to keep customers in their stores.

Although originally created as homage to the popular cinematic horror monster, the zombie walk has been transformed into a space that calls into question many of the social norms and values that permeate our society. The zombie walk is based within the do-it-yourself counterculture of this era. Beginning with handmade flyers tacked to streetlights in downtown Toronto and word-of-mouth promotion, the zombie walk since its inception has closely resembled the Situationists' *détournement*. The zombie walkers have reclaimed public spaces—previously delineated as sites of commerce, rationality and production—and have turned them upside down to reveal the (literal) horrors that lie beneath. Also, by performing the very thing that modern cities wish to expel the most (the dead), the zombie walk situates the abject, monstrous and horrific qualities found at the margins of our culture within the centre, where they cannot be ignored. The dead (whether fake or not) slump down our streets, enter our movie theatres and shopping centres, and rub their rotting corpses along our windows. They reclaim those spaces, if only for a moment, through the fear that they instill in us: through the fears that always exist within our culture, but that we are never able to see to their fullest.

Performance that is removed from the theatre, that takes place out on the streets of our cities, is imbued with the potential to be radical. Such performances can engage the tensions that circulate in our culture, "revealing how many established ideas, theories, traditions and practices have been shaken fundamentally by tectonic shifts in the cultural, social and political disorder of the late twentieth century" (Kershaw 1999, 16). Because of their space in between clearly established borders, such performances can also temporarily subvert dominant ideologies and in the process reclaim public spaces, ideas and objects for their own means. The zombie walks that occur in cities across North America and Western Europe are one example of horrific play used as a means of challenging modernist notions. Within the performance of the undead, but performing the abject to its fullest potential, bystanders are called to recognize the horror that their community is built upon. By recognizing the horror and questioning many of the values that uphold our culture, the zombie walk can temporarily reclaim the city space for the zombie walkers' own desires. And in that moment of panic, when the undead rise from their graves and stagger slowly toward their next victims, the rational city is overturned, while rampant freedom, play and joy remain.

REFERENCES

Alexander, Jeffrey C. and Jason L. Mast. 2006. "Introduction: Symbolic Action in Theory and Practice: The Cultural Pragmatics of Symbolic Action." In *Social Performance: Symbolic Action, Cultural Pragmatics, and Ritual,* edited by Jeffrey C. Alexander, Bernhard Giesen, and Jason L. Mast, 1–28. Cambridge, UK: Cambridge University Press.

Austen, Jane and Seth Grahame-Smith. 2009. *Pride and Prejudice and Zombies.* Philadelphia: Quirk Productions.

Boyle, Danny, dir. 2002. *28 Days Later.* DNA Films.

Brietenstien, Todd. 2001. Zombies!!! Twilight Creations.

Brooks, Max. 2003. *The Zombie Survival Guide: Complete Protection from the Living Dead.* New York: Three Rivers Press.

Caillois, Roger. 1961. "The Classification of Games." In *Man, Play, and Games,* translated by Meyer Barash, 11–35. Urbana: University of Illinois Press.

Carlson, Marvin. 2004. *Performance: A Critical Introduction.* 2nd ed. New York: Routledge.

Dalgetty, Greg. 2007. "The Dead Walk! A Dispatch from Toronto's Record-Breaking Zombie Walk." *Penny Blood: Horror and Cult Entertainment Magazine,* 21 October, http://www.pennyblood.com/zombiewalk1.html.

Dead Rising. 2006. Capcom Production Studio 1.

Dendle, Peter. 2007. "The Zombie as Barometer of Cultural Anxiety." In *Monsters and the Monstrous: Myths and Metaphors of Enduring Evil,* edited by Niall Scott, 45–57. New York: Rodopi.

Franck, Karen A. and Quentin Stevens. 2007. "Tying Down Loose Space." In *Loose Space: Possibility and Diversity in Urban Life,* edited by Karen A. Franck and Quentin Stevens, 1–33. Oxon: Routledge.

Goffman, Erving. 1959. "Performances." In *The Presentation of Self in Everyday Life,* by Erving Goffman, 17–76. New York: Doubleday.

Hill, Jason. 2007. Last Night on Earth. Flying Frog Productions and Heidelberger Spieleverlag.

HorrorPops, The. 2005. "Walk like a Zombie." *Bring It On!* Hellcat Records.

Hutcheon, Linda. 2002. *The Politics of Postmodernism.* 1989; reprinted, London: Routledge.

Johns, Geoff. *Blackest Night.* DC Comics.

Kershaw, Baz. 1999. *The Radical in Performance: Between Brecht and Baudrillard.* London: Routledge.

Kirkman, Robert. *The Walking Dead.* Image Comics.

Left 4 Dead. 2008. Valve Corporation and Certain Affinity.

Liacas, Tom. 2005. "101 Tricks to Play with the Mainstream: Culture Jamming as Subversive Recreation." In *Autonomous Media: Activating Resistance and Dissent,* edited by Andrea Langlois and Frédéric Dubois, 60–72. Montreal: Cumulus Press.

Low, Setha M. 2003. "The Edge and the Center: Gated Communities and the Discourse of Urban Fear." In *The Anthropology of Space and Place: Locating Culture,* edited by Setha M. Low and Denise Lawrence-Zúñiga, 387–407. Oxford: Blackwell Publishing.

Marcus, Greil. 2002. "The Long Walk of the Situationist International." In *Guy Debord and the Situationist International: Text and Documents,* edited by Tom McDonough, 1–20. Cambridge, MA: MIT Press.

McIntosh, Shawn. 2008. "The Evolution of the Zombie: The Monster that Keeps Coming Back." In *Zombie Culture: Autopsies of the Living Dead,* edited by Shawn McIntosh and Marc Leverette, 1–17. Lanham: Scarecrow Press.

Merrifield, Andy. 2005. *Guy Debord.* London: Reaktion Books.

Morley, David. 1996. "Postmodernism: The Rough Guide." In *Cultural Studies and Communications,* edited by James Curran, David Morley, and Valerie Walkerdine, 50–65. London: Arnold.

Nichols, Joshua. 2008. "*Lacan, the City, and the Utopian Symptom: An Analysis of Abject Urban Spaces.*" Space and Culture 11, 4: 459–74.

Plant, Sadie. 1992. *The Most Radical Gesture: The Situationist International in a Postmodern Age.* London: Routledge.

Raimi, Sam, dir. 1992. *Army of Darkness.* Dino De Laurentiis Company.

Raunig, Gerald. 2007. *Art and Revolution: Transversal Activism in the Long Twentieth Century.* Translated by Aileen Derieg. Los Angeles: Semiotext(e).

Resident Evil. 1996. Capcom Production Studio 4, Westwood Studios, and Nextech.

Romero, George A., dir. 1968. *Night of the Living Dead.* Image Ten.

———. 1978. *Dawn of the Dead.* Laurel Group.

———. 1985. *Day of the Dead.* United Film Distribution Company.

Rotten, Rob, dir. 2006. *Porn of the Dead.* Punk Productions.

Stevens, Quentin. 2007. *The Ludic City: Exploring the Potential of Public Spaces.* Oxon: Routledge.

Wright, Edgar, dir. 2004. *Shaun of the Dead.* Studio Canal.

Zombie Pinups. 2010, 18 March. www.zombiepinups.com.

A PRELIMINARY REPORT ON THE FIRST EXCAVATION SEASON

(1 JUNE-15 JULY 2047) AT ZOMBIE ASSAULT SITE UK56, NEWPORT, SOUTH WALES

MELISSA BEATTIE
(EXCAVATION TEAM LEADER)

The global catastrophe of the 11 January 2012 zombie assault is one that we still do not fully understand, nor have we even remotely recovered from it, even in the most well-funded reclamation areas. Although studies have been done by researchers in fields as diverse as chemistry, epidemiology, comparative religions and philosophy, our recent excavation season of two zones of the city of Newport, South Wales, marks the first use of archaeology to help us better understand the events of that night. Although our findings are specific to Newport, we believe that this study will provide the basis for similar projects in other locations in the United Kingdom and elsewhere.

The decision to release this preliminary report so quickly was twofold. First, we believed that the public should always be informed and involved in matters relating to their communities. Much as with our sister discipline of history, archaeology influences cultural identity by telling a community about its past, and that heritage is communal, not something reserved only for those who formally study it. Second, we wanted to help archaeologists and other researchers who wish to engage in similar studies. Historically, publication of sites has occurred at a snail's pace, and access to some journals can be difficult, impeding study; matters only become worse if one is looking for studies outside one's field. Because this event touched every part of the globe, we wanted to make certain that every researcher who wants or needs our data is able to access it. This is also why we are attempting to be as free from unexplained jargon as possible. There are drawbacks, of course, to our rapidity; most of our official maps and drawings are not yet available, so a few illustrations, mostly scans of our hand-drawn field sketches, will have to suffice.

We begin with a summary of events as we know them. Beginning at sundown all along the International Date Line on 11 January 2012, the dead began to rise from their graves. As the sun set on each area of Earth, the same thing happened. The zombies, ravenous and moving slowly, assaulted telecommunications and transport links as soon as they rose, presumably to avoid others being warned. This suggests that there was some intelligence controlling them, as is the case in the "traditional" Vodou zombie, though what or who has defied all attempts at identification to this day. Still, this strategy was quite effective; though sporadic and confused reports of "rioting" leaked out of Oceania and then Asia, it was not until the crisis reached Europe and Africa that the magnitude of the problem began to be realized, and even then it was not believed. At sunset GMT, an almost completely unprepared United Kingdom found its dead rising from their graves, attacking any living beings they came across. Anyone who died that night from any cause, zombie contact or not, became a zombie not long after death. Once the sun rose, however, all remaining zombies simply fell where they were, never to be animate again. As many bodies as could be found were collected and burned—fire and destruction of the head being the only ways to kill them—but zombie corpses were found for months after the event as the world slowly began to clean up from its night of horror.

The world has not yet finished this recovery, however. Large areas remain barren or simply bulldozed over; this is the case in much of Newport, though in early 2012 it was the third largest city in Wales. It was deemed by Westminster to be of "lesser importance" than other cities in the United Kingdom, a decision that, though strongly protested by local lawmakers and residents, does allow for archaeological investigation without interference from modern structures. Newport was also reportedly the site of some of the fiercest fighting against the zombies in the United Kingdom, and we were guided by historical records and the odd interview.

Because there was so much coverage of the disaster, most of which is still usable and accessible, one might well ask why an archaeological excavation was important or indeed necessary. Unlike ancient sites and cultures where we have little or no written information left to us—what most people think of as typical archaeology—we have a great deal of historical data that can be sifted through, as some critics of the project have remarked. Why, they have asked, should we feel the need to unearth these skeletons from our recent past? What could archaeology contribute?

The best answers to those questions come not from a textbook or lecture, but from a film. As the fictional archaeologist Indiana Jones remarks in his first film, archaeology is concerned with facts. Although Indiana is hardly a typical archaeologist—his methodology seems to be closer to grave robbing, though, to be fair, much of the non-fictional archaeology of the 1940s would be considered anywhere from irresponsible to illegal under current standards of practice—he is correct on this point. The study of material remains, though still subject to some bias when interpreted, is far more objective in many ways. As anyone who has more than a passing familiarity with the historical records of the zombie assaults is aware, the reports vary widely even when dealing with the same area and sometimes even contradict each other. This can happen for many reasons, such as eyewitnesses not remembering events accurately after the fact, witnesses being unaware of certain aspects of the events as they were happening, or even rare occasions of intentional distortion.

Archaeology, on the other hand, gives us some practical data with which to work; if we are told by one source that a building in a certain location was destroyed by fire, but by another that it collapsed but did not burn, theoretically we can excavate the

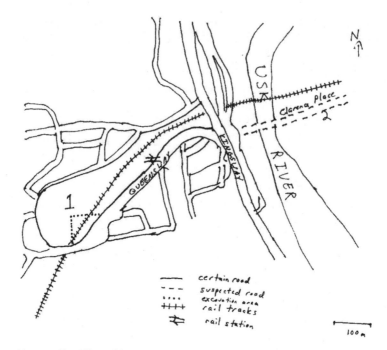

Map 12.1 The Affected Area.

remains from that area and determine at least a partial answer. Interpreting the results of this excavation would show that there either was a building at that location or there wasn't; if there was a building, then it should show signs of having been in a fire if it were burned down. We might not be able to determine exactly why the building collapsed if there was no fire, but we can at least eliminate one possibility from one historical source. If we find no building at all, then we know that there is a major discrepancy in both records. Thus, in addition to providing its own insights, as will become apparent in our discussion of this particular site, archaeology serves as a way of testing what eyewitness histories say.

According to the historical records available to us in the area of the city we are interested in, the zombies rose from the main cemetery, located approximately 1.5 kilometres southwest of the rail and coach stations. This meant that they could easily assault both stations, cutting off the humans and swelling their own ranks as they killed the humans. They then advanced from the station across a bridge over the river Usk. By this point, however, police had realized that something was wrong and, soon followed by local citizens, they began to engage in street battles, forcing the zombies back toward the rail station, and at least some of them were forced into construction trenches and then burned. As with everywhere else on Earth, at daybreak the zombies suddenly fell still and did not rise again. The attack was further complicated by weather conditions; the entire United Kingdom was dealing with snow and ice, which, while hampering the zombies, also worked against the humans.

Based upon these reports and maps of the old city, we determined two zones to dig our test trenches, though we only had survey equipment for one, as discussed below. Both of these locations can be seen in Map 12.1. On the western side, roads still exist, though the area is uninhabited and overgrown; the courses of the streets are shown with solid lines. The routes over the Usk and onto the eastern bank of the river have been lost. This area is utter waste ground, and the one route of which we are reasonably certain is given in dashed lines. It does correspond with earlier maps, at any rate.

The first zone was along the course of the "burn pit," the trench made by construction equipment located near the rail station in which at least some zombies were herded and set ablaze. We are unsure if this was an attempt to flank the zombies or if it was done by an independent unit; as with most cases around the world, resistance was mostly uncoordinated though extremely fierce and uncommonly successful in Newport. In this trench, we wanted to find at least some reasonably intact (though obviously burned) zombie bones in the hope of somehow differentiating them from regular human bones. We turned up some surprising data. First of all, we realized that none of the non-invasive geophysical methods of prospection that archaeologists often use—and that will be described later—would be possible due to the old rail lines and wet soil conditions. We did, however, have the historical records to draw on, all of which stated that the burn pit had been dug by a JCB (also known as a backhoe or mechanical excavator) going east to west, in a large area approximately 250 metres southwest of the rail station, which had been undergoing construction at the time of the attack, and that the trench was about ten metres long, five metres wide and six metres deep, extending from the carpark at the west to the rail lines at the east. Two articles from local news outlets and one reputable online source all gave approximate directions; the online source also had photographs and what was said to be a sketch made that night of where in the field the burn pit was.

The accounts did not all tally, however, with several inconsistencies about distances. Still, most studies of the battle in Newport cite these items as being the most reliable, and we thus used them to determine three areas in which to dig our test trenches, based upon interpretation of the data. We believed that the burn pit should be located somewhere between fifty and seventy-five metres north of the southernmost end of the area, and within seventy-five metres of the eastern edge at that point; the dotted lines on Map 12.1 delineate this area. Because the zombie remains were covered by both the dirt dug by the JCB and a trench collapse, we expected that the strata, or layers of dirt, would be inconsistent across the area; what we did not anticipate was just how far off the historical records (and our extrapolations) were. The trench was in fact dug from the northeast to the southwest, and was only fifteen metres from the eastern edge of the area at its closest point, where our excavation encountered it. In fact, only one of our three test trenches in this section, Trench 3, successfully intersected the burn pit, and that at an angle. Therefore, we are unsure how wide or long the pit actually is—Trench 3 intersected it diagonally for approximately five metres on one side, seven metres on the other, and four metres in width—and the depth we found averaged only three metres. The historical sources also say that dozens of zombies were pushed in and burned. Because of the burning and subsequent bulldozing of the area, most of the bones are in small pieces and difficult to identify. Therefore, as our osteologist identified five femurs (thigh bones) and three crania (skulls), we determined that there were at least three individual zombies in this section.

Figure 12.1 is a diagram of the area within the dotted lines of Map 12.1; that is, it shows the relationship between the

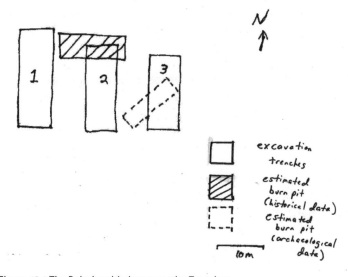

Figure 12.1 The Relationship between the Trenches.

trenches in the area we were excavating (features such as the rail line have been left out in order to make the diagram more clear; they can be seen on Map 12.1). The area marked with diagonal lines is where we thought the burn pit would be; our trenches are shown with solid lines and the believed actual course of the burn pit is delineated by dashed lines. As you can see, there is a significant difference between where the records suggested the burn pit was and where our actual findings showed it to be. This is hardly uncommon for archaeology, even when there are eyewitness reports of an event written immediately after; for example, battlefield archaeology frequently shows heavy concentrations of bullets and other artillery (i.e., areas of heavy fire during a battle) in locations far different and distant from those given in the historical reports.

Since we know that anyone who died for any reason on 11 January 2012 became a zombie, regardless of whether a zombie was responsible for the death, we were fairly certain that there was no disease involved. This was confirmed by tests of bones, teeth and the surrounding soil, all of which would have contained some trace of any pathogen. We did find a large amount of petrol residue in the soil, suggesting that it was used as an accelerant in the burning. This is unsurprising, since the human body is not easy to set on fire and the snowstorm that hit the United Kingdom that night would have hindered combustion.

There was also no appreciable difference between zombie bones and those of normal humans, though there were a few instances of what appear to be human teeth marks on bone, suggesting that these are the remains of humans who were killed by zombies that night (and subsequently became part of the zombie horde). We might have discovered at least a partial reason for that. We considered doing carbon-14 testing to determine an exact date; this type of dating, however, works at minimum on organic items at least 300 years old, and that is problematic; however, just by observing the bones, they did not appear to have been in the ground for centuries. We realized, however, that almost all the zombies in any given area were local, which meant that we could look at the graves. To prevent the zombie uprising from ever happening again, all remaining graves in most areas of the world were dug up and the remains cremated; in the United Kingdom, lists were made of those who were burned in order to return the ashes to the families. Thus, all we had to do was go to the records office and find these lists, then cross-check them with cemetery records. Names on the cemetery register but not on the list of cremations were therefore those of people who had risen as zombies.

By looking at their listed dates of death, we determined that the oldest zombies from this area were between five and six years past death. This is probably because most older bodies, apart from the specially preserved, such as Egyptian mummies (who did rise), would have decomposed to the point where there was not enough connective tissue (skin, muscle and joints) to allow them to move. The rate of decomposition varies from place to place, however, and we have very little data on how long it takes for an embalmed body to decompose in any case, but we would be unsurprised to find that virtually all zombies in the United Kingdom were under ten years buried. We have put forward a proposal to several organizations to fund a project that will compare cemetery registers and cremation lists from several regions of the United Kingdom over the next year better to determine the maximum and average ages of zombies. The fact that we can even consider obtaining such data underscores how fortunate we are to have the resource of complete records and registers, often lacking in the study of earlier periods.

Our second zone of study was approximately 0.7 kilometres away, in the wasteland that now covers Clarence Place, what Queensway is called east of the river Usk. This street was the site of a fierce battle between humans and zombies. According to the histories, after taking out the rail and coach stations, the zombie hordes began to cross the Usk at various points, one of which was here. This road, after crossing the Usk, led to a street with mostly commercial structures, many of which were still doing business at the time of the assault. When the zombies began attacking those in the streets and entering the various businesses, however, the inhabitants mounted a fierce struggle against them. The zombies managed to make it to a fork in the road, identified on old maps as Caerleon Road (North) and Chepstow Road (South), which is where the humans blocked them. Because of a combination of the weather—the streets were covered in ice; zombies, of course, cannot heal if they slip and break a limb—and a fire that broke out through unknown means, the zombies not only suffered heavy losses, but also were pushed back across the Usk by the early hours of the morning. Humans then successfully guarded the east bank of the river at that crossing until dawn, to prevent more zombies from coming, as well as at various other points along the street. Between the fire and the fighting, however, the entire area was considered a total loss. It was almost immediately bulldozed and covered with several metres of soil; the area has not yet been redeveloped.

We began by performing a geophysical survey in this area. There are three main types of survey, but we already knew that there was too much metal debris buried there for the type that uses electromagnetic fields (magnetometry) and that the ground was too wet for the type that makes maps by looking at how much resistance to electricity things in the soil have compared with the soil itself (geo-electric prospection), so we opted for ground-penetrating radar, which we call GPR. It works by sending radar waves into the ground and analyzing what lies beneath the surface based on how it reflects these radar waves. Ideally, this creates a picture that we can analyze with computer technology and turn into a map that shows us where walls and structures are buried before we start digging. Since we had only the one GPR unit, it was determined that Clarence Place would probably give us better results as well as a guide for the next excavation season. Unfortunately, because the soil used to cover the whole area was abundant in clay (various officials believed that clay, being the most impermeable to water and other fluids, might help to seal in any potential contagion), our picture was not particularly clear even when compared with photographs and maps from the early twenty-first century. We chose what seemed a likely looking area on the map, believing it to intersect two distinct structures. This, unfortunately, was not the case. Our trench was fully inside a single structure, albeit one with two distinct areas; we believe that one section was a bar and the other a stage, though because of the positioning of the trench we do not yet have even a preliminary ground plan. This is not an ideal outcome, of course, and we will attempt to determine a more viable area of excavation for future seasons.

Because of our limited time and resources, we could only put in the one trench in this area; if our funding applications are successful, then we intend to put a much larger team in the field next year. Although our GPR maps were not entirely clear, we could at least get an estimated depth on what we determined was a full structure. Because there were over seven metres of overlying compacted soil, we brought in a JCB to remove most of it; as soon as we saw that we had reached the destruction layer (i.e., parts of the bulldozed building), we changed to more traditional methods. Going down by units of ten centimetres at a time (unless we found a reason to stop, such as a change in soil or debris type) with small pick-axes, brushes and trowels, we managed to uncover a vast amount of useful data. Although complete details will be listed in the subsequent full publication, we do wish to address some of the most important points.

One of the most perplexing questions about this particular region is the fire. Some histories call it accidental, while others say it was an intentional act to destroy the zombies. The exact location of the source is similarly unknown. We had hoped to shed light on this, but because we found ourselves excavating in only one structure we cannot make any real determination. The building was heavily damaged by fire along its north-facing frontage, but this damage did not extend deep into the building; the structure's roof collapsed beyond that, perhaps creating a natural fire break or allowing the snow in and preventing further burning. It could even be that someone extinguished the fire in order to save the structure. As is so often the case in archaeology, we simply do not have enough data.

This excavation has allowed us to shed some light on one peculiarity of the Newport assault, however: the witness reports of a few "Roman zombies" taking part in the street battle, something not seen anywhere else in the United Kingdom. Although we cannot use carbon-14 dating for the reasons discussed above, we do know that in most cases there is too much decomposition for effective movement for anyone dead more than a few decades. This has led to any number of theories, most of which involve the classical predecessors of the zombie. I will give a brief explanation of each of these predecessors for those who are not familiar with them. They include the shades of the underworld in Homer's *Odyssey*, who needed blood before they could speak, and Alcestis and Eurydice, who were both returned from the underworld, though Eurydice was lost before she reached the surface. Alcestis, however, is unable to speak without a purification ritual and waiting three days. There is also the Roman rite of *devotio*, in which a soldier throws himself at the enemy as a representative of the army, and his death is intended as a sacrifice to gain victory from the gods. If the soldier survives, then a larger-than-life-size statue must be buried in his place, with a blood sacrifice made over it, and the soldier is no longer able to offer any sacrifice public or private, which suggests that he is legally or religiously in some sort of undead state.

None of these predecessors, however, adequately explains the reports and blurred pictures from Newport of zombies wearing togas and crowns of laurel. Although some doubt has been expressed over the years by those who accurately point out that the Roman wardrobe contained far more commonly worn items than the toga, our excavation can now shed light on this mystery based upon one of the findings from the trench in area 2. We discovered the remains of one male whose clothing and some soft tissue had partially survived thanks to being waterlogged; based upon the volume of water, the proximity to the remains of pipes and the internal structure of the building as reconstructed by old photographs, we believe that he had been killed in the fight near the lavatory facilities. The pipes burst, creating a large and fairly deep puddle into which the body fell. The roof subsequently collapsed nearby, letting in the snow and partially burying him; bulldozing the debris sealed him in. When the clay-rich soil was heaped on top,

Figure 12.2. Artist's Interpretation of "Roman" Zombie.

it created an even better seal, allowing for some of the fabric to survive. The garment remains can be interpreted as a toga, and the battered skull had pieces of what appeared to be a crown. The soft tissue results were inconclusive, since anyone turned into a zombie suffered immediate decomposition of the flesh, as we were able to see in photographs from the night.

Testing on the fabric of the toga, however, revealed it to be cotton, rather than linen, or perhaps wool, as we would have expected; it also did not have the wear one would expect from being from the Roman period. The pieces of crown that had penetrated the skull were also made of plastic, and the body showed bone-deep human toothmarks. Because of all these factors, we can say with confidence that these "Roman" zombies were in fact people coming from or going to a toga party who were killed and became zombies that night rather than zombies who dated from the period of Roman Britain. Our team illustrator, Emily Stilwell, gives an artist's interpretation in Figure 12.2 based upon our findings.

We might never know for certain how or why on that fateful night in January 2012 the dead rose from their graves to attack us. This small excavation, however, has revealed to us many things. We now have more evidence that, whatever the cause, it was not biological. We have found at least some suggestion about what age these zombies were and have managed to solve at least one mystery, that of the "Roman zombies of Newport." We have been able to integrate history with archaeology, sometimes to be used to correct errors and sometimes to be used as an invaluable guide. There are, admittedly, some questions we cannot answer yet, such as the nature and direction of the fire, but we hope that, with continued excavation here in Newport and elsewhere in the world we can, someday, explain this disaster. All archaeology, even contemporary, takes time.

STRATEGIC INTELLIGENCE ANALYSIS OF A ZOMBIE ATTACK

HARRIS DELEEUW

The zombies in this chapter are fictional and loosely based upon those in the films of George A. Romero.

> Intelligence is not a science, certainly not a natural science. It is an art or a craft, and as such it cannot be governed by the basic tenets of logic. Intelligence officers must be gifted with imagination and creativity, enabling them to peer behind the curtain of apparent reality. (Halevi 2004, 21)

SCENARIO

It happened on a Sunday morning on a clear, mild day. News Talk Radio received and broadcast a report from a listener in Ruralville, an outlying, semi-rural suburb in the southeast of Capital City. The quality of the mobile telephone call was not good. The signal kept breaking up and there were background noises that drowned out the speaker. Thinking it was a laugh, the radio station decided to play the audio track with minimal cleanup or editing. The speaker was a man, possibly elderly. He did not give his name.

> *Caller:* "Hello, hello. I'm calling from Ruralville. There's kids here. A mob. A gang." Crashes, bangs and some unintelligible shouts broke up the call. "They're animals. Animals."
>
> *Announcer:* "Sir, are you saying the animals are attacking some kids?"
>
> *Caller:* "No, no. The kids. They are the animals. They're at the door. Oh, my God, no!"
>
> There were sounds of a struggle.
>
> *Announcer:* "Sir, sir, can you hear me? Sir?"
>
> The recording ended with a screech and what sounded like gurgling.

News Talk Radio played the recording a few times. Other radio stations and internet news sites picked the story up, all treating it as a joke. The local police learned of the incident from listening to the radio stations. A local police officer called News Talk Radio for more details and was told the station's Sunday breakfast show was playing it as though it was a hoax. The nearby agricultural college had recently started the new academic term with the traditional student shenanigans, which might have included making a hoax call to the radio station or spooking local residents.

A police car with two officers was despatched to try to locate where the incident might have occurred. After cruising around the market farms, the police saw a group of people on a property near a barn and a house. The police approached warily, reporting it in, but they had few details. The road was a muddy single track with fences on both sides, making it hard for the officers to see the group clearly. The police stopped and one of the officers left the car, his handgun drawn. He called out to the mob to announce the police presence.

The driver watched intently, but only saw the attacker lurch out from behind a wall when it was too late to warn his partner. Horrified, he watched as a large man attacked his partner. The driver switched on the siren and lights, and screamed into the radio, "Officer down, officer down!" As others joined the big man in the attack on the police officer, the driver realized that some of the attackers were reacting to the noise of the siren and were beginning to move toward the source. The officer drove in reverse at speed away from the farm. The mob was slow-moving and he escaped, but he was shaken by what he had seen. His report noted,

Attended Market Farm 3 in routine patrol. Officer 2 set upon by large white male possibly armed with a knife. Unknown white male joined by group of about 4 adults, all possibly armed with knives or similar cutting weapons. Blood was on their clothes. Officer 2 unable to protect himself. Officer 1 called in "Officer down" alert. Armed group started to attack police vehicle. Officer 1 decided to initiate withdrawal procedures and is now monitoring entrance to Market Farm 3. Assistance urgently required. This is not a hoax.

Within the hour of that report being made, City Police Central Command received a report about a gang of men and women trespassing on a property north of Capital City. When asked to describe them, the caller, an elderly woman, said,

"There are about a dozen of them. They are roughly dressed, unkempt. They seem to have blood on them as though they've been injured, but they don't seem to be seeking help. They are menacing my property, young man."

"Are they armed, ma'am?"

"I can't see and it's plainly unsafe for me to investigate. That's your job."

A patrol car was dispatched. The officers located a group of people who attacked the car, but both officers escaped. They were sure that among the attackers was the old lady who owned the property.

On the basis of the two reports, the City Police commander on duty activated the Emergency Security Protocols (ESP) for Capital City. The teams were contacted and the first shift made their way to the City Police Central Command building.

The Emergency Security Protocols demand a fast response with on-duty police teams quickly deployed to the scene or scenes, and the Command and Control (C&C) team reporting for duty at the City Police Central Command building a few kilometres from the centre of Capital City. The C&C team coordinates the teams in the field and provides logistical support such as food, water and equipment. They also schedule and contact personnel for shifts. They make decisions about numbers of teams and their locations, and the equipment to be deployed, informed by intelligence analysis. Assessed and prioritized intelligence enables the C&C team to make decisions based upon a more complete view of the situation than just reacting to news on the ground as it happens, a natural human reaction in times of stress.

INTELLIGENCE GATHERING AND ANALYSIS

We tend to form early impressions from the limited facts as we know them, with imperfect reference to our past experience. This almost instant summation enables us to make the core decision: fight or flight? This suits individual reactions to immediate life-and-death situations but is not so good for everyday situations. Our evolving sophistication means we know these instinctive, hard-wired decisions are fallible if we rely only on our immediate conclusions. For example, our instinct is to treat difference with suspicion, particularly if people who look different or behave differently from us are acting in what we perceive to be a threatening manner. Those of us who live in a typical early twenty-first century urban environment might realize that the rowdy teenagers hanging about outside the corner shop are unlikely to pose any real danger, but we will tend to be more wary of them should they be of a different ethnicity and we do not know them personally. Our individual behaviour can be, and has been, writ large on the international stage. Intelligence analysis, particularly in military decision-making, has developed methods to limit this fallibility.

The earliest surviving mention of intelligence exists in the sixth-century BCE Chinese text, credited to Sun Tzu, on war and military strategy. Sir Francis Walsingham in the court of England's Queen Elizabeth I was responsible for formalizing intelligence gathering for the state. Both intelligence gathering and its analysis became progressively more important as the world developed nation states and the stakes for which countries went to war became more significant. The Napoleonic wars, for example, are widely credited with professionalizing modern military intelligence, and it was from them that most European nations created some kind of secret police or spying capability to protect their empires. In a somewhat amusing historical joke, Great Britain left it quite late to form its famous espionage apparatus, known worldwide as MI5 (1909) and MI6 (1909). Countries such as France and Germany believed that Britain had had an exceptionally effective system in place through most of the eighteenth and nineteenth centuries because they had never been able to detect British spies (Andrew 2009). During both twentieth century world wars and the Cold War, and most recently during the so-called War on Terror, intelligence grew exponentially in importance for most modern countries. As a direct result, there were moves to further professionalize analysis of the enormous datasets becoming available, particularly during the Cold War, when the stakes were to avert a global nuclear war. The US Central Intelligence Agency (CIA), for example, published an extensive array of documents about intelligence analysis, and even now it openly debates the discipline's history and current state of affairs. A growing number of books exploring these and similar themes have been published, particularly during the 1980s and 2000s (see the bibliography for examples).

Police forces in many Western liberal democracies started to apply intelligence analysis in their operations against crime during the 1970s. Don McDowell, an Australian who codified strategic intelligence analysis for law enforcement in the 1990s, wrote that "concepts of espionage and critical analysis are often confused as if they were all part of the same entity. *Espionage* is about gathering data in the intrusive and invasive environment of spying. *Intelligence* and *analysis* is a wider concept of problem solving that involves data gathering and analysis, interpretation and speculative consideration of future developments, patterns, threats, risks and opportunities" (1998, 6). Civilian law enforcement is more about the latter, whereas international relations, which includes both the threat of and actual war, is balanced between the two strands.

The drive for police and law enforcement to introduce intelligence-led policing is simple to explain. Policing illegal alcohol, drugs, other forms of organized crime, serial rape and murder, and theft has led to demands for policing to be less reactive to reports of crime and to focus instead on prevention. A common approach is geographic profiling of where certain crimes occur. Police analysts identify "hotspots," so called from mapping software that illustrates clusters of crimes. Geographic profiling can be applied at several different levels: across a whole country, province or state, city, town or within a local area. Each level is analyzed for different reasons, with results intended for different decision-makers. For example, the strategic levels looking at crime rates across a country or city are used most often for deciding overall responses by the state law and order apparatus to crime hotspots. Problems can occur when unsophisticated analyses indicate that crime rates might be reducible to race or based upon an oversimplified association with poorer areas. This can feed the biases held by police, particularly if they are from a social group distinct from those they are policing.[1] Geographic profiling is also applied at the local or tactical level when reports of, say, a series of rapes with a similar *modus operandi* is plotted in the software according to when and where they occurred. Advances in forensic science have meant better identification of criminals from their fingerprints, foot (shoe) prints and DNA. Traces left at scenes of crimes enable refined hotspot mapping to link events to particular offenders. Viewers of any of the CSI series and other forensic science series are familiar with the types of forensic tools available. Factoring in when the crimes occurred allows community police to target both an area and times when crimes are more likely to occur, as well as advise residents when to be

1 Historical and sociological studies have shown many examples of where police had been drawn from a particular social group with implications for law enforcement. Examples include the former Royal Ulster Constabulary in Northern Ireland, who were almost exclusively Protestant. They were replaced by the Police Service of Northern Ireland with a concerted effort to recruit Catholic and other police as part of the process of reconciliation. Other UK police forces now actively try to recruit from local Black, South Asian and gay and lesbian communities in an effort to break institutional racism and prejudice based on sexual orientation.

more careful. These sorts of basic techniques have been successfully used by the US Federal Bureau of Investigation (FBI) in its work against serial sex offenders, as popularized in fictional TV series such as *Criminal Minds* and the movie and book *The Silence of the Lambs.* The FBI has added an understanding of psychology to its arsenal of knowledge and analytical tools. Non-fictional accounts from a number of former special agents are readily available (see the bibliography for a selection).

Racial profiling, when people are grouped according to their skin colour, ethnicity, nationality, religious affiliation or any other type of classification, can cause law enforcement serious problems, and modern police tend to try to avoid it as far as possible. Police have made an effort to learn from the statistically corroborated incidents when police in predominantly white areas use stop-and-search powers against black or other visible ethnic minorities out of any reasonable proportion. Numerous academic studies and official enquiries into institutional racism have provided insights into these problems, the findings of which have been incorporated into intelligence analysis training for law enforcement. However, it has not been evenly applied and while there have been demonstrable improvements in many countries there is no single police force that has eradicated prejudice from its work. Intelligence analysis needs to guard continually against prejudicial responses, because they are likely to curtail the number of lines of enquiry and can lead to a failure to respond appropriately. For example, counterterrorist profiling that suggests Islam correlates to Arab terrorists leads to faulty security systems where non-Arab terrorists plotting in the name of Islam are not stopped but innocent Muslims are denied their rights, or worse.

Counterterrorism intelligence overlaps both criminal intelligence and that engaged during conventional war. Terrorism is often an act of war, declared or otherwise, but it is defined differently from conventional war because of the inherent politics involved in the types of conflict in which terror is used as a tactic. This also affects how states respond to terrorist attacks. In most liberal democracies, the civil police are first-level responders to a terror-inducing attack and take control of the emergency, with other services taking part in the coordination of medical and fire control. Security and intelligence agencies such as the UK's MI5 and the Australian Security and Intelligence Organization (ASIO), and often military intelligence, play a part in obtaining, assessing and reporting intelligence to the police and government decision-makers in the event of an emergency such as a terrorist bombing.

COUNTERING THE ZOMBIE ATTACK

The above is the setup, broadly speaking, for our fictitious liberal democracy. Among the teams assembling at the City Police Central Command are two teams of intelligence analysts. Most, including the team leaders, work for the City Police. The City Police hold jurisdictional responsibility for first response to a declared emergency, regardless of what caused it. The intelligence analysts are trained to respond to a known or suspected terrorist incident but can be called out for any emergency in which a human agency is suspected. Other members of the teams are from the National Police (NP), Military Intelligence (MI) and the Domestic Intelligence Security Service (DISS). Both intelligence teams have access to all of the information available to the police, military and security service. One group is dedicated to looking at the immediate tactical picture (the Tactical Intelligence Group or TIG), the other to the strategic or longer-term view (the Strategic Intelligence Analysis Group or SIAG).

The TIG is staffed mostly by City Police with some National Police and Military Intelligence personnel. They are charged with immediate responses to requests for information from the operational teams in the field. Maps are vital, complete with information about what is in the areas affected. Things such as population centres, places that store weapons or things that can be made into weapons, hospitals and so on are important because they pose risks of escalation. Although it is desirable that these data are kept up to date, this is not always the case. An urgent task is therefore to update information, particularly relating to the geographic area or areas in which the incident is occurring. The TIG tries to assess the immediate level of the threat. Based upon police and media reports, the reported mobs might be using bladed hand weapons, but not firearms.

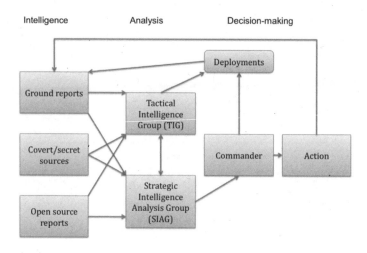

Figure 13.1 Intelligence Flow in Command and Control.

They have appeared in apparently random parts of Capital City and its immediate surrounds. One common factor is proximity to university and college campuses. The TIG feeds its findings to the SIAG as well as directly to the forward command posts (see Figure 13.1).

The SIAG has a less reactive role. It is led by a City Police analyst of suitable seniority: the rank of detective inspector, or shift captain, or the equivalent. In this case, the first SIAG leader is a civilian analyst. Among the day shift are another two City Police strategic analysts, one a counterterrorism specialist. A National Police analyst, a Military Intelligence officer and a member of the DISS form the rest of this team. Unlike the TIG, the SIAG is a smaller, specialist team whose security clearance is at the highest level. Both teams apply what is often referred to as the intelligence cycle (see Figure 13.2), which, broadly speaking, is based on project planning.

The SIAG settles in quickly. It's a relatively small pool that supplies the SIAG with its staff, mostly due to the security vetting. Because of the high cost of terrorist attacks or other serious emergencies, training all of those involved in responding is taken seriously. The analysts have worked with the protocols before and are familiar with the process and forms. The

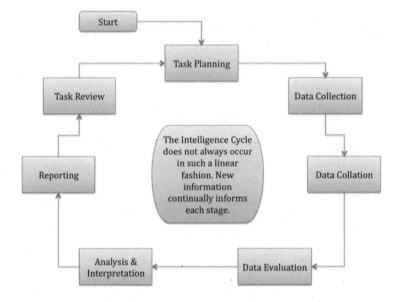

Figure 13.2 The Intelligence Cycle.

team leader is responsible for reporting a summary of all intelligence findings and a likely scenario of how the event is to unfold to the City Police commander every two hours. The SIAG does not have much time before the first briefing needs to be given.

The first task for the SIAG is to define the problem. In a quick-time situation, the SIAG needs to identify what the group members already know and the areas where they know they lack knowledge or understanding, and a particularly incisive team can uncover things they didn't know they know. They will also know there is an unquantifiable amount they don't know. If that sounds at all familiar, it was infamously referred to by former US Secretary of Defense Donald Rumsfeld in the early 2000s.

Table 13.1 First Stage of Problem Definition

What we know we know	What we know we don't know
What we don't know we know	What we don't know we don't know

Brainstorming is an exceptionally useful tool to capture information already known by the SIAG, including uncovering things the group members know individually but not as a group. For brainstorming to be effective, there are rules to follow. The main rule is that ideas flow without fear of criticism. The ideas should not get "bogged down" in detail or flow too far from the problem at hand. Due to the time constraints in such a situation, the SIAG is likely to use already formulated basic questions to guide the brainstorming more than might occur when the tool is used in, say, unstructured business planning. What is going on? Who is doing it? Why are they doing it (motives)? Where is it happening? How is it happening? What is the likely prognosis or development? There are several ways to capture the information generated from brainstorming, and one of the most effective for quick-time intelligence analysis is known as mind mapping (see Figure 13.3 for a simplified example). Using Post-It notes and a laminated or plastic board means that ideas can be moved around as the event unfolds and as their knowledge and understanding become more comprehensive. Computer software also exists and can be used projected onto a wall.

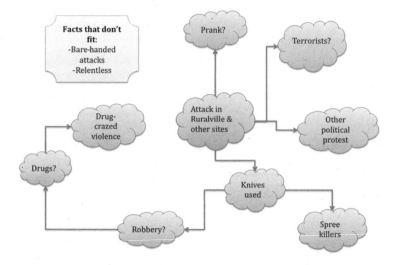

Figure 13.3 Mind Map (Simplified).

One of the main underlying reasons for this problem definition stage is the need to identify bias and try to limit its effects on the analysis and thus decision-making. Even though intelligence analysis is designed to facilitate robust decision-making, it is far from infallible, and intelligence failures often make the news in a way that successes do not. The consequences of intelligence failure can be horrific: the terrorist attacks in the United States on 11 September 2001, the Yom Kippur War of 1973 when Israel was surprised by an attack by Egypt and Syria, Operation Barbarossa when Hitler attacked the USSR in 1941, and the Japanese attack on Pearl Harbor also in 1941 are often cited as examples of intelligence failure with devastating consequences. In these cases, all of which have been examined extensively, biased or prejudiced opinion at either the analyst or the decision-maker stage, or both, was found to have played a part in the intelligence failure.

The very makeup of the SIAG is a step to counter natural human bias. The DISS analyst, for example, automatically favours the hypothesis that the incidents of mob violence are some kind of admittedly unusual terrorist event, whereas the police favour a theory of robbery or, more likely, some kind of violence-inducing drug such as PCP.[2] These examples are both indications of "groupthink," when an organization's reason for being "blinkers" its intelligence analysts against fully exploring what might be happening. Groupthink was arguably one reason why Western governments missed the beginnings of the collapse of the Soviet Union in the late 1980s. Agencies such as the CIA were formed to oppose Soviet Communism; they could not conceive a world where the enemy did not exist (Haines and Leggett 2003).

SIAG analysts, regardless of their home agencies, tend to have further education degrees and/or extensive operational experience. Degrees in psychology, statistics, modern history, geography, politics, criminology and law are fairly typical.

---

2 PCP, also known as "angel dust," is an illegal drug linked to users who inflict extreme violence against others and who apparently have an increased pain threshold, so they can seem invincible.

Police intelligence analysts understand, for example, the limitation of witness observation. Numerous studies indicate that people "see" things they expect to see, which explains the phenomenon of multiple, varying descriptions of a single perpetrator of a crime by numerous eyewitnesses, regardless of whether they are trained observers or everyday folk. In the Ruralville incident, the first police responder thought he saw a knife used in the murder of his colleague, and this was reported. The City Police intelligence analysts in the SIAG might give that reported observation undue weight only because it came from a police officer, one of their colleagues. The sole report of a knife would alert the SIAG as a whole to be wary of the observation, and, while the analysts examine the attacks with the assumption that the perpetrators are armed, scenarios in which the perpetrators are not armed will also be explored as part of the continuing process of problem definition, hypothesis development and testing.

Time pressure means that SIAG members must conceptualize their current thoughts on the situation, record them and move on quickly. The collective experience of the group and the strength of the tested, straightforward Emergency Security Protocols timetable and reporting enable the group to note issues for research, thus allowing a focused yet open-minded analysis. Already the basic scientific precept of testing hypotheses dominates. Analysts of the calibre usually assigned to a SIAG apply the hypothesis –> indicator –> general area –> general question –> refined question –> specific question sequence without consciously thinking that this is what they are doing.

The next phase is research: the data collection, collation and evaluation stages of the intelligence cycle. The easiest division of labour is along areas of expertise and access to information sources. The room in which the SIAG is based has secure data lines to the different agencies that comprise the SIAG. This simply means that the DISS officer has access to DISS systems, the police to theirs and so on. All agencies look for recorded events that might be similar to what is occurring in Capital City. From her experience, the MI officer knows that military systems do not hold such information, so she applies her skills as a generalist researcher to search the internet. The internet is a major boon in many ways to the intelligence community in providing access to what is described as "open-source information," meaning that it has not come from secret or privileged information sources. As any researcher who uses the internet knows, the quality and accuracy of much of the vast array of human knowledge and opinion online are variable. Intelligence agencies have formulated ways to quickly show the levels to which pieces of information can be trusted as credible. One of the most widely used is the NATO Admiralty System of Evaluation, also used by Australia and New Zealand (see Table 13.2). This type of alphanumeric code is easy to apply to any particular information snippet, and an example of how it is typically used is included in the SIAG briefing form (see Figure 13.4). For the police and DISS, the databases they are searching will have had an evaluation applied by the original reporting officer. In a similar manner, the MI officer will apply her knowledge to assess both the reliability of the information source and the credibility of the information. Experience means that the MI officer will first go to trusted sources such as already known news websites or blogs. As they are progressively exhausted during the event, she will start to look at sources with unknown reliability and therefore will likely be rated an "F6," at least initially. If the information echoes that in more reliable sources, then the credibility of the information can be rated higher.

After an hour of research, the SIAG comes back together to conduct a second round of formal analysis. The analysts use the quickest and easiest tools, and the ones with which they are most familiar. In this case, they conduct more focused brainstorming to amend the mind map they have already begun. In an effort to save time, the SIAG leader types their findings as they go into the predeveloped form (see Figure 13.4). The most relevant intelligence reports can either be copied into the form verbatim or summarized with reference to the original. Depending on the outcome of the incident, these documents will be used in court (be it the coroner's, a criminal or some other legal process) and therefore need to be clear about apparent fact and the group's opinion. Decisions and countering arguments also need to be recorded accurately.

Table 13.2 NATO Admiralty System of Evaluation

Reliability of the source of information:	Credibility of the information:
A = completely reliable	1 = confirmed
B = usually reliable	2 = probably true
C = fairly reliable	3 = possibly true
D = not usually reliable	4 = doubtful
E = unreliable	5 = improbable
F = not known	6 = cannot be judged

At this early stage, only two hours into the emergency, the information is sketchy and full of contradictions. SIAG analysts begin with the known facts of the current event, identify and isolate the unique factors at work, identify the logical antecedents and consequences of the event, and develop scenarios as plausible narratives. In an event such as this, in which the unique factors outweigh the known typical antecedents of terrorist or criminal acts, the SIAG will work both backward to seek explanation of how the situation developed and forward to map a future outcome. Because this situation is outside the normal extreme events for which the SIAG is trained, the key priority is to find and draw on historical precedents, but the need to be wary of analogies becomes important. No two events, no matter how similar they seem, are identical and while analogies are a useful tool they are open to subjective interpretation and can distract even experienced intelligence analysts from other credible possibilities.

Some of the analysts, not just from DISS, favour a terrorist incident as the dominant hypothesis. The SIAG leader forces the issue by running a devil's advocate session with three members of the team looking at each of the isolated facts and components of that narrative, and actively developing counterfactual arguments. The key points confirmed are: no political group has claimed responsibility, there is no secret intelligence indicating any monitored political group might be behind the attacks, and these attacks follow no known prior pattern. The SIAG members agree that the terrorist scenario is unlikely. At the same time, the remainder of the group explores the motive of robbery using Situation Appreciation, in which each analyst asks "so what does that signify?" of each factor until it quickly exhausts the known facts about robbery. All of the reports do describe attacks on property (and people), but none indicates any type of theft. When the group members come back together, the SIAG concludes that the violence is extreme, unplanned and apparently random. Spree killing is a possibility, but the National Police analyst voices her skepticism on the basis of her knowledge of such crimes. They overwhelmingly feature lone or paired killers, usually using firearms, not crowds that might or might not be armed with knives. The City Police analysts suggested that a drug such as PCP taken by students might have resulted in the mob violence. Since this idea came late in this first-reporting cycle, the chance to analyze it before the SIAG leader briefs the police commander is unrealized. They note it in the Further Intelligence Requirements section.

Using the Briefing Form as a crib, the SIAG leader verbally reports the current situation and possible scenarios to the commander. The first SIAG report is important for capturing what is known at the time in the assessed summary (the situation report, or sit-rep) as well as eliminating typical terrorist and spree killer incidents as the least likely scenarios. This means the C&C team can avoid directing resources to operating standard responses to those types of incident.

SIAG Briefing 1	Start date/time of incident: 09/09/2012 06:00 (24 hr)
Officers:	City Police: SIAG leader and 3 analysts National Police: 1 analyst Military Intelligence: 1 analyst DISS: 1 analyst Others: nil

Summary of Facts (rolling situation report—most recent first):
Date/time of report: 09/09/2012 11:00 hrs

At approximately 06:00 hrs the media (radio) reported an incident in Ruralville involving an unknown number of offenders threatening residents. (F6)

At 07:13 hrs a City Police patrol (Car RV7) radioed that an officer had been attacked and killed by a mob of civilians at Market Farm 3 in Ruralville.

Knives suspected. Second officer left immediate scene for safety reasons. Full report at IR9-683-89. (B3)

At 07:52 hrs City Police Central Command received a call from an elderly woman to the north of Capital City about 12 vagrants trespassing on her property. Local police patrol (Car N42) dispatched. Attacked by vagrants, including one who looked like the owner of the property. Full report at IR4-665-15. (B4)

Current Assessment (most recent first):
Date/time of report: 09/09/2012 11:00 hrs

Based upon the available intelligence and initial assessment, a terrorist incident can be ruled out. There has been no declaration from known political groups and the attacks do not follow any form of terrorist attack previously in any other country, including ours.

Robbery as a motive also does not appear validated by the intelligence picture.

Spree killing is a possible explanation, but also does not follow the usual patterns of lone or duo perpetrators with firearms.

Ferocity and tenacity of attacks in Ruralville against a police officer suggest drug use such as PCP. A tainted batch of the drug might explain the other incidents in other parts of the city. Caution required as (1) PCP is not widely used in Capital City, and (2) batches are normally found in less apparently randomized geographic locations.

Potential Scenarios (most recent first), rated in terms of likelihood (probable, possible, not likely):
Date/time of report: 09/09/2012 11:00 hrs

Too early for developed scenarios. Two broad scenarios.
1. Incidents are unrelated.
2. Incidents are related.

Further Intelligence Requirements (most recent first):
Date/time of report: 09/09/2012 11:00 hrs

Drug angle
Other causes
Continue monitoring for political motivation.

Figure 13.4 Mock-Up of SIAG Briefing Form for First Two Hours

Table 13.3 A Selection of Tools and Techniques Used in Intelligence Analysis

Competing Hypotheses	The playoff between various dominant hypotheses, which might involve techniques such as "Red Teaming" and "Devil's Advocate," is designed to force thorough considerations of all the positives, negatives and "grey areas" of each hypothesis. Richards J. Heuer Jr. (1999) developed this in greater detail in *Psychology of Intelligence Analysis*.
Devil's Advocate	Individuals deliberately try to counter all the points raised by the team.
Drill Down	As the name suggests, this approach involves exploring deeper and deeper into each facet of the hypothesis.
Future's Wheel	This is a bit like a mind map, only asking "what would happen if ...?" to develop each idea. It is normally limited to three ideas out from the central question.
Occam's Razor	This is the principle that the simplest explanation tends to be the best one and is also known as the law of succinctness. It is used to pare down the problem to its simplest form.
PESTELOM	A simple check that aids the gathering of information from a variety of sources. The *aide memoire* stands for political, economic, social, technical, environmental, legal, organizational and media. There are variations on these strands.
Problem Identification	This involves repeatedly asking why the problem exists until the issue is exhausted. Think of a typical annoying six-year-old child always asking "why?" until the conversation enters the ridiculous and emulate that behaviour. This breaks the situation down, but keeps attention focused on the problem at hand (very helpful with brainstorming and mind mapping). Summarizing the problem concisely—preferably in two words—sharpens the process.
Provocation	Adapted from Edward de Bono's business-improvement techniques, this involves lateral thinking to generate an original starting point for creative thinking. A deliberately stupid comment is made relating to the problem and then explored seriously, but with judgment suspended.

Red Teaming or Red Cell Thinking	A sub-team is formed to try to come at the problem deliberately from the adversary's point of view.
Situation Appreciation	This involves stating an observed situation and asking "so what?"

While the SIAG leader is briefing the commander, the SIAG members are redefining their priorities in light of their conclusions at this stage. They must fully explore the drug angle, continue to monitor the possibility of political motivation and, very importantly, continue to develop other hypotheses to test. Information is now flowing into the Command Centre as police in numbers attend the sites. A third incident was identified between 10:30 and 11:00 to the near west of Capital City. The TIG identifies a second common denominator beyond proximity to university and college campuses. Each site is near a large cemetery, which for Site Three the TIG notes is a large tract of open land within a built-up suburban and light industry zone.

The SIAG favours the drug scenario. The team is now three hours (plus travel) into a day on a weekend after most of them have put in a full five-day week. It is a day involving intense pressure to use their imaginations and knowledge, and thoroughly to conduct research that can effectively test their hypotheses to explain the scenario. The temptation to cut corners and concentrate on the one scenario is enormous. However, the SIAG leader understands these dangers when they are still at a relatively early stage. The leader therefore splits the group in two: one half will continue to develop hypotheses independent of the drug scenario and methods to test them, and the other half will concentrate on exhausting all the possibilities relating to some kind of behaviour-modifying substance. They widen the scope of this scenario beyond PCP and break the theory down using various questioning techniques (see Table 13.3 for a selection).

Role playing enables the SIAG to question the problem from as many different perspectives as possible. New information from the TIG and the SIAG research informs this continuing analysis, which eliminates PCP and the other main known illegal drugs from being the cause of the mob violence. However, the idea of a biological or chemical agent changing people's behaviour remains the most logical explanation and is not being contradicted by new knowledge. The analysts start to refer to this unknown agent as "Factor Z." Among the reports coming in are increasing numbers of incidents in which apparent victims of the violence have joined the mobs. It defies rational explanation, but, when considered as an indicator of some kind of agent of transmission, it cannot be dismissed easily. The analysts begin to think of these reports as indicating that the victims thought killed were in fact injured and infected. The SIAG leader draws the group together when it becomes apparent that the scenario as a whole is more resistant to the analytical assault than any other scenario.

TV programs such as *24, Flash Forward* and *[spooks]*,[3] as well as the James Bond films, suggest that people involved in intelligence work in a ticking-time-bomb scenario are virtually superhuman. Emergency situations do mean the entire TIG and SIAG cannot take breaks at the same time. Meal times are staggered so that there are always enough people working in case there is a sudden turn of events when a pivotal fact is discovered. The temptation is for people to eat and work, but experience has informed the rule that group members take a half-hour lunch break from the job to recharge, which is vital for their work.

At 13:00 hrs, the second briefing occurs. The commander's primary concern is about the potential for more outbreaks and where they might occur. The SIAG leader can tell him that they are in a position to try to answer that question now that they have determined Factor Z as the likely cause. They still need to identify the agent, prove the links to the universities and colleges, and determine if there are any cures. The commander is satisfied with that response.

On return to the SIAG, the leader tasks one of the City Police analysts with reviewing all of the intelligence they have gathered to date and their analyses. During this two-hour block, this analyst realizes a basic question has not, in fact, been answered or properly explored: the identities of the original attackers.

3   *MI5* in the United States.

SIAG Briefing 2	Start date/time of incident: 09/09/2012 06:00 (24 hr)
Officers:	City Police: SIAG leader and 3 analysts National Police: 1 analyst Military Intelligence: 1 analyst DISS: 1 analyst Others: nil

Date/time of report: 09/09/2012 13:00 hrs

Numerous reports are being recorded onto the CCP systems. TIG is recording full log.

At approximately 10:49 hrs, Western College reported an incident of violence quickly determined to fit the pattern of the attacks at Ruralville and in the north. Full details at IR7-467-74. (B2)

Date/time of report: 09/09/2012 11:00 hrs

At approximately 06:00 hrs the media (radio) reported an incident in Ruralville involving an unknown number of offenders threatening residents. (F6)

At 07:13 hrs a City Police patrol (Car RV7) radioed that an officer had been attacked and killed by a mob of civilians at Market Farm 3 in Ruralville. Knives suspected. Second officer left immediate scene for safety reasons. Full report at IR9-683-89. (B3)

At 07:52 hrs City Police Central Command received a call from an elderly woman to the north of Capital City about 12 vagrants trespassing on her property. Local police patrol (Car N42) dispatched. Attacked by vagrants, including one who looked like the owner of the property. Full report at IR4-665-15. (B4)

Current Assessment (most recent first):
Date/time of report: 09/09/2012 13:00 hrs

The most promising scenario is an unidentified agent—Factor Z—that causes human beings to act with extreme violence against unaffected human beings.

All previous scenarios have been effectively disproved on the basis of available information.

Date/time of report: 09/09/2012 11:00 hrs

Based on the available intelligence and initial assessment, a terrorist incident can be ruled out. There have been no declarations from known political groups and the attacks do not follow any form of terrorist attack previously in any other country, including ours.

Robbery as a motive also does not appear validated by the intelligence picture.

Spree killing is a possible explanation, but also does not follow the usual patterns of lone or duo perpetrators with firearms.

Ferocity and tenacity of attacks in Ruralville against a police officer suggest drug use such as PCP. A tainted batch of the drug might explain the other incidents in other parts of the city. Caution required as (1) PCP is not widely used in Capital City, and (2) batches are normally found in less apparently randomized geographic locations.

Potential Scenarios (most recent first), rated in terms of likelihood (probable, possible, not likely):
Date/time of report: 09/09/2012 13:00 hrs

Most probable scenario is that the incidents are related and caused by an as-yet-unidentified infectious agent: Factor Z.

Date/time of report: 09/09/2012 11:00 hrs

Too early for developed scenarios. Two broad scenarios.
1. Incidents are unrelated.
2. Incidents are related.

Further Intelligence Requirements (most recent first):
Date/time of report: 09/09/2012 13:00 hrs

Identifying Factor Z
Other causes

Date/time of report: 09/09/2012 11:00 hrs
Drug angle
Other causes
Continue monitoring for political motivation.

Figure 13.5 Mock-Up of SIAG Briefing Form for Second Two Hours

Are they students from the university campus, as everyone first supposed? The analyst informs the SIAG leader, who agrees that it is an important oversight. The analyst's job now is to obtain pictures and to speak to the TIG to try to identify the original offenders.

Risk assessment is now an important tool for the SIAG to test the elements of its reviewed hypothesis to better answer the commander's needs. Risk assessment involves estimating the risk or likelihood of a threat happening and then assessing the likely impacts by multiplying the likelihood by the amount that it will cost to put right. Tables 13.4 and 13.5 are examples of how risk is assessed. For example, the SIAG will need to determine the likelihood of further sites where people might become infected with Factor Z. Their determinations will use their acquired knowledge of the original sites of infection; at this stage, sites they consider as almost certain sites are those near where attacks have taken place and likely as those near universities and colleges. They will factor in the proximity to population sites (i.e., where there are large numbers of people vulnerable to infection) to determine the potential impact of each risk. This provides a measure that can then guide the commander's decision-making.

Table 13.4 Likelihood of a Risk Occurring

Measure	Traffic Light	Definition
Almost certain	Red	Almost certain to occur in the immediate or near future
Likely	Amber/red	Likely to occur in the near future
Possible	Amber	Possible at some point
Unlikely	Green/amber	Unlikely to occur at any given point
Rare	Green	Highly unlikely to occur

Reports continue to flow into the teams. The police forward-command teams report that gunshots do not stop the offenders, although their bodies are damaged by the shots. The SIAG leader notes the odd phrasing in the reports where they refer to "damaged" rather than "injured." One report is submitted about the accidental decapitation of one of the perpetrators. That act stops the offender dead, but no other injuries seem to be able to stop those affected by Factor Z and committing the violent offences. This seems to be an important lead. The DISS and police search their systems and find no other similar event; the DISS officer extends his search to files that DISS can access on international events and submits a request that the International Relations Department search classified databases from allied countries. The MI officer finds a conspiracy theory website that has reports of an eerily similar type of mob violence manifestation some decades earlier in a small town in a distant, impoverished country. This website refers to the attackers as "zombies," describing them as "reanimated corpses from cemeteries and relentless in pursuit of living human flesh." The only way this other country was able to solve the problem was by decapitating each one. The MI officer files the report because of its close likeness to what they are seeing in Capital City, but she rates it as F6. On learning of the reports of decapitation in Capital City, she amends the report rating to F3 and shares it with the SIAG. The DISS analyst submits another search to foreign sources to test the validity of the website the MI officer has found.

Table 13.5 Potential Impact of Each Risk

Measure	Traffic Light	Definition
Catastrophic	Red	Catastrophic impact and/or damage
Major	Amber/red	Major impact and/or damage
Moderate	Amber	Moderate impact and/or damage
Minor	Green/amber	Minor impact and/or damage
Insignificant	Green	Insignificant impact and/or damage

Eureka moments like this are often a sudden drawing together of apparently disparate events in a way that makes sense even if the solution remains preposterous. The SIAG team members test each part of this new theory while they wait, and the SIAG leader decides to be cautious when briefing the commander at 15:00 hrs and tells him they are nearing a fuller explanation that needs to be verified. He tells the commander they are waiting on that verification, but they can answer the questions he posed at 13:00 hrs about the likelihood of more outbreaks of mob violence. They now consider proximity to cemeteries important and the task to identify the first offenders has become crucial. Proximity to institutions of higher learning with experimental chemical laboratories remains important. There are no other sites like that in Capital City beyond those where the attacks have already occurred. The main problem is infections of others caused by the offenders from the original three sites.

Later the DISS analyst is able to verify an unusual event in the country mentioned in the website. A little after that, the CP officer is able to identify some of the offenders caught on camera by the police car to first respond to the reports in Ruralville. Two are identical to victims of a road accident who had died from internal injuries. They had been buried in the cemetery nearest the agricultural college, which the SIAG now suspects is the source of the contagion. The SIAG leader confirms to the commander the apparently impossible: the offenders are reanimated corpses that can only be stopped by decapitation.

CONCLUSION
It is usually the case that the real nature of an emergency situation is not known when an emergency response is called. For this reason, intelligence analysis cells such as the TIG and SIAG in this fictional example are called in to help determine the nature of the event. Therefore, their immediate role is to quickly gather as much information as possible and to pull apart, or analyze, what they know about the matter at hand. The SIAG's role in particular is important for developing scenarios and risk assessments to help the commander's decision-making about where to deploy resources. The SIAG's role is also important for recording events as they unfold and vital for the inevitable legal process following the event.

The example in this chapter shows how intelligence analysis is applied in a real-time emergency situation in which the perpetrators—zombies, in this case—are not a known threat. Similar techniques are used in everyday police work, but without the intense time pressure caused by an initial risk or threat assessment employed when deciding to call an emergency.

BIBLIOGRAPHY
Andrew, Christopher. 2009. *The Defence of the Realm: The Authorised History of MI5.* London: Allen Lane (Penguin).

Australian National Security Framework. http://www.ag.gov.au/agd/
www/nationalsecurity.nsf/AllDocs/85A16ADB86A23AD1CA256FC6
00072E6B?OpenDocument.

Bar-Joseph, Uri. 2003. "Intelligence Failure and the Need for Cognitive
Closure: The Case of Yom Kippur." In *Paradoxes of Strategic
Intelligence: Essays in Honor of Michael I. Handel,* edited by Richard
K. Betts and Thomas G. Mahnken, 166–89. London: Frank Cass.

Bruce, James B. and Roger Z. George, eds. 2008. *Analyzing Intelligence:
Origins, Obstacles, and Innovations.* Washington, DC: Georgetown
University Press.

Canter, David. 2003. *Mapping Murder: The Secrets of Geographical
Profiling.* London: Virgin.

Charters, David A., Stuart Farson and Glenn P. Hastedt. 1996.
Intelligence Analysis and Assessment. London: Frank Cass.

DeLong, Candice. 2001. *Special Agent: My Life on the Front Lines of the
FBI.* London: Headline Book Publishing.

Douglas, John E. and Mark Olshaker. 1995. *Mindhunter: Inside the FBI's
Elite Serial Crime Unit.* New York: Scribner.

———. 1997. *Journey into Darkness.* New York: Scribner.

———. 1998. *Obsession: The FBI's Legendary Profiler Probes the
Psyches of Killers, Rapists, and Stalkers and Their Victims and Tells
How to Fight Back.* New York: Scribner.

———. 1999. *The Anatomy of Motive: The FBI's Legendary Mindhunter
Explores the Key to Understanding and Catching Violent Criminals.*
New York: Scribner.

Douglas, John E. and Johnny Dodd. 2007. *Inside the Mind of BTK: The
True Story behind the Thirty-Year Hunt for the Notorious Wichita
Serial Killer.* San Francisco: Jossey-Bass.

George, Roger Z. 2006. "Fixing the Problem of Analytical Mindsets:
Alternative Analysis." In *Intelligence and the National Security
Strategist: Enduring Issues and Challenges,* edited by Roger Z.
George and Robert D. Kline. Lanham: Rowman and Littlefield
Publishers.

Gill, Peter and Mark Pythian. 2006. *Intelligence in an Insecure World.*
Cambridge: Polity Press.

Haines, Gerald K. and Robert E. Leggett, eds. 2003. *Watching the Bear:
Essays on CIA's Analysis of the Soviet Union.* https://www.cia.gov/
library/center-for-the-study-of-intelligence/csi-publications/
books-and-monographs.

Halevy, Efraim. 2004. "In Defence of the Intelligence Services." *The Economist,* 31 July, 21.

Heuer, Richards J. Jr. 1999. *Psychology of Intelligence Analysis.* Washington, DC: Center for the Study of Intelligence, CIA.

Johnston, Rob. c. 2003. "Integrating Methodologists into Teams of Substantive Experts: Reducing Analytic Error." *Studies in Intelligence* 47, 1. https://www.cia.gov/library/center-for-the-study-of-intelligence/csi-publications/csi-studies/studies/vol47-no1/article06.htm.

Kuhns, Woodrow J. 2003. "Intelligence Failures: Forecasting and Lessons of Epistemology." In *Paradoxes of Strategic Intelligence: Essays in Honor of Michael I. Handel,* edited by Richard K. Betts and Thomas G. Mahnken, 80–100. London: Frank Cass.

McDowell, Don. 1998. *Strategic Intelligence: A Handbook for Practitioners, Managers, and Users.* Cooma: Istana Enterprises.

McCrary, Gregg O. 2003. *The Unknown Darkness: Profiling the Predators among Us: A Former FBI Profiler Examines His Most Fascinating—and Haunting—Cases.* New York: HarperCollins.

Ratcliffe, Jerry H. 2008. *Intelligence-Led Policing.* Cullompton: Willan Publishing.

———, ed. 2004. *Strategic Thinking in Criminal Intelligence.* Sydney: Federation Press.

Ressler, Robert K. 1992. *Whoever Fights Monsters: My Twenty Years Tracking Serial Killers for the FBI.* New York: St. Martin's Press.

Ressler, Robert K., Ann W. Burgess and John E. Douglas. 1988. *Sexual Homicide: Patterns and Motives.* Lexington, MA: Lexington Books.

Rieber, Steven and Neil Thomason. 2007. *Creation of a National Institute for Analytic Method: Toward Improving Intelligence Analysis.* https://www.cia.gov/library/center-for-the-study-of-intelligence/csi-publications/csi-studies/studies/vol49no4/Analytic_Methods_7.htm.

EVOLUTION OF THE MODERN ZOMBIE

PHILIP MUNZ AND PHILIPPE P. VACHON

INTRODUCTION

In an earlier paper on the subject of mathematical modelling of infectious disease (Munz et al. 2009), the authors warned that "only quick, aggressive attacks can stave off the dooms- day scenario" and that "only ever-increasing attacks, with in- creasing force, will result in eradication [of zombies], assuming the available resources can be mustered in time." What hap- pens when our governments do not heed these words and do not prepare for the potentially apocalyptic zombie attack? How can the average Joe or Joan prepare for such an attack? Through the heroic works of George A. Romero and the scien- tific expertise on zombies (Delorme and Day n.d.), a substantial base of knowledge and understanding is being built up to as- sist individuals ranging from high-level policy-makers through to bored housewives playing EverQuest. Zombies have become ubiquitous as antagonists in a number of different forms of en- tertainment, such as movies, video games and novels. To un- derstand best how the modern horror zombie came to be what it is today, it's important to understand what its ancestors were and how zombies have evolved over the years.

Evolution is an extremely important biological concept, and is the cornerstone of modern understanding of how flora and fauna on Earth came to be in the states they are today. In its most basic sense, evolution can be thought of as describing a change in a species over time. It is considered as the process of change by which new species develop from pre-existing species, sometimes through selective breeding, descent with modification or survival of the fittest. Over many generations of a species, mutations will produce successive, small changes in traits (Futuyama 2005), generally favouring traits that better ensure the survival or adaptation of a species. Descent with modification simply means changes in the properties of organisms over generations and it tries to account only for the similarities among creatures (Mayr 2001).

Speciation is the formation of new species as a result of geographic, physiological, anatomical or behavioural factors. With respect to zombies, different species arise due to writers, directors, producers and burning social issues of the times in which the particular variant zombies are conceived.

The archetypal modern horror zombies, more commonly known as "the living dead" (Romero 1968), are reanimated human corpses that mindlessly wander in hordes and terrorize the living. These zombies have a single, horrifying goal: to feast on living flesh, usually with some variation on the ability to turn normal humans into other zombies (O'Bannon 1985). Generally, the zombie horde is portrayed as mindless, though perhaps demonstrating some level of collective awareness or a common goal. Typically, if any collective goal is sought, the nature of the goal is entirely determined by the living dead's appetite for live human flesh (Romero 2005; Wright 2002).

Physically, most zombies show signs of decomposition, discoloured eyes, open wounds and missing limbs or other body parts. Zombies are often seen wearing a burial suit, as one of the finest sources for candidate zombies (or the beginning of a zombie apocalypse) is the existing dead, torn from their final resting places. Later portrayals have suggested that zombies are the harbingers of the fall of civilization as we know it and are often related to the apocalypse (an excellent recounting can be found in *World War Z* [Brooks 2006]).

No one specific cause is shared by all portrayals; the origin of the zombie is redefined almost every time. These origins include the use of science—radiation, scientific experimentation, genetic mutation (Keiji 2006)—as a scapegoat; mutation of another known virus, specifically Creutzfeldt-Jakob (mad cow) disease (Fleischer 2009); Hell running out of room and the dead walking the Earth (Romero 1978); and living beings of pure evil dying and becoming undead (Wirkola 2009).

The best-known sightings of zombies by the masses occur in the cinema, where the zombie as it is known today was born. As a popular means to educate the public on how to react in the event of a zombie apocalypse, the cinema has ensured that millions have seen how to deal with the zombie horror. However, in recent years, improvements in video-game technology have enabled the creation of extremely realistic zombie simulators. As one character from *Diary of the Dead* (2007) claims, we will "learn to survive by watching others survive."

Any video game in which the antagonists satisfy the above definition of a zombie is considered useful for our discussion. Video games can be thought of as training simulations (in fact, there are already some non-zombie training simulations being considered or used by the American Army, including *Virtual Battlespace 2*) to prepare for the next inevitable zombie outbreak. Technology has improved so much over the years that users now enjoy near-lifelike special effects, graphics and a level of realism not previously experienced. This technology enables game creators (such as Valve and Capcom) to prepare more comprehensive and applicable simulations as new information on zombie outbreaks becomes available.

Video games have evolved rapidly in the past few decades, ranging from classic eight-bit video games on the Atari and the Nintendo Entertainment System (NES) to the extremely realistic modern PC and console video games, such as *Left 4 Dead*. As the uptake of zombie-related video games increases, an army of millions of individuals is exposed to zombie identification exercises, eradication exercises and some basic zombie biology. This training will assist in ensuring that at least some portion of humanity will survive a zombie apocalypse and possibly reduce the amount of potential zombie fodder.[1]

Popular music and the written media can also be used to educate the masses about the zombie threat and how to respond to it. In recent years, there has been an influx of zombie "fiction." Some of these works of so-called fiction are posed as literature to help with survival training (*The Zombie Survival Guide* [Brooks 2003]). Others serve as a recounting of the horrors experienced by survivors of a zombie outbreak and a commentary on social issues before, during and after the fact (*World War Z* [Brooks 2006]). One notable musician, Rob Zombie, has incorporated zombie aesthetics and innuendo into so much of his work that, were it not for the fact that he can sing (if one believes that what he does can actually be considered singing), he would likely have already been identified as a zombie.[2]

ZOMBIE ORIGINS

The word *zombie* has been used to describe many different phenomena throughout human history. The word is said to have come from the late 1800s in the Afro-Caribbean spiritual belief system of Vodou (anglicized as "voodoo"), for which the term was originally the name of a snake "god," *nzambi*. Later the word was associated in the voodoo cult with the meaning of reanimated corpse. It is also said to have come from a Louisiana Creole word meaning phantom or ghost. In the early 1900s, it was used as a slang term to mean "slow-witted person." Although this is an important description of a zombie, we want to ensure that it is not confused with the image of a horror zombie.

Zombies have been present in horror films since the 1930s.

---

1 We should point out that excessive consumption of fast foods and potato chips while performing such training is counterproductive for those wishing to deal effectively with the impending zombie apocalypse.

2 We hold no opinion on whether or not Rob Zombie's music is good so please do not contact us on this matter.

The first recorded zombie movie was *White Zombie* (Halperin 1932). The zombie characters were individuals given a drug that turned them into mindless beings that the antagonist enslaved. Many zombie movies of the 1930s–60s followed a similar formula, in which the zombies were created by mad scientists (*The Walking Dead*, 1936), voodoo practices (*Voodoo Man*, 1944; *The Plague of the Zombies*, 1966), magic (*Teenage Zombies*, 1959) and hypnosis (*Tales of Terror*, 1962). Others labelled zombie flicks were borderline science-fiction stories with the zombie-like characters providing many of the scares. Examples are *Plan 9 from Outer Space* (1959) and *The Earth Dies Screaming* (1965), in both of which the zombies are deceased humans brought back to life by alien invaders.

When we use the term "zombie," we are referring exclusively to the modern horror zombie. This type of zombie was introduced in George A. Romero's *Night of the Living Dead* (1968). What makes this movie the origin of the modern horror zombie? The zombies in earlier movies were more akin to the original definition of a historical zombie: that of the Afro-Caribbean, Haitian or Creole cultures and not the reanimated corpses that Romero describes. It was actually in *Night of the Living Dead* that zombies were presented as flesh eaters for the first time. There was also a gritty realism displayed in the film not seen before. The zombies were much more believable and terrifying than those raised by alien invaders. These zombies were not controlled by a mad scientist or voodoo priest, but were autonomous, following their own will to find and consume flesh. These characteristics of Romero's zombies heavily influenced many works since, making this movie the obvious choice as the origin of the modern horror zombie.

ROMERO ZOMBIES

Night of the Living Dead was our introduction to the modern horror zombie and it is worth noting that not once in the film was the term "zombie" used to describe the creatures. According to one source (Kay 2008), the dead were modelled after ghouls and not traditional zombies. These creatures, however, became the very embodiment of the archetypal modern horror zombie: mindless monsters devoid of intelligence with an appetite for human flesh; unlike the traditional zombie (voodoo), they were not under anyone's control.

The film revealed one hypothesis about the cause of the zombie horror: that a virus was caused by radiation from a Venusian space probe. This was briefly mentioned only once in the movie and never further elaborated.

We were also informed, through the characters' experiences, as well as through newscasts that appear in the background during a variety of scenes in the movie, that the zombie outbreak was not an isolated incident. Throughout the movie, there were many occurrences of similar attacks all over the eastern seaboard. This showed that the zombie problem can become overwhelming in a short period of time.

This film showcased several weaknesses of these zombies. Luckily, zombies have not evolved enough (yet) to eliminate these potential means of eradication. For instance, it was shown that zombies would be killed if their heads were removed or their brains destroyed, either one essentially impairing their inexplicably restored motor functions. These zombies showed signs of physical decomposition and were likely more fragile than the average human, thus making them easy to destroy one on one. "If you have a gun, shoot 'em in the head, that's a sure way to kill them. If you don't, get yourself a club or a torch. Beat 'em or burn 'em, they go up pretty easy." Without these vulnerabilities, zombies would likely have already established themselves as the dominant species on the planet, given the virtually unlimited sources of corpses to be reanimated and their lack of fear for their own existence.

After being the first to encounter the modern horror zombie, Romero went on to discover more about them. Since *Night of the Living Dead,* he has built upon the modern horror zombie concept to horrify and educate millions of people.

In *Day of the Dead* (Romero 1985), zombies have overrun most of the world. Few living humans remain, including a group of soldiers and scientists in the process of studying zombies. One of the survivors, a mad scientist named Logan, has developed a friendship with one of his specimens and has given him the name Bub. Bub is the first zombie to display the evolutionary trend we will call "zombie consciousness," or the rudimentary understanding zombies have about their surroundings and what drives them to be the horrifying monsters we see in the movies. Bub shows signs of deeper emotions than any other zombie in his connection with Logan. For instance, he does not show any desire to eat Logan and even shows affection for the scientist when he exacts revenge (the only way a zombie can) on the human who killed his friend. Bub also shows evidence that he possesses distant memories of his past life when he mimicks the use of a razor to shave his face, flips through the pages of a book as if he is reading and points a gun at an intended victim.

The evolution of zombie consciousness did not end with Bub. In Romero's subsequent film, *Land of the Dead* (2005), development of concepts of leadership and autonomy within the zombie hordes are evident. In addition, several zombies begin to show signs of remembering rudimentary skills from when they were alive, all pertaining to the different lifestyles they had before becoming infected. Zombies pump gas, play a musical instrument, shoot a gun, lift and carry larger objects and use them for some purpose. The horde of zombies also appoints a leader, referred to as "Big Daddy" in the end credits of the movie, and follows him through the film to its climax. Big Daddy shows further signs of the evolved Romero zombie when he produces guttural cries of despair and rage in apparent recognition of different situations. The guttural sounds also seem to be a form of communication among zombies. This indicates a development of awareness in zombies of their surroundings, quite an improvement over their "ancestors," who stumbled aimlessly into or around things. This poses a serious problem: if zombies can recognize situations, or learn from similar experiences, they can adapt their "hunting" strategies. They will also be harder to destroy since they can remember past events and likely will not fall for the same tricks and/or traps.

ZOMBIES WITH MULLETS WEARING SPANDEX

As moviegoers became more cynical, it was apparent that more realistic, gory and action-packed zombie films needed to be made. In the 1980s, Daniel O'Bannon stepped up to the plate with *The Return of the Living Dead*. It alluded to the fact that Romero's film *Night of the Living Dead* was a dramatization of real events and that zombies pose a real threat. The source of the zombies was an experimental chemical called Trioxin, which would slowly kill any living person who came into contact with it and subsequently raise him or her from the dead. The film was released within weeks of Romero's *Day of the Dead* and featured a more dramatic evolutionary turn in the zombies than Bub. The zombies could not be stopped by being impaled in the brain, and they could move around even when in multiple pieces (with each piece having some mobility). They were also the first zombies able to speak, albeit slowly and usually with just one word: *braaaiiinnnsss*. It should come as no surprise, then, that their diet also had a disturbing evolutionary change. While still interested in feeding on flesh, the zombies altered their palates to include brains. There are a few hypotheses about this; perhaps these zombies considered brains a delicacy.[3] A more pessimistic thought is that zombies might know that consuming a human's brain would leave that person dead, thus leaving the flesh of the deceased to be easily consumed later.

After *The Return of the Living Dead*, zombies' newly evolved characteristics continued to be recognized in the *Living Dead* sequels as well as other accounts of zombie-related chaos. For example, the brain-eating frenzy has shown up in many other film projects, and is becoming an influential and well-known component of the zombie canon. It was best described in a recent literary work by Grahame-Smith (2009): "It is a truth universally acknowledged that a zombie in possession of brains must be in want of more brains." *Day of the Dead* and *Return of the Living Dead* were released around the same time, and both identified a similar evolutionary advancement. It seems that zombies were meant to communicate, however unbelievable that might seem.

In 1983, a most unexpected evolutionary leap occurred. It was found that, under specific conditions, zombies could dance.

3 We have not had the chance to conduct any interviews with these zombies, leaving us with only speculation at this time.

During the production of Michael Jackson's music video *Thriller*, it was discovered that, by combining Jackson's music with Vincent Price's voice, zombies could rise from their graves. Once Jackson became a zombie as well, the undead in the music video could follow his dance steps in sync. While dancing, the zombies appeared rather mobile, with no appendages lost in all the gyrating. This quality did not change the fact that, when not dancing, they still shuffled along, following the classic zombie stereotype. Due to the deaths of both Price and Jackson, it is unlikely that such a situation will ever be encountered again.

REANIMATING THE UNDEAD

Video games have been around since 1972 with the Magnavox Odyssey (Wolf 2001). However, it was not until the mid-1990s, when gaming consoles became ubiquitous in households, that any video game had a recognizable zombie theme (White 1984). *Resident Evil* (1996) was the first and began a recurring theme in video games. In recent years, the rate at which zombies appear as antagonists in video games continues to climb, with more than nine games released in 2009.

Video games enable the user to feel more like a participant and not just an observer, which makes them ideal training devices for dealing with zombies. This is evidenced by the fact that many such games (simulations) are played from the first-person perspective (Booth 2008) and are, to some effect, of the role-playing variety. To play a game from the first-person perspective means that the graphics on the screen represent what the individual would see if it was actually in front of him or her. Role playing—in the context of games—asserts that many of the events in the game are driven by the decisions and actions of the user-controlled character.

Some zombie games, such as *Zombies Ate My Neighbours* (Ebert 1993), use a third-person camera (similar to observing the scene from a distance) to follow the user-controlled character and give her a broader sense of her surroundings. Other games have been referenced in movies (e.g., the trampoline jumping in *Zombies Ate My Neighbours* was referenced in *Shaun of the Dead*) or been a source of inspiration for movies, such as

Resident Evil. The games themselves have generally evolved into a grittier, scarier and more realistic first-person perspective simulation.

VIDEO GAMES AND THE HORRORS OF THE 1990S[4]

In the 1990s, zombie movie evolution seemed to plateau. While zombies still made occasional appearances (e.g., *Brain-dead,* 1993), there were no new significant evolutionary leaps made in the genre. This allowed the video-game industry to introduce and improve on zombie outbreak simulations with their own classes of zombie. Early titles developed zombie antagonists much like those already seen in film. The main differences between the video-game simulation and the film medium were that game graphics were pixellated, murky and generally unrealistic, their storylines were contrived and overused, and the goal of the game was to produce entertainment rather than scare audiences.

There were a few exceptions during this period: *Zombie Nation* (Seuo 1991) and *Zombies Ate My Neighbours.* In *Zombie Nation,* magnetic rays from a crashed meteor turn humans into zombies. Although this might seem like a common cause, there is an additional development: the meteor "zombifies" inanimate objects, the most influential being the Statue of Liberty. However unrealistic this might seem, the idea does create the possibility for zombies to find another way to increase their numbers, a very disconcerting thought.

Zombies Ate My Neighbours shows another interesting though possibly unrealistic attribute of zombies: their ability to work with supernatural creatures such as vampires, werewolves and evil dolls. These zombies work with the legions of classic cult horror figures, to the dismay of the in-game protagonists. At no point are the zombie characters so much in need of flesh that they attack a vampire, werewolf or one of their own. This is the first example of zombies working with nonzombies. However, this new teamwork should not be cause

4 We do not consider the evolution of zombies as the greatest horror of this decade; instead, we hand that award unceremoniously to the Spice Girls.

for alarm as the idea of evil dolls is so farfetched it borders on hilarious.

The House of the Dead series (Atsushi 1996) became first and foremost a tool against zombies rather than a new zombie evolutionary turn. It provided the opportunity for humans to prepare for a zombie outbreak in ways their earlier counterparts could not. *The House of the Dead* offered not only a first-person account, but also a more hands-on experience requiring the user to fire plastic guns at the screen, simulating an actual firing of the weapon. At the time of its initial public release in 1996, it was the most effective survival simulation available. The three subsequent games in the series (released in 1998, 2002 and 2005) continued to use plastic guns for game play and gave the user an improved experience through better graphics. This franchise has helped to pave the way for other video-game survival-horror scenarios such as *Resident Evil* and *Left 4 Dead*.

The *Resident Evil* zombies were created through a virus called the T-virus, a scientific experiment of the Umbrella corporation. With the added influence of science, an individual infected with the zombie T-virus could be altered into something much different from the standard zombie. One character, Nemesis, seen in *Resident Evil 3* (Kazuhiro 1999) and the film *Resident Evil Apocalypse* (Witt 2004), should be considered the first instance of zombie mutation. Nemesis was very different from most zombies encountered in the *Resident Evil* series. He had the ability to run and use weapons, and was more nimble than conventional zombies. He was autonomous and bent on utter destruction, rather than consumption, of in-simulation characters. Although Nemesis might have had a great impact on zombie evolution, he should serve as a warning to humanity to tread lightly when using zombies for research and experimentation.

In 2005, Wideload Games Developers decided to implement a different kind of zombie-training simulation. It was called *Stubbs the Zombie in Rebel without a Pulse* (Seropian 2005). Instead of using the game to simulate a survival scenario in a zombie outbreak, they decided to simulate what to do if you became a zombie. The player-controlled character, Stubbs, returned from the dead to exact revenge on his rival. The game play required the zombie character to cause as much chaos, and to turn as many people into zombies, as possible.

Stubbs gained new evolutionary qualities to help him in his quest. That he would try to exact revenge at all was not seen before in zombies. He had memories of his life before he died and became a zombie, consistent with the idea of zombie consciousness as seen in the Romero zombie species. Stubbs could communicate with his fellow zombies (which he was responsible for creating) through speech that consisted of only the word *brains* said in many tones with limited gestures. This was not entirely new; however, it reinforced the possibility of zombie communication. Stubbs could also use parts of his body as weapons. For example, he used flatulence to stun enemies, threw grenade-like gut bombs and used his head as an explosive bowling ball. This gave players of the game the wrong impression of what it is like to become a zombie. Stubbs was the only zombie who had the ability to perform such acts; the legions of undead that he created behaved like the zombies from *Return of the Living Dead* and *Thriller.* They were able to say "brains" and followed Stubbs as their predecessors did Jackson.

THE LIGHTER SIDE OF ZOMBIES

There has evolved a new classification of zombie-related media and literature in recent years. The term "zombie comedy" (or "zom-com") has been coined to describe movies that blend modern zombie horror with slapstick comedy or dark humour.

Stubbs was a good example of the comedy zombie. His unique abilities were not consistent with those of any other zombie and were created more for entertainment than anything else. His quest of chaos and revenge became a running joke that played out over the course of the story. Part of his mission was to find the woman he once loved and, when the two were reunited, he promptly ate her brain, thus turning her into a zombie.[5] Although we cannot dispute that Stubbs is an improvement on the zombie archetype, the fact that the game

5 We find it difficult to determine if she was a willing participant in this act.

exists to make fun of such a terrible situation as a zombie outbreak reduces the impact and concern that one day zombies will use gut grenades against unsuspecting victims.

The film *Shaun of the Dead*[6] made fun of practically everything about the classical zombie stereotype, yet still remained true to the zombie canon. Although most of the humour was provided by the uninfected characters, there was still a recognizable contribution from the zombie population. The film was an important example of what will happen to humanity if we do not prepare for the next zombie outbreak. The human population was slowly eradicated over the first half of the film because they did not recognize the signs.

Some curious zombie characters appeared in this film. For example, there was a documented instance of a zombie using a wheelchair to chase a human character, and zombie twins were sighted, both occurrences providing a dark comical element. A humorous solution to the problem of what to do with the remaining zombies was also suggested by this film: the zombies that remained after the climax were given menial service industry jobs that fit their abilities. A similar idea was used in another zom-com, *Fido* (Currie 2007).

In one of the more surprising and humorous turns of events in zombie history, two of the men responsible for *Shaun of the Dead* (actor Simon Pegg and director Edgar Wright) found themselves in Romero's *Land of the Dead*. At the conclusion of *Shaun of the Dead*, both men had seemingly survived the outbreak, yet only fourteen months later, in *Land of the Dead*, we witnessed them wreaking havoc as zombies. To some, it seemed tragic, but surely to the zombies it was so ironic that it became funny.[7]

Although the classic television program *The Simpsons* is not live action, it has become such a large part of North American culture in its past twenty seasons that anything it has not

---

6 The first zombie comedy to upgrade to "zom-rom-com," or zombie romantic comedy.

7 We wish to point out that they find this turn of events absolutely hilarious. Does that mean the authors are closeted zombies, seeing that such an event in a movie is surely intended to grab zombie audiences?

lampooned is likely not real. In one of its Hallowe'en episodes, *Treehouse of Horror III* (Baeza 1992), Bart accidentally calls zombies from their graves using a cult book he acquired at the library. It is documented in this episode that zombies prefer to be called "the living impaired." Evidence is provided to corroborate the hypotheses of O'Bannon, for the zombies speak well and are interested only in brains. In the first example of a zombie's selective consumption, Homer is spared by the zombies because he does not have enough brains to provide them with sustenance. It is somewhat interesting that many of the most important men in history were unable to avoid being turned into zombies, as George Washington, Albert Einstein and William Shakespeare, all zombified, converge on Homer. However, in spite of their importance to human history, they are ultimately destroyed in the exciting conclusion.

Two forces, powerful and complementary, converge, creating one horrifying mess. This is why, for many directors and video-game designers, a zombie crossed with a clown must be included somewhere. By combining two of the most frightening concepts known to humanity, the zombified clown becomes a critical element in *Zombieland*, as the characters find themselves in a zombie-infested carnival. Zombie clowns were also found in *Left 4 Dead 2* (Faliszek 2009), when the protagonists' fond childhood memories of visiting the carnival were shattered by the horror the undead had wrought there.

The horror of a clown, with a big red nose, running at you with bared teeth, crazy red hair and oversized ruby-red shoes is enough to make even the most hardy of veterans wet their pants. Add the fact that this clown does not want to make you laugh (but is very interested in what you have between your ears, for food purposes) and you have one of the most horrific elements of zombie cinema and video games.

THE TWENTY-FIRST CENTURY ZOMBIE

Whether the increased interest in the zom-com genre at the turn of the century necessitated another evolutionary turn for the modern zombie, or whether the timing was purely coincidental, a new development was inevitable and began showing in earnest in the mid-2000s.

The 2004 remake of *Dawn of the Dead* (Snyder 2004) introduced a disturbing new feature: these zombies were capable of running. They were actually able to retain many more of their physical attributes after succumbing to the zombie virus, physical strength and speed being the most notable.

How can zombies run? It might seem absurd when trying to picture the classical zombie running after its prey. With the physical decomposition sustained by the archetypal zombie, one would likely conclude that a running zombie would surely shatter its tibia and fibula.[8] This additional information shows that zombies have evolved substantially from the classical Romero interpretation.

Slower decomposition had implications for pregnant women. Snyder showed that women late in their pregnancies and subsequently infected by a zombie could still carry their zombie offspring to term.[9] This should not lead us to conclude, however, that zombies can become pregnant, nor can it tell us whether a woman in her first trimester can still produce a zombie baby.

With this slowed physical decomposition, it has been shown through other sources that zombies can also climb, fight and break glass without using an object or some sort of protection against bodily harm. Video-game simulations have also corroborated this trend in zombie evolution and have hinted at further, even more horrifying developments in the capabilities of zombies.

The *Left 4 Dead* series of simulations initially seemed like a general postapocalyptic scenario of survival against archetypal zombies: the foes appeared slow and vacant. At least until they became aware of your presence and ran at you with murderous

8 Being of mathematical and computing persuasions, we had to look up these names in *Gray's Anatomy* to be certain we hadn't mixed them up with other bones in the human/zombie body.

9 We believe the only explanation is that, since the child is still part of its mother and dependent on her immune system for protection, anything that the virus does to the mother it does to the unborn child. When the mother "dies" and becomes undead, so does the child. This is pure speculation, of course, but it makes sense, right?

intent and speed. If you were not armed and ready, this zombie onslaught was debilitating, knocking the in-game character off his feet, leaving him open to further attacks by zombies.

There is another facet of the *Left 4 Dead* series to be considered, one just as terrifying as the ability of zombies to run. It is claimed in the opening sequence that two weeks have passed since the outbreak of the zombie infestation, and during this time some zombies have been able to mutate into different classifications, possibly caused by the lifestyle or nature of the individual before zombification.[10]

Although the Nemesis-like mutation was present in *Left 4 Dead*, the attributes and behaviours of these zombies differed from those of the Nemesis character. Recall, from *Resident Evil 3*, that Nemesis worked alone and was autonomous from the other zombies in the series. Each mutated zombie in *Left 4 Dead* still worked as part of the mob, satisfying a key characteristic of the modern horror zombie. Although the special capabilities of these mutated characters were unique to each and differed from those of the standard zombie, the goal was the same: to use non-zombies as a food source[11] and transmit their mutagens to susceptible individuals whom they did not eat alive. Nemesis did not attack a human with the intention of eating her flesh; he was intent instead on utterly destroying his prey with weapons. Although both types of zombie characters spell doom for humanity, the mutated zombies of the *Left 4 Dead* series are closer to the zombie canon and redefine some aspects of it, making it even more imperative that the human race prepares itself for the zombie apocalypse.[12]

THE OUTLOOK FOR THE ZOMBIE APOCALYPSE

Through evolution, the traits of the horror zombie have contin-

10 We find it amusing to speculate on which mutation the stereotypical basement-dwelling video gamer would develop into.

11 How else could they have survived for two weeks?

12 We find it disturbing that strong emphasis was placed on preparing to deal with the inevitable evolution of H1N1, while almost no documented evidence exists to indicate that there were any such measures put in place to deal with zombies and their continuing evolution.

ued to become increasingly frightening. With the addition of mutations within the zombie genus itself, along with the increasing physical capabilities of zombies (due, presumably, to decreasing the rate at which the zombie decays), it is clear that the zombie threat has become even more menacing.

The significance of these evolutionary leaps has a different impact on how the different media portray zombies. With film, the slower decomposition of zombies that contributes to these new characteristics has a stronger impact on audiences, hopefully inspiring fear and a desire to be prepared for the coming zombie apocalypse. Zombies represent the epitome of fear, and when *Shaun of the Dead* and other titles poke fun at the slower-moving monsters it lowers people's desire to be prepared for the coming of zombies. It is terrifying to know that humans are no longer at the top of the food chain. Even scarier is that, with zombies moving as fast as humans, it is now harder to avoid becoming their next meal.

A similar argument holds for video-game simulations. To be properly trained, the user must be able to cope with the gruesomeness of the zombie apocalypse scenario. Unfortunately, users have not evolved at the same pace as zombies. Mutated classes of zombies with special abilities bring an element into the game play that the typical gamer has minimal experience with and which is likely to horrify even the hardest of veterans. This takes advantage of the inherent human fear of the unknown: a player who might be proficient at eliminating the common zombie, or even Nemesis, is now forced to face a horror that he or she likely has never encountered before.

Through analysis of the horror zombie over the ages, not only is there a clear evolution of the traits of the undead, but also there are clearly different families or species of zombies, each with its own subset of characteristics. It is fair to assume that the term "zombie" has evolved in its own right and should be considered to define a category of creatures rather than one specific type. There have been documented cases in recent history in which humans have encountered zombies and these tales have been turned into lessons for the moviegoing or video-game-playing public. These lessons are intended to inform people about how to identify and survive a zombie apocalypse and how to destroy the undead before being destroyed themselves, be it through insatiable hunger for brains or through special, evolved capabilities. By not recognizing these abilities, we are ill prepared for the coming apocalypse.

It might seem like a daunting task to evaluate just how effective the media have been in educating the public, including which sources provide the most accurate information about this ever-present threat. Even developing a benchmark for this is difficult; in the case of movies, box office profits are one means to evaluate the success of a film. However, does a film's box office success relate directly into the accuracy and quality of its content? For video games, one might be inclined to select from Microsoft's "Platinum Hits" or Sony's "Greatest Hits" titles,[13] but even then some of what we consider the best sources of information (*Left 4 Dead*) are not on these lists.

A consideration of the evolution of the modern zombie over the past forty years leads us to believe that zombies will not stop evolving anytime soon. What does it mean for human survival if our predators can adapt and evolve faster than we can? What is the tipping point in zombie evolution at which humanity will ultimately succumb? These questions are difficult for us to answer even now; only time will tell, but we have some rough ideas of how things might go.

13 Included in these elite classes are titles such as *Dead Rising* and the *Resident Evil* series.

ACKNOWLEDGEMENTS
We wish to thank George Romero, Simon Pegg and all the other creators for their zombie influences. Special thanks go to Robert Smith? for his invitation to be part of this book and to Craig Olinksi for the helpful suggestions and for all his time listening to us ramble on about zombies.

REFERENCES
Atsushi Seimiya. 1996. *The House of the Dead.*
Baeza, Carlos, dir. 1992. "Treehouse of Horror III: Dial 'Z' for Zombies." *The Simpsons.*
Brooks, Max. 2003. *The Zombie Survival Guide: Complete Protection from the Living Dead.* New York: Three Rivers Press.
———. 2006. *World War Z: An Oral History of the Zombie War.* New York: Three Rivers Press.
Delorme, Mike and Troy Day. N.d. "The Efficacy of Vaccination for the Eradication of Rage-Virus Mediated Zombieism." Unpublished manuscript.
Currie, Andrew, dir. 2007. *Fido.*
Ebert, Mike, designer, and LucasArts. 1993. *Zombies Ate My Neighbours.*
Faliszek, Chet, writer. 2008. *Left 4 Dead.*
———. 2009. *Left 4 Dead 2.*
Fleischer, Ruben, dir. 2009. *Zombieland.*
Futuyama, Douglas J. 2005. *Evolution.* Sunderland, MA: Sinauer Associates.
Grahame-Smith, Seth and Jane Austen. 2009. *Pride and Prejudice and Zombies.* Philadelphia: Quirk Productions.
Halperin, Victor, dir. 1932. *White Zombie.*
Jackson, Michael. 1983. *Thriller.* Directed by John Landis. Music video.
Kay, Glenn. 2008. *Zombie Movies: The Ultimate Guide.* Chicago: Chicago Review Press.
Kazuhiro Aoyama, dir. 1999. *Resident Evil 3: Nemesis.*
Keiji Inafune, creator. 2006. *Dead Rising.*
Mayr, Ernst. 2001. *What Evolution Is.* New York: Basic Books.
Munz, Philip, Ioan Hudea, Joe Imad and Robert Smith? 2009. "When Zombies Attack! Mathematical Modelling of an Outbreak of Zombie Infection." In *Infectious Disease Modelling Research Progress*, edited by J.M. Tchuenche and C. Chiyaka, 133–50. Hauppauge, NY: Nova Science Publishers.

O'Bannon, Dan, dir. 1985. *The Return of the Living Dead.*

Romero, George A., dir. 1968. *Night of the Living Dead.*

———. 1978. *Dawn of the Dead.*

———. 1985. *Day of the Dead.*

———. 2005. *Land of the Dead.*

———. 2007. *Diary of the Dead.*

Seropian, Alex, designer. 2005. *Stubbs the Zombie in Rebel without a Pulse.*

Seuo Sekizawa. 1991. *Zombie Nation.*

Shinji Mikami, creator. 1996. *Resident Evil.*

Snyder, Zack, dir. 2004. *Dawn of the Dead.*

White, Sandy, creator. 1984. *Zombie, Zombie.*

Wirkola, Tommy, dir. 2009. *Dead Snow.*

Witt, Alexander, dir. 2004. *Resident Evil Apocalypse.*

Wolf, Mark J.P., ed. 2001. *The Medium of the Video Game.* Austin: University of Texas Press.

Wright, Edgar, dir. 2002. *Shaun of the Dead.*

DAWN OF THE SHOPPING DEAD

MATT BAILEY

In 1978, George A. Romero released the second of his cult classic zombie films, *Dawn of the Dead*. Set in an out-of-town mall, the movie critiqued a shopping culture that had become central to American life. Romero parodied those who were magnetically drawn to the mall, lured by trinkets and bright lights into a wonderland of consumption. But he also appreciated the mall's social importance. A thread of memory calls his zombies back even though they are dead to material pleasure. They roam the movie mall's carpark and stumble through its darkened, unpowered interior. Malls were suburban America's great social site and here, in a post-zombie-attack landscape, they continue their key role of drawing the surrounding population to a central location.

This chapter uses *Dawn of the Dead* as an avenue to explore the recent past. Such usage of popular culture is a relatively new addition to historical studies. Historians made forays into folk culture in the 1920s and 1930s, while the 1960s saw examinations of popular culture by historians interested in reclaiming a voice for the working class. In the 1970s and 1980s, social historians further emphasized the importance of popular culture for ordinary people. Cultural historians have since focused even more specifically on cultural productions—from sports to music to movies—using them to discuss and analyze broad social and cultural changes. Following in this tradition, I use *Dawn of the Dead* here to explore the development of the shopping mall and its place in postwar consumer society.

The movie opens with America in crisis. Zombies have risen violently to overtake and disrupt all facets of everyday life. Nowhere is safe. It is against the law to remain in a private residence, however secure. The media continue to operate, but broadcasts are inconsistent and chaotic. Anarchy rules. For the movie's key characters, the situation is becoming unbearable. Francine and her fiancé, Stephen, work in a television station. As it descends into chaos, Stephen persuades her to flee with him in the station's helicopter. Their friend Roger is a member of a SWAT team. During a particularly bloody and traumatic zombie cleanout of an apartment block, he meets Peter, another SWAT officer. Recognizing a shared inner pain at the carnage they daily witness and deliver, Roger offers Peter a seat in the helicopter on which he, too, plans to escape the city.

The four meet on the roof of the station and fly into the night. The next day they pass over "redneck" hunting parties shooting zombies for sport before landing at a small abandoned airport. They procure fuel, but also attract roaming zombies that must be fought off. There is no safe ground; they must keep running. Returning to the air in search of a secure refuge, the four argue, unable to agree on a direction or plan. Another night passes, but daylight brings a change of fortune. Below, a sprawling carpark surrounds a windowless, box-like structure. "What the hell is it?" asks Peter. "Looks like a ... shopping center," Stephen replies. "One of those big indoor malls." Peter might have spent too much time in the city because, by the late 1970s, malls covered the American suburban landscape.

Every civilization has its great monuments: the pyramids, the Agora, the Great Wall, castles, canals, temples, churches and so on. America, and now much of the rest of the world, has malls. After fifty years of North American dominance, the world's largest malls are now in Asia, reflecting both the spread of consumerism and a changing world order. Malls cater to Asia's rising middle class and its explosion in car use. On a smaller scale, malls served the same function in 1950s America, where widespread car use saw the population move out from the city into what we now call suburban sprawl. Like Fran, Stephen, Peter and Roger, the motivations for flight were the poor conditions and decay of the urban core, and the hope for a better life beyond it.

Many postwar American cities faced problems with traffic congestion, inadequate parking, aging buildings and declining property values. The Great Depression and World War II had seen little maintenance or upgrade of building stock. A high demand for accommodation brought cheap subdivisions of existing apartments, while much new construction had been substandard. Cars, even as they spread the population outward, brought congestion and pollution to central business districts that struggled to provide parking facilities.

Suburbanites in the 1950s and 1960s sought space, comfort and security beyond the city. On cheap land, they built houses of their own and turned them into homes, purchasing mass-produced consumer durables, furniture and televisions. This largely white relocation from the city to the suburbs was one of the great internal migration flows of postwar America. The other was the Black migration from the South, which saw the African American population of northern and western cities rise from around four percent in 1940 to sixteen percent in 1970. One city that attracted considerable black migration from Alabama was Pittsburgh, fifteen miles from Monroeville Mall in which *Dawn of the Dead* was filmed. By 1980, about two-thirds of metropolitan African Americans lived in central cities compared with about one-third of metropolitan whites.

Suburbanization, then, was a new form of segregation. The racialized and oppressed of 1950s and 1960s America, like the zombies in *Dawn of the Dead*, were left behind in the urban core, which in many cities began to crumble. This decline is highlighted in the scene where Peter and Roger meet. They are sent to a decaying, overcrowded building where violence and crime accompany poverty and degradation. After fighting off the living upstairs, they find dead bodies packed in a basement. As these bodies reanimate, the two men are forced to shoot them down in a repetitious and bloody execution. The zombies are fictional, but the social breakdown that surrounded them was a lived reality for the most marginalized in the twentieth century's most powerful democracy.

Well before these depths were reached, the suburbs were booming. Their population grew at four times the rate of the city through the 1950s. In many manufacturing belt cities, including Pittsburgh, the city population actually declined. Pittsburgh lost eleven percent of its population during the 1950s, even as its suburbs grew by twenty-two percent. Low unemployment, rising wages, widespread credit facilities and government-assisted housing schemes fuelled affluence and created a ready market for big retailers that followed their customers out from the city. Department stores opened suburban branches before the war and escalated their expansion programs after it. Congregations of other retailers and chain stores formed around them in major suburban locations. This brought ready access to shops but also created problems. Just as zombies emerge at the airfield where the group refuel, congestion, noise and pollution resurfaced in the suburbs. Shopping became difficult, at times unpleasant and even dangerous.

Big retailers and developers responded to suburban congestion by constructing malls—often outside established commercial districts—with parking lots that separated pedestrians from cars. One of the first malls to offer extensive free parking was the J.C. Nichols Country Club Plaza, which opened up four miles south of Kansas City in 1923. Other developments followed, but the Great Depression and World War II slowed further development. In 1946, there were only eight major shopping centres in the United States. The 1950s suburban boom, though, brought significant development as well as the arrival of Victor Gruen, the father of the modern mall.

Gruen had grown up in Vienna, and the European city maintained a strong and nostalgic hold on his memory. When he encountered the vast sprawl of American suburbia, he was shocked. It seemed inhumane. If Romero envisaged wandering zombies in this terrain, Gruen saw displaced people, disconnected from each other and their environment. He recalled the vibrant public life of his childhood city and foresaw the mall as a new social space, which business would provide in return for the healthy profits to be gained from mixing commerce with culture and social activity. For Gruen, the mall continued a long history of such space: the medieval market square, for example, housed markets, was generally close to the church and was used as a space for people to congregate and interact.

Gruen focused his philosophies on Southdale, which opened in Edina, Minnesota, in 1956. If its developers undermined its more altruistic elements, it still cemented Gruen's place in American architectural and retail history. Gruen had designed the first completely internalized mall in a conscious attempt to create an urban environment for suburbanites. It brought the city's lights, colour, bustle, variety and crowds but without their unwanted accompaniments: noise, dirt, chaos, congestion, "danger" and racial complexity. The mall had parking for over 5,000 cars, 139 specialty shops, two department stores and a monumental central court. It was fully air-conditioned, and its internal design meant that shops opened onto internal concourses, leaving sheer, largely blank walls on the exterior.

The mall in *Dawn of the Dead* is a descendent of Southdale: an internalized, two-storey, air-conditioned retail behemoth. It boasts department store anchors, hundreds of specialty shops, a bank, games arcade, fountain, internal gardens and ice-skating rink. Stephen lands the helicopter on its roof, out of reach of zombies wandering randomly across the carpark's empty tarmac. There are zombies inside the mall too. Fran asks Stephen why they come there. He replies, "It's a kind of instinct ... memory.... [It's] what they used to do. This was an important place in their lives." The living dead of the late 1970s had grown up on mall culture. Eight out of ten new stores opened inside one of the 18,000 shopping centres then scattered across the country. Malls were social institutions, particularly for youth. They were sites of leisure, entertainment, collective interaction, employment, distraction and shopping: the pastime of consumer society.

The zombies in *Dawn of the Dead* are drawn back to the mall by a deeply embedded sense of place. Otherwise, we know little about them or the reasons for their rise. Earlier movies had drawn on the historical roots of zombies in Haitian Vodoun, where sorcerers, or *bokors,* turned people into mindless chattels under their control. In *White Zombie* (1932) and *I Walked with a Zombie* (1943), both set in Haiti, zombies were depicted as people controlled by an external "master." Other films maintained this characterization but used new locations, including America. In the 1950s and 1960s, flesh-eating zombies were introduced; *The Plague of the Zombies* (1965) pioneered the decayed, stuttering forms that would follow in later movies. It was Romero, though, who defined the zombie for the modern cinema audience. In his first major film, *Night of the Living Dead* (1968), zombies (or "ghouls") appeared as mindless human forms, with some basic instinctual responses, stiffly stumbling in search of fresh flesh. They were raised from the dead, but not by any individual, and one could only "kill" them by destroying their brains. There were few zombie movies following *Night of the Living Dead* that were not influenced by it in some way.

It was eleven years before Romero returned to the zombie genre with *Dawn of the Dead.* In it, his zombies maintain their basic characteristics and form, though their movements are a little jerkier and their features more decayed. They have no personalities; only their clothes indicate what they might once have been. Stripped bare, they are the ultimate consumers, engorgement on the living their only goal. The mall, though, still appeals to them. Even prior to the arrival of the foursome, when there is no human flesh on which to feed, it still calls them, as it did the living.

Breaking through a skylight, Peter, Roger, Stephen and Fran set up base in an upstairs storeroom before the two SWAT men head off to explore the mall and find supplies. They head through a dirty, narrow, back service corridor: the functional reality behind the mall's glittering façade. After arriving in a central control room, they find a bunch of "keys to the kingdom," as Roger calls them. Flicking switches, the men bring the mall to life: lights come up, music fills the previously silent void, fountains begin pumping, and escalators kick back into operation. It is showtime again. The effect on the zombies is comical. Their stuttering legs cannot cope with escalators: there are falls and collisions and a few of the dead land in the pond around the fountain. They might be drawn there, but death has rendered them incapable of navigating the mall, a site that had become almost natural to postwar Americans.

Peter and Roger dash past them, finding refuge in a department store. Locked glass doors keep the zombies at bay while the men—after a perilous two-day helicopter ride fleeing their collapsing city—go on a shopping spree. "Let's get the stuff we need," cries Peter. "I'll get a television and a radio." Still acclimatizing, Roger replies, "Right … lighter fluid … chocolate … chocolate." A little later, after locating screwdrivers to break into heating ducts that run above the ceiling, he laughs: "One-stop shopping. Everything you need, right at your fingertips."

Convenience was a central premise of the mall. Shoppers arriving in cars could park at a single destination and have everything they needed, as Roger says, "at their fingertips." Women with small children only had to bundle them in and out of the car once. There were public toilets, baby change rooms and even child-care facilities. Developers organized strategic tenancy mixes to ensure that all mainstream needs and wants were catered to. As these changed over time, centralized management gave malls the organizational capacity to keep pace with fashion and customer expectations. Entertainment facilities, such as cinemas and *Dawn of the Dead*'s ice rink, kept people amused and extended their visits. Food outlets did the same, allowing customers to shop for longer. Banks and other services rounded out the facilities. The mall was designed to ensure that people need never shop anywhere else; for most customers, it really was a practical solution to their shopping needs.

As Roger and Peter loot the department store, Stephen follows them, enjoying some uninhibited consumption of his own. Returning to Fran, who has been attacked by a Hare Krishna zombie that found its way upstairs, he consoles her, "You should see all the great stuff we got, Frannie. All kinds of stuff. This place is terrific. It really is … it, it's perfect." He voices a core promise of the shopping centre: perfection through abundance and exclusion. Malls sanitized commercial space to remove all impediments to consumption; they were clean, convenient, stacked with goods and without weather, "undesirables," noise or congestion to distract the customer. Appropriated by the group, the mall's utility remains undiminished. Undesirables will be excluded (or killed) and its material bounty seems limitless. Roger, for one, is sold: "We've really got it made here, Frannie," he continues. Able to choose from the mall's vast array of goods, the group fills empty bellies with caviar and crackers, which the men wash down with Jack Daniels. In the background, the president's message is repeated on a transistor radio brought up from the department store: it is against the law to occupy any private residence, however safe or well protected.

The mall offers a secure haven to *Dawn of the Dead*'s central characters. From the time they land on its roof, Peter and Roger recognize its value as a fortress: a modern castle, provisioned for years, with a carpark moat. Malls have always been promoted as safe places for women and children to shop: convenient car parking, clean toilets, baby change rooms and privatized security were advertised, while the exclusion of undesirables was implied. Malls were privatized social and commercial enclaves. In a zombie-infested landscape, the physical logic of their design—high walls, small entrances, a centralized control room, alarms, security cameras, bolted doors and internal gates—becomes more apparent.

The men decide to secure the complex by blocking its entrances with delivery trucks and killing the zombies left inside. It is a big operation that goes smoothly until Roger is attacked while hot-wiring a truck. Close physical fighting ensues, with Roger revelling in the danger. He appears to get carried away, becomes reckless. He fights off one attack and drives his truck from the delivery docks around to the front of the mall. Parking across its doors, he is picked up by Peter in another truck, kicking off clawing zombies in the process. Roger, though, has left his bag behind. With the wealth of the mall waiting, it is a trifle, but his attachment and wilfulness send him back to claim it. It is his! And it costs him his life. Bitten, he is doomed. Back in the mall's upstairs storeroom, lying in a makeshift bed with his leg rotting away, he deliriously calls to Peter, "We whipped 'em, didn't we? We whipped 'em and we got it all."

This was the offer of the mall: the promise of plenty in an environment that tempted at every turn. The process by which this occurred became known as the "Gruen transfer": the point at which the mall, as a kind of architectural *bokor,* combined its layout, music and visual marketing to entrance the customer. This was a far cry from his intentions. Gruen had designed Southdale with non-commercial spaces: points at which people could sit or congregate without being inundated with marketing and visual merchandising. In his previous centre, Northland, there were landscaped gardens for the same purpose. He envisaged the businessman as the twentieth-century Renaissance prince—a patron of the arts, a member of a beneficent elite—and was bitterly disappointed when, twenty years later, he looked back to see nothing but the commercial components of his designs remaining. The one-stop social/commercial complex became one big shop with a perpetual and intensive drive for sales. The complete commercialization of the mall was reflected in the broader society as consumerism came to infiltrate all aspects of modern life.

With the zombies dispatched and the mall secured, Peter, Roger, Stephen and Fran bask in the joys of consumer goods. Anything on display is theirs for the taking. Peter and Stephen raid the bank and pose for its cameras. Fran models clothes; Stephen browses for a jacket, shrugging at a price tag. Even Roger, who must now be wheeled around in a barrow, tries on hats and practises his golf putt in a store aisle. Fran goes skating; Peter and Roger play ball; the three men immerse themselves in arcade games, racing cars and shooting alien invaders in a retreat from the real-life carnage they have been dishing out to the dead. The treats, trinkets and luxuries of the mall are all sampled. Armloads are collected and brought upstairs to the foursome's new abode.

Zombies, meanwhile, claw the glass outer doors, desperate to enter the magic kingdom. Observing them, Roger worries, "They're after us." Peter disagrees. "They're after the place," he replies. "They don't know why, they just remember.... Remember that they want to be in here." When Fran asks "What the hell are they?" Peter makes the link between the ravenous hordes, the mall and the consuming public: "They're us, that's all." The link becomes clearer and a sense of empathy grows as Roger, lying in his bed, succumbs, dies and rises red eyed and ash grey. Peter, willing himself to have the strength, shoots him from the other side of the room. His companions bury Roger in the mall's indoor garden.

The group continues to accumulate resources. Fran is pregnant and the upstairs storeroom becomes a nest decked out in department store finery. With a television, stereo, plush red lounge, hanging plants and glass-topped table, it looks like a dream suburban home, albeit with braces of rifles from the mall's gun shop on the wall. Embedded in the mall, their home is suburbia contained, intensified and magnified. Malls were the public spaces of suburbia and reflected many of its ideals: they were safe, comfortable social sites providing consumables around which social relations revolved. The suburbs brought home ownership, backyards and privacy, but also created isolation, particularly for women. Shortages of public transport, social infrastructure, employment and retail facilities often meant long commutes for men and long days at home for women. The mall was offered as a solution, but, emptied of shoppers and stripped back to its essentials in *Dawn of the Dead,* it is a gilded cage. Peter maintains a quiet rage, belting countless tennis balls against a wall on the roof. Fran and Stephen slip into lethargy. The television in their designer lounge room emits only static, a constant reminder of their isolation. "What have we done to ourselves?" Fran whispers hoarsely.

Numerous commentators have suggested that suburbanization brought a retreat from public life, that a focus on family and consumer goods coincided with a decline in broader social networks. This was partly to do with working hours. As people spent more, women entered the paid workforce in increasing numbers and everyone worked longer hours. Consumables offered time-poor workers convenience, entertainment and meaning. But the law of diminishing returns suggests that the more people spend the less happiness they get for their dollar. A family's first television might bring great satisfaction. But a second? And a third?

Life for *Dawn of the Dead'*s characters inside the mall, despite security and an endless supply of goods, becomes mundane and dull. At one point, Fran layers herself in makeup. Indolent, she gazes at the mirror, loosely twirling a small ivory-handled revolver. Glutted and isolated, she has become apathetic. She, Stephen and Peter are cut off from humanity and drowning in abundance. The hideout has become a home, but life is meaningless. The delight of commodity consumption has lost its flavour because, it seems, commodities in themselves have no intrinsic value. The earlier raid on the bank provided Peter and Stephen with worthless banknotes because the economic collapse triggered by the zombie rising means they cannot be spent. Consumer goods, however well made or wondrous, are also rendered meaningless after their social context has been destroyed.

Romero's critique of consumer culture held particular resonance at the time the film was released. In the 1970s, industrialized countries were undergoing a period of turmoil and change. The postwar boom came to an abrupt halt with the oil crisis late in 1973, which quadrupled the price of oil the following year. Economies built on cheap oil ground slowly on, but were hit by other broad economic and political changes. The confidence in lasting affluence that had developed through the 1960s was badly shaken. Capitalism had long been wracked by boom-and-bust cycles, but consumerism—with its seemingly endless round of production and consumption—had seemed a saviour. It was widely argued that mass consumption, by creating employment and driving economic growth, would create a more equitable society. Unprecedented levels of growth in the 1950s and 1960s seemed to prove the argument. Business boomed and wages escalated.

When high levels of growth vanished in the 1970s, but wages kept rising, conflict was inevitable. Manufacturing headed offshore in search of cheaper labour, causing unemployment to rise at home. Critiques of the status quo were also emerging. They began in 1960s counterculture and were continued into the 1970s by anti-war activists, feminists, environmentalists and equal rights campaigners. They highlighted the dark side of consumer capitalism: the military-industrial complex that bullied and killed for business interests across the globe; its patriarchal structure and the confinement of women to the private sphere; the environmental destruction wrought by mass production; and the illusion that affluence meant equality for all.

When a conservative remake of *Dawn of the Dead* was released in 2004, times were very different. Consumerism was widely accepted, propped up with massive levels of personal debt, and if the threat of "terror" was worrying it was more likely to affirm the status quo than generate critique. But when Romero was making the movie in the late 1970s, consumerism's promise of more for all (in the mall) seemed hollow. So much so that Peter and Fran kill themselves in the film's original ending, though this was changed during production to leave a glimmer of hope.

The mundane but secure existence of *Dawn of the Dead*'s central characters is violently interrupted when a gang of bikers observe Fran training with Stephen in the helicopter above the mall. Realizing the group have secured the mall, they plan a night-time invasion to take it for themselves. Peter picks up radio calls from the bikers and organizes a defence. He and Stephen close and lock the mall's internal roller gates and are heading back upstairs when the bikers smash through the outer doors. Driven mad by abundance at their fingertips, they smash, loot and consume all they can get their hands on.

Stephen snaps. Instead of hiding upstairs as planned, he opens fire, muttering, "It's ours. We took it, it's ours." A pitched battle breaks out: the bikers are dispatched, the zombies overrun the mall, and Stephen is devoured, left to die in a lift. Peter and Fran flee in the helicopter. Although at times succumbing to the mall's allure, they alone have kept their heads throughout. They escape its embrace because they maintain self-control. It is Romero's warning against the mall's invitation to addiction and excess.

As the level-headed flee the mall, zombies shuffle and stumble through its broken gates and shop windows. A mindless, homogeneous crowd, they sample its delights. Stuttering across the ice rink, some fall to their knees, but keep clawing their way forward. The collapse of order seems to bring life to the undead. Their faint living memories coach them to try on clothes and sample the mall's delights. Like Fran, Stephen,

Peter and Roger, as well as the bikers, they too cannot resist the products on display. Excess breeds chaos as the mall descends into madness.

Romero uses zombies to tell the story of the mall's place in American society and what that society might become if it loses its grip on its humanity. The zombies are us, not only because they were once living, but also because we too can debase ourselves through mindless consumption. Malls developed in response to consumer needs, but their design was almost too perfect. More than a solution to existing needs, they became a driving force in the cultural economy of consumer capitalism.

The mall is a symbol of our age: cheaply constructed along standardized designs; filled to the brim with goods; promising happiness in commodities, fulfillment through their purchase; privately controlled and operated yet publicly accessible to those who conform to its values and regulations. It is our most recognizable site of mass consumption, and it is mass consumption, more than anything else, that underpins our culture, social interactions and economy. What this means for us as individuals and as a society is open to question, but it is a question that merits exploration.

At the point in the movie when Peter is forced to shoot Roger, there is a great buildup of tension. As Roger slowly sits up in his bed, rising to join the living dead, and Peter grips his gun, forcing himself to remain in control, Stephen and Fran sit in the next room glued to the television. On it, a heated debate over how to deal with the zombie plague rises in volume. A scientist being interviewed is arguing for rationality. When Peter pulls the trigger, the tension snaps. In the void it leaves, the scientist insists that "We've got to remain rational ... logical ... logical ... there's no choice. It's that or the end." A dissenter argues, "Scientists always think in those types of terms. It doesn't work. It's not how people really are." This might be Romero's take on the human condition: succumb to base desire, or use reason to steer a path through fear, envy and greed. The behaviour of *Dawn of the Dead*'s characters in the mall reveals this to be a particularly thorny dilemma in a culture built on desire.

AND THE DEAD SHALL WALK, BUT HOW?

ANTHONY TONGEN, CAITLIN V. JOHNSON AND SEAN M. FRANCIS

INTRODUCTION

The key term in the title is walk; zombies cannot run! (Brooks 2003, 13). Therefore, to better equip the reader for a zombie attack, we will dissect (not literally) the walking behaviour of a zombie from a biomechanical viewpoint. During a zombie attack, instead of wondering about your chances of survival, you should ask, "Is it possible to outrun a zombie?" or "Is it better to run uphill or downhill?" or "Will the zombie jump over this fairly low obstacle?" This chapter will better equip you to escape a pursuing zombie. We will also consider the intriguing question, from a biomechanical framework, of whether or not Frankenstein is a zombie. Interestingly, if Frankenstein is a zombie, then we need to be able to outmanoeuvre him; however, if Frankenstein is not a zombie, then he is susceptible to a zombie bite and can become a zombie. Therefore, we might need to outmanoeuvre a creature that will hereafter be referred to as Zombiestein.

Biomechanics is the study of the mechanics of a living (or possibly reanimated) organism; particularly, it examines how external forces such as muscles, gravity and decaying limbs affect the skeletal structure. The unusual form of movement of zombies and Frankenstein is one of their striking characteristics; their unusual gait provides an excellent opportunity to examine limb use during locomotion. From a biomechanical standpoint, the following information is important for our study of zombies.

> Zombies have, literally, no physical sensations. All nerve receptors throughout the body remain dead after reanimation.... Undead physiology has been proven to possess no powers of regeneration.... This inability to self-repair, something that we as living beings take for granted, is a severe disadvantage to the undead.... Ghouls [zombies] possess the same brute force as the living.... The one solid advantage the living dead do possess is amazing stamina. Imagine working out, or any other act of physical exertion. Chances are that pain and exhaustion will dictate limits. These factors do not apply to the dead. They will continue to act, with the same dynamic energy, until the muscles supporting it literally disintegrate.... The "walking" dead tend to move at a slouch or limp. Even without injuries or advanced decomposition, their lack of coordination makes for an unsteady stride. Speed is mainly determined by leg length. Taller ghouls have longer strides than their shorter counterparts. Zombies appear to be incapable of running. The fastest have been observed to move at a rate of barely one step per 1.5 seconds. Again, as with strength, the dead's advantage over the living is their tirelessness. Humans who believe they have outrun their undead pursuers might do well to remember the story of the tortoise and the hare, adding, of course, that in this instance the hare stands a good chance of being eaten alive.... The average living human possesses a dexterity level 90% greater than the strongest ghoul. Some of this comes from the general stiffness of necrotic muscle tissue (hence their awkward stride).... No one has ever observed a zombie jumping or swimming. (Brooks 2003, 9–14)

Human locomotion is unique within the animal world in that we move on two extended legs. Human gaits can be described using a few simple terms, which are also illustrated in Figure 16.1. The gait cycle consists of two phases, stance phase (A-E) and swing phase. Stance phase begins with a touchdown when the heel strikes the ground (stage A). At heel strike, the centre of gravity of the body is at its lowest point. At mid-stance, where the hip is directly over the knee and ankle, the centre of gravity is at its highest (stage C). The centre of gravity falls in the second half of the stance phase that ends with toe-off (stage E). The period from the touchdown of a limb to the subsequent touchdown of the same limb is called a stride. Speed or velocity is the amount of time it takes an individual to go a particular distance. In general, animals and people shorten the stance phase to increase speed. At higher speeds, humans change from a walking gait to a running gait in which there is a period when no feet are on the ground, also referred to as an aerial phase.

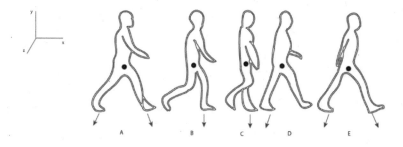

Figure 16.1 Diagram of Human Walking. A human walking step begins with a heel strike (A), where the centre of mass is low, then the centre of mass rises and the body passes over the foot like an inverted pendulum to the point of mid-stance (C), the centre of mass falls again and the step ends at toe-off (E). The grey dot represents the approximate location of the centre of mass during a typical stride.

Humans have long legs relative to their height compared to other mammals, affording humans long stride lengths. Human stride lengths are additionally lengthened by the foot rollover that occurs from heel strike to toe-off (Alexander 1992). By increasing the path length traversed by the effectively longer limb, this foot rollover not only allows the centre of mass to cover a longer distance, but also reduces the mechanical work required at the step-to-step transitions to change the direction of the centre of mass (Adamczyk et al. 2006). During *walking*, the centre of mass rises and falls during each walking step like an inverted pendulum. This rise and fall of the centre of mass affords an exchange of kinetic and potential energy during human and animal walking (Ahn 2004; Cavagna 1977).

As the centre of mass rises in the first half of the stance phase, potential energy increases while kinetic energy decreases. With the fall of the centre of mass in the second half of the stance phase, kinetic energy increases while potential energy decreases. At the transition from one step to the next, mechanical work is required to redirect the centre of mass from one inverted pendulum to the next. This costs metabolic energy because the front leg does negative work to redirect the centre of mass movement and the back leg does positive work to continue the centre of mass moving forward (Donelan et al. 2002a, 2002b, 2005). Nonetheless, it seems that the vertical fluctuation of the centre of mass does more to save energy; experimental tests have demonstrated that inverted pendulum walking is less metabolically expensive than flat-trajectory walking (Ortega and Farley 2005).

When humans are *running*, say from a zombie, there is an aerial phase in which no limbs are touching the ground and a stance phase in which only one limb is touching the ground. The compliance (think bending) of this limb during landing serves to attenuate peak ground reaction forces that can cause damaging strains on the bones of the lower limb. This compliance can also stretch tendons and ligaments such that they can "spring" back, putting stored elastic energy back into the system (Alexander and Bennet-Clark 1977; McMahon et al. 1987).

Zombies walk with stiff legs and sway mediolaterally side to side. Mediolateral swaying was initially thought to increase energy expenditure in animals such as penguins, who sway or waddle as a regular part of their locomotion. Griffin and Kram (2000), however, demonstrated that the mediolateral sway or waddle of penguins does not account for their high metabolic cost of locomotion.

Although energy conservation is important to living animals, energy expenditure is of little concern in zombies because they have infinite energy that does not seem to be restricted with respect to metabolic costs. However, as their limbs are continuously decomposing and vulnerable to dismemberment, high peak forces can present a significant danger to zombies. During both walking and running gaits, humans experience ground reaction forces that are potentially damaging to their musculoskeletal system. Peak ground reaction forces increase shock through the skeleton of the lower limb and therefore increase strain to skeletal structures (Bennell et al. 1999; Burr et al. 1996). Bone is living tissue that bends under force, which produces strain. It is such strain that stimulates bone remodelling, but high levels of strain can cause injuries. Peak force and free moment have been associated with injuries such as stress fractures in humans (Milner et al. 2006). Humans attenuate these forces with a controlled rollover process during walking (Donelan et al. 2004), and compliant limbs, muscles and tendons during running (Ferris et al. 1998; Gross and Nelson 1988; McMahon and Cheng 1990; Roberts 2002; Voloshin and Wosk 1982). Bone remodelling in response to load over time can also serve to attenuate high loads in the lower limbs of humans (Burr et al. 1985; Lanyon 1984; Morris et al. 1997).

Zombies, however, are in a constant state of decomposition and cannot remodel their skeletons in response to load. Their stiff limb posture suggests a lack of compliance of the total limb or individual joints. Frankenstein also walks with stiff legs, and his unusually large size is likely to impose high skeletal forces during locomotion. Taken together, these features suggest that zombies and Frankenstein should move in a manner to minimize peak loads on the skeleton. At least for zombies, this reduction in load can come at any energy cost since energy is not of concern to them.

The study of movement and the forces involved in producing it is called kinetics. We can measure the forces involved in the stance phase of running using a force plate. When we step on the ground, we apply a force into the ground. This force has a direction that is downward and slightly forward. The ground applies a reaction force that is equal and opposite (Newton's third law of motion!) to that force. Therefore, the ground reaction force (GRF) has a direction that is upward (keeping a walker from going through the ground) and backward (a "braking" force that slows our forward movement). Force plates measure this ground reaction force and break it into its orthogonal components.

Consider a three-dimensional coordinate system with orthogonal directions x, y and z. Corresponding to Figure 16.1, imagine walking along the x-axis, with the y-axis pointing toward the sky. Now think about the forces that the ground imparts on your every step as equal and opposite reactions; these are the forces measured by a force plate. The force with the largest magnitude that the ground imparts on your body is the vertical ground reaction force (VGRF), which is in the y-direction. The antero-posterior (fore-aft or braking-propulsive) force, in the x-direction, is less than the VGRF by approximately a factor of 10. The medial-lateral force (MGRF), in the z-direction, is less than the VGRF by approximately a factor of 100 in both running and walking. Due to their magnitude, VGRF data will be the focus of this chapter; however, due to the mediolateral sway of the zombies, we will also examine MGRF.

In this project, we examine whether the unusual walking gaits of zombies and Frankenstein contribute to the reduction of peak forces and centre of mass movements. As discussed above, centre of mass movements are different in human walking and running, and the fluctuating inverted-pendulum-type movements of the centre of mass during walking have been associated with reduction in metabolic costs (Ortega and Farley 2005). We ask how constant decomposition and other physiological anomalies of zombies have affected their movement dynamics. First, we hypothesize that, since zombies possess limitless energy, their walking pattern might not reflect mechanisms for energy conservation to the extent seen in humans. Although we cannot directly measure energy expenditure or energy exchange using the methods described here, we will use centre of mass movement data to develop hypotheses for future analysis. Second, we suggest that zombies' walking form will reflect an emphasis on reduction of peak ground reaction forces. These peak forces put strains on the skeleton that put it at risk of fracture. As zombies are in a constant state of decomposition, they will be losing bone strength and not remodelling their skeletal system, so it would be beneficial to them to moderate peak forces on their musculoskeletal system.

METHODS

We collected ground-reaction force data on four adult human subjects walking normally, walking like Frankenstein and walking like zombies. Walking like a zombie was defined as emulating a typical zombie walk with all limbs intact and moderate joint stiffness while moving with stiff legs and swaying mediolaterally. Walking like Frankenstein was defined as walking with stiff legs while leaning forward. Each walking type was practised prior to performance for data collection, and trials in which gaits were not judged to be acceptable by the researchers were repeated. Each gait type was performed at two different speeds (seventy steps per minute and one hundred steps per minute) that were controlled using a metronome. Although using a metronome ensures consistent step rates, our subjects exhibited a large range of step lengths due to differences in leg length, so overall speed might not have been consistent across subjects. Subjects were asked to walk the length of a laboratory runway in which a force plate was embedded flush with the floor. They were advised not to target the force plate, and each subject walked at least four steps before and after hitting the force plate to ensure steady state locomotion rather than acceleration or deceleration during the step on the plate. Each trial was performed three times.

Ground reaction forces were collected using a Kistler 9286A force plate (Kistler Instrument Corporation, Amherst, NY). The force plate collects ground reaction forces in three orthogonal directions: vertical (F_y), fore-aft horizontal (F_x) and mediolateral (F_z). Ground reaction forces (mass × acceleration) were used to determine acceleration in the vertical (a_y) direction. These values were integrated to find velocity and integrated again to determine the position of the centre of mass. As our goal was only to compare the total vertical movement of the centre of mass during the step, the initial centre of mass position was adjusted to a position of (0,0) for each step. Although this is only an estimate for the lowest point of the centre of mass—and

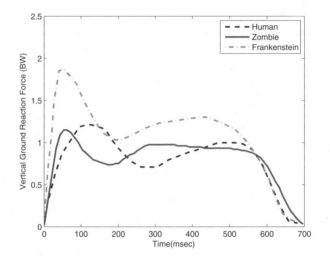

Figure 16.2 Vertical Ground Reaction Forces from One Individual Using All Three Gait Types Moving at the Higher Speed. Forces are presented on the y-axis in body weights and the x-axis represents time in milliseconds. Note the high peak force during Frankenstein walking and the more moderate peak forces in human and zombie walking. All curves exhibit the double hump typical of inverted pendular walking.

arbitrarily assigned a point of (0,0)—because an entire step was not collected, double support phase is usually a low point in the centre of mass (Alexander and Jayes 1978), and heel strike is the beginning of this double support phase.

Peak ground reaction forces, the maximum force in each direction, were compared across speeds and gait types to assess force attenuation mechanisms. A one-way repeated measures analysis of variance (ANOVA) was used to assess variation across gait types and within gait types across speeds. Tukey's HSD post-hoc comparisons were used to assess significant differences between individual gait types. Subjects and repeated trials were considered random effects and were tested for any potential contribution.

RESULTS
PEAK GROUND REACTION FORCE
Peak *vertical* ground reaction forces were significantly ($p < 0.05$)

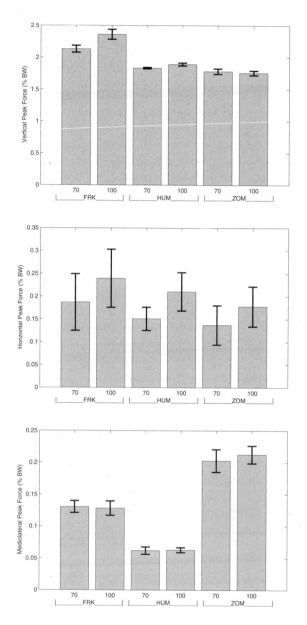

Figure 16.3 Comparisons of Peak Ground Reaction Forces in the Three Gait Types (FRK = Frankenstein; HUM = Human; ZOM = Zombie) at Two Speeds (70 Beats Per Minute, 100 Beats Per Minute).

higher during Frankenstein walking than during human walking at both measured speeds and significantly higher than both zombie and human walking at the higher speed ($p < 0.01$, Figures 16.2, 16.3a).

Peak *horizontal* (fore-aft) ground reaction forces were significantly higher during Frankenstein walking than during zombie walking ($p < 0.05$) during slow and fast walking, but neither differed significantly from human walking (Figure 16.3b). The greatest differences in peak forces were found in peak *mediolateral* ground reaction forces. Humans exhibited the lowest mediolateral ground reaction forces. Zombie walking produced higher peak mediolateral ground reaction forces than either human or Frankenstein walking ($p < 0.01$, Figure 16.3c). Frankenstein walking also produced significantly higher mediolateral ground reaction forces than human walking ($p < 0.01$, Figure 16.3c).

CENTRE OF MASS MOVEMENT

Centre of mass movement in the vertical and mediolateral directions has a similar magnitude in humans and Frankenstein. Zombie walking, however, is remarkably high in mediolateral movement (as we can see from the characteristic mediolateral sway), but low in overall vertical movement (Figure 16.4)

DISCUSSION

Zombies (or at least humans walking like zombies) exhibit vertical peak forces consistent with human vertical peak forces; however, Frankenstein has extremely high peak vertical ground reaction forces (Figures 16.2, 16.3a). Because of his locked knees, Frankenstein takes shorter steps in which the centre of mass takes a much shorter path over the foot from heel strike to toe-off. The initial heel strike is performed at a larger angle relative to the ground, resulting in a ground reaction force with a relatively larger vertical component compared to humans.

Although zombies have a nearly identical vertical force to humans, their mediolateral peak force is significantly higher because of the side-to-side swaying of their bodies, as evidenced by their large mediolateral centre of mass fluctuations. Emperor penguins have been observed to waddle or sway back

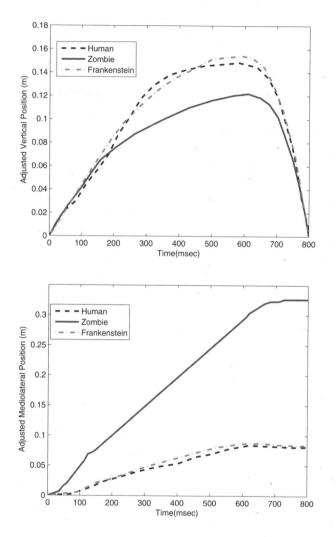

Figure 16.4 (a) Vertical and (b) Mediolateral Changes in the Centre of Mass Position for All Three Gait Types in One Individual Moving at the Faster Pace. Centre of mass positions have been adjusted so that all begin at zero. Note the low vertical and high mediolateral movement of the centre of mass during zombie walking.

and forth as well. This sway was previously associated with the high cost of locomotion in emperor penguins; however, Griffin and Kram (2000) demonstrated that it is their short legs, rather than their waddle, that causes increased energy requirements. Donelan et al. (2004) demonstrated that mechanical and metabolic energy increases with step width because of the disproportionate increase in costs required to reorient the centre of mass at the step-to-step transition with wider step lengths. Zombies use a wide step width that results in their mediolateral sway, and this can increase energy costs in zombies or humans walking like them. Of course, energy loss might not be an issue for zombies, who have infinite energy and therefore should not be concerned with the efficiency of their gait.

On the other hand, zombies lack the necessary regenerative capabilities that humans have, such as bone remodelling. This is the process by which old bone is broken down while the foundation for new bone is being laid, at which point the bone has been regenerated. Bone remodelling is well known to occur in response to mechanical strain (Lanyon 1984; Lanyon and Rubin 1984), microdamage (Burr et al. 1985), as well as a variety of other autocrine functions, such as growth hormone (Komarova et al. 2003). This is a continual process that restores approximately ten percent of the skeleton per year and is essential in the face of continual microdamage. Zombies lack this process of regeneration, so high skeletal strain can be destructive to their skeletons. We did not test zombies at a running speed because running is not conducive to their deteriorating life form. To have a faster gait, peak forces must increase because contact time has to decrease. This would be harmful to a zombie because it would cause the forces on the limb to be detrimentally high.

Biomechanically, Frankenstein is not a zombie! He exhibits a gait pattern very different from that of zombies, including a larger peak vertical force and a smaller peak mediolateral force. Frankenstein might be able to remodel his bones in response to mechanical load. Since he is a reanimation of a human life form and is capable of human biological functions, such as hormone secretion and bone remodelling, the high peak forces might not be as detrimental as they are for a zombie.

CONCLUSION

For perhaps the last time, we have put to rest the debate and we declare that Frankenstein is not a zombie, at least biomechanically! However, this conclusion means that a monster such as Zombiestein is a distinct possibility. Although we did not simulate Zombiestein's gait experimentally, the message boards might soon be abuzz with what Zombiestein's gait would resemble.

Returning to our initial questions, it is possible to outrun zombies, especially since they don't run. However, without concern for energy expenditure and with their low-impact gait, they can keep going and going as "Energizer Zombies." Although this topic might need to be addressed in the future in a separate zombie-related chapter, we hypothesize that changing the terrain often (e.g., going uphill and downhill) will cause zombies to slow their progression toward their next meal. These high-impact activities would compromise the structural integrity of these creatures, whose skeleton is unable to respond to high-load environments. Also, since zombies cannot jump, any obstacle that causes them to alter their gait should slow their progress. So, instead of using an oil slick to avoid a zombie, you should go over and under as many fences, tables or other obstacles as possible that will make the zombies change their gait. We hope these tips will help you in the unfortunate event of a zombie and/or Zombiestein invasion!

ACKNOWLEDGEMENT

The authors thank Roshna Wunderlich for her assistance with this project.

REFERENCES

Adamczyk, P.G., S.H. Collins, and A.D. Kuo. 2006. "The Advantages of a Rolling Foot in Human Walking." *Journal of Experimental Biology* 209: 3953–63.

Adamczyk, P.G. and A.D. Kuo. 2009. "Redirection of Center-of-Mass Velocity during the Step-to-Step Transition of Human Walking." *Journal of Experimental Biology* 212: 2668–78.

Ahn, A.N., E. Furrow and A.A. Biewener. 2004. "Walking and Running in the Red-Legged Running Frog, *Kassina maculata.*" *Journal of Experimental Biology* 207: 399.

Alexander, R.M. 1991. "Energy-Saving Mechanisms in Walking and Running." *Journal of Experimental Biology* 160: 55–69.

———. 1992. "A Model of Bipedal Locomotion on Compliant Legs." *Philosopical Transactions of the Royal Society of London* 338: 189–98.

Alexander, R.M. and H.C. Bennet-Clark. 1977. "Storage of Elastic Strain Energy in Muscle and Other Tissues." *Nature* 265: 114–17.

Alexander, R.M. and A.S. Jayes. 1978. "Vertical Movements in Walking and Running." *Journal of Zoology London* 185: 27–40.

Bennell, K., G. Matheson, W. Meeuwisse and P. Brukner. 1999. "Risk Factors for Stress Fractures." *Sports Medicine* 28, 2: 91–122.

Brooks, M. 2003. *The Zombie Survival Guide: Complete Protection from the Living Dead.* New York: Three Rivers Press.

Burr, D.B., R. Bruce Martin, M.B. Schaffler and E.L. Radin. 1985. "Bone Remodeling in Response to In Vivo Fatigue Microdamage." *Journal of Biomechanics* 18, 3: 189–200.

Burr, D.B., C. Milgrom, D. Fyhrie, M. Forwood, M. Nyska, A. Finestone, et al. 1996. "In Vivo Measurement of Human Tibial Strains during Vigorous Activity." *Bone* 18, 5: 405–10.

Cavagna, G.A., N.C. Heglund and C.R. Taylor. 1977. "Mechanical Work in Terrestrial Locomotion: Two Basic Mechanisms for Minimizing Energy Expenditure." *American Journal of Physiology* 233: R243–61.

Donelan, J.M., R. Kram and A.D. Kuo. 2002a. "Mechanical Work for Step-to-Step Transitions Is a Major Determinant of the Metabolic Cost of Human Walking." *Journal of Experimental Biology* 205: 3717–27.

———. 2002b. "Simultaneous Positive and Negative External Mechanical Work in Human Walking." *Journal of Biomechanics* 35, 1: 117–24.

Donelan, J.M., D.W. Shipman, R. Kram and A.D. Kuo. 2004. "Mechanical and Metabolic Requirements for Active Lateral Stabilization in Human Walking." *Journal of Biomechanics* 37, 6: 827-35.

Ferris, D.P., M. Louie and C.T. Farley. 1998. "Running in the Real World: Adjusting Leg Stiffness for Different Surfaces." *Proceedings of the Royal Society B* 265: 989–94.

Griffin, T.M. and R. Kram. 2000. "Penguin Waddling Is Not Wasteful." *Macmillan Magazines* 408: 929.

Gross, T.S. and R.C. Nelson. 1988. "The Shock Attenuation Role of the Ankle during Landing from a Vertical Jump." *Medicine and Science in Sports and Exercise* 20, 5: 506–14.

Komarova, S.V., R.J. Smith, S.J. Dixon, S.M. Sims and L.M. Wahl. 2003. "Mathematical Model Predicts a Critical Role for Osteoclast Autocrine Regulation in the Control of Bone Remodelling." *Bone* 33, 2: 206–15.

Lanyon, L.E. 1984. "Functional Strain as a Determinant for Bone Remodelling." *Calcified Tissue International* 36, 1: S56–61.

Lanyon, L.E. and C.T. Rubin. 1984. "Static versus Dynamic Loads as an Influence on Bone Remodelling." *Journal of Biomechanics* 17, 12: 897–905.

McMahon, T.A. and G.C. Cheng. 1990. "The Mechanics of Running: How Does Stiffness Couple with Speed?" *Journal of Biomechanics* 23: 65–78.

McMahon, T.A., G. Valiant and E.C. Frederick. 1987. "Groucho Running." *Journal of Applied Physiology* 62: 2326–37.

Milner, C.E., I.S. Davis and J. Hamill. 2006. "Free Moments as a Predictor of Tibial Stress Fracture in Distance Runners." *Journal of Biomechanics* 22: 2819–25.

Morris, F.L., G.A. Naughton, J.L. Gibbs, J.S. Carlson and J.D. Wark. 1997. "Prospective Ten-Month Exercise Intervention in Premenarcheal Girls: Positive Effects on Bone and Lean Mass." *Journal of Bone and Mineral Research* 12, 9: 1453–62.

Ortega, J.D. and C.T. Farley. 2005. "Minimizing Center of Mass Vertical Movement Increases Metabolic Cost in Walking." *Journal of Applied Physiology* 99, 6: 2099–2107.

Roberts, T.J. 2002. "The Integrated Function of Muscles and Tendons during Locomotion." *Comparative Biochemistry and Physiology: A Molecular and Integrative Physiology* 133, 4: 1087–99.

Voloshin, A. and J. Wosk. 1982. "An In Vivo Study of Low Back Pain and Shock Absorption in the Human Locomotor System." *Journal of Biomechanics* 15, 1: 21–27.

BECOMING ZOMBIE GRRRLS ON AND OFF SCREEN

NATASHA PATTERSON

THE ZOMBIE AND I

In the past decade, there has been a notable resurgence in the zombie film, a sub-genre of horror. Indeed, the zombie has successfully infiltrated all areas of popular culture, resulting in the proliferation of cultural products for our consumptive pleasures. No longer solely the property of the geeky fanboy, zombies have found their way into the hearts and braaaiiinnnsss of men and women, young and old, and those who otherwise might never have considered themselves "horror fans." Clearly, the popularity of the zombie illustrates its resonance with/for fans and consumers. However, what draws us to the zombie surely varies from person to person. The first time I saw George A. Romero's classic and genre-breaking film, *Night of the Living Dead* (1968), I was hooked. Since then, zombies have gradually made their presence known to me, in the form of DVDs, comics and graphic novels, posters, as well as movie figurines, all scattered throughout my humble abode. The zombie and I share a (mostly) peaceful existence. As a (feminist) fan of the zombie film, I find myself in a particularly unsettling position, for my relationship with the cannibalistic creature is not a straightforward one of blind adoration but one characterized by a process of ongoing negotiation (the not-so-peaceful part). This is the lot of the feminist pop culture critic.

The zombie figure, as (re)envisioned by Romero in the late twentieth century, has been copied, parodied, and reworked over and over again, causing much debate among fan-critics. A number of films, from *28 Days Later* (2002) to the *Dawn of the Dead* (2004) remake, presented a reworked zombie capable of running at high speeds, a move that irked many Romero purists (me included). Chalking it up to the influence of video games on the film industry, I was quick to dismiss these creatures as not "real" zombies. However, in recent years, another filmic zombie representation has popped up, elevating the fast-paced zombie to a fully functioning subject capable of speech but not immune to the effects of zombification (i.e., cannibalistic drive, decomposing body). Interestingly, I find myself drawn to these most recent offspring of the zombie sub-genre, especially as some of the more compelling stories are told through the figure of the female zombie in films written and directed by women.

In this chapter, I explore the significance of two recent representations of female zombies through close textual analyses of the independently produced films *Graveyard Alive* (2003) and *American Zombie* (2007). These films are a welcome departure from the typical (Hollywood) zombie film since they openly grapple with questions of identity and pleasure, and how undergoing zombification complicates these concepts, especially as they intersect with sexuality, race and gender. Following my discussion and analysis of the films, I draw on my "lived experience" to examine the links between the on-screen female zombie subject and the off-screen fan practice of performing, through costume and makeup, an articulation of zombification as (feminist) identity. My desire to cultivate a "femi-zombie" persona can be partially attributed to my frustration with a postfeminist media culture that works to render feminism passé and unnecessary, and instead encourages us to find solutions to complex social problems (e.g., gender inequality) in our engagements with consumer culture (Tasker and Negra

2007, 6). The concept of postfeminism, as it manifests itself in popular culture, is best understood as a sensibility that produces a neoliberal femininity "which present[s] women as autonomous agents no longer constrained by any inequalities or power imbalance whatsoever" (Gill 2007, 153). There are, however, places within popular culture that offer women alternative and oppositional identifications still indebted to, and clearly engaged with, a critical yet pleasurable feminist standpoint, sometimes where you least expect it.

SETTING THE STAGE

Although there is still a dearth of literature focusing exclusively on zombies, especially with regard to gender representation, there is no shortage of literature on the horror film. The horror film, as a cultural text, is a useful site from which to enter debates about the politics of gender representation. Films, like all cultural productions, are not ahistorical and self-contained entities with predetermined and fixed meanings; rather, they are constantly evolving to reflect shifting attitudes about men and women, and even feminism. For many critics, this focus on gender is central to horror's success as a genre. As horror film scholar Barry Keith Grant writes, "whether one prefers to examine horror films in terms of universal fears or historically determined cultural anxieties, issues of gender remain central to the genre. For gender, as recent theory has argued, is, like horror itself, both universal and historical, biological and cultural" (1996a). Film scholars such as Linda Williams (1984) and Barbara Creed (1993) exemplify how feminist cultural critics have long been fascinated with the genre's treatment of women, especially how horror films have dealt with questions of sexual difference, paying attention to how such films (negatively) construct women/femininity as monstrous other and/or code monstrosity as a feminized position (e.g., *Videodrome*, 1983; *Aliens*, 1986).

Feminist scholarship within this field of study often draws on cine-psychoanalytic approaches to analyze gender representation, often with the presumption that this approach will (and does) produce the "correct" interpretation. Moreover, cine-psychoanalytic readings often overlook audience reception, instead arguing that the film structures the audience response, which reinforces the notion of the passive viewer who (unproblematically) accepts the dominant message presented in the film. Proponents of audience studies argue that reception is integral to the meaning(s) generated about any given film and that these meanings must be contextualized as viewer preferences and readings change over time. Situating the reception and criticism of horror film within its cultural and historical context(s) makes it possible for a variety of readings, including feminist ones. Finally, the literature has been criticized for interpreting films through a gender-binary lens that privileges only two subject positions, on and off screen: male/masculine and female/feminine (see Gaines 1999; hooks 1992; Stacey 1987; Weiss 1992). In other words, cine-psychoanalysis, rooted in theories of sexual difference, ignores other categories of difference such as class, race, sexuality, ability and so on, leaving many viewers invisible and/or underrepresented.

Recognizing these limitations, a number of feminist film critics have sought out different techniques to understand the cultural significance of horror films and how these films, rather than simply objectifying and victimizing women, have often reflected on contemporary social issues and problems. Notably, Carol Clover's (1992) work on the slasher film made great gains in this area. Her work proffered a rather contentious notion (at the time): horror films are not merely the by-products of a misogynistic nightmare, but actively negotiate with prevailing ideas and debates of the day, especially feminist challenges to patriarchal definitions of gender. For instance, Clover showed how the slasher film, despite constantly being criticized for victimizing women, often portrayed the hero, dubbed the Final Girl, as female. The Final Girl, having no one else to rely on (e.g., father, policeman), had to save herself by killing the psycho murderer. For Clover, this courageous female figure was a feminist symbol of empowerment and intellect. The Final Girl might also be read as a postfeminist figure since she refuses to become a victim, like her (dead) "sisters," wielding her brand of (individualistic) power and looking sexy as she saves herself. Although Clover's analysis opens up the possibility of a resistant and/or pleasurable spectating position for women in/and horror, Clover ultimately dismisses this by focusing on what it means for the male spectator (as the presumed audience and consumer of the slasher film), who is able to switch back and forth between identifying with the monstrous killer and the Final Girl.

The Final Girl has also made her way into the zombie film. Discussions of gender in zombie films have tended to focus on representations of the male and female survivors, notably in Romero's *"Dead"* trilogy. Early on, scholars debated and analyzed how Romero's special brand of flesh-eating hordes function as a social critique of the dominant institutions (e.g., the family, consumer culture) of patriarchal capitalism (see McLarty 1984; Wood 1986). Later, critics expanded these discussions by pointing out that Romero's women tap into feminist discourses of empowerment and independence, challenging patriarchal constructions of women as passive, irrational and (physically and intellectually) weak (see Grant 1996b; Patterson 2008). Furthermore, whereas the gender order has long placed men within the realm(s) of strength, rationality and action, Romero's men are often portrayed as incompetent, overbearing, condescending and (unjustifiably) entitled. Thus, his zombie films offer a social critique of the patriarchal-capitalist system while providing female viewers with pleasurable (and feminist-inspired) representations of women who are just as capable of, if not better at, surviving a zombie apocalypse as men are.

Patterson (2008) has also suggested that, aside from Romero's "positive" depictions of women, part of the pleasure derived from his films rests on the zombie figure itself, which becomes a site of critical exploration, inviting us to take immense pleasure in its destructive and deconstructing ways. The presence of zombies renders the patriarchal-capitalist social order obsolete as both men and women are called on to step outside their prescribed gender roles to ensure the survival of humanity. For men, this means they must act more cooperatively and selflessly; for women, this often results in courageousness and assertiveness. Indeed, the need for collective action overrides all personal and individual needs and desires, a concept that I embrace as a feminist one. This "Romerian" notion has even pervaded video games; the recently released *Left 4*

Dead 2, a game premised on a zombie apocalypse, requires players to work together in a cooperative and communicative manner, as opposed to the single-player shooter mode common to most games. These traits are considered the keys to success. *Left 4 Dead 2*, developed by Valve Corporation and released for PC and Xbox 360 in 2009, also gives players the opportunity to take on the role of monster, creating a range of identificatory positions beyond male and female, something this zombie fan relishes.

In contrast, some readings of Barbara, the lead female character in *Night of the Living Dead*, have placed her firmly as the antithesis to the Final Girl, for she acquiesces to the lead male character, Ben, turning into a frightened, incoherent mess, almost zombie-like. However, I argue that Barbara symbolizes more than "woman as victim." After all, she is merely behaving in a way appropriate for a woman at that time (late 1960s). Instead, her breakdown reveals just how "deadly" the patriarchal feminine social script is for women, especially when faced with danger. Her investment in, and performance of, a passive (and therefore respectable) femininity literally hurts her. Unable to protect herself, Barbara eventually succumbs to the zombie hordes. *Night of the Living Dead* parallels the destructiveness associated with patriarchal constructions of femininity with zombification. In short, negative social constructions of women and womanhood are tantamount to a life lived (un)dead. Therefore, the movie possibly acts as a warning to women: it is not in our best interests to invest, without reservations or questions, in such narrow definitions of femininity; our survival depends on it! Although these earlier films addressed femininity and feminism through the figure of the female survivor, newer films, such as *Graveyard Alive* and *American Zombie*, grapple with these issues by displacing them onto the zombie figure. Patriarchal constructions of femininity are no longer critiqued for producing a "zombie-like" quality in women; rather, they are now represented in a female/feminine zombie subject, contributing to a sub-generic shift that revolves around the zombie rather than the survivor. Look out, Final Girl, there's a new gal on the scene and she's not afraid to get ugly.

regular food, and begins to change her appearance by wearing makeup, removing her eyeglasses and cultivating a "sexy nurse" look. She also starts to become more assertive and is no longer shy about expressing herself sexually; we see her aggressively flirt with men at work, and in turn they begin to notice and desire her. Patsy happily embodies and performs a hyper-sexualized femininity, which ends up propelling her from a passive subject position to an active one. As director Elza Kephart muses, "We wanted to make a point that the sexual female, even though she's a monster, is victorious. She's better off being a zombie. She's not necessarily happier, but now she's aware of the power she can have. She's probably sadder, but at least she's active" (Ladouceur 2005, 48). If Patsy is sadder, perhaps it stems from the fact that zombification has effectively "killed off" her lifelong dream of a utopian hetero-romantic fantasy.

Patsy finds her life suddenly in overdrive as she is able to live the life she had always wanted instead of reading about it in romance novels. However, her new empowered position is the result of zombification, suggesting that it was only once she left the world of the living and became a member of the undead that her "life," ironically, began. Media studies scholar Marc Leverette posits that the liminal (in-between) space occupied by the zombie is ultimately a transgressive one, for it calls into question "the boundaries of our individual subjectivity," allowing the audience to "celebrate a different and unknowable Other" (2008, 196). With this in mind, I posit that zombie Patsy's "liminal persona" (Leverette's term) is constructed as an empowering (subject) position that offers pleasure for the female viewer. Patsy does not mourn the loss of her old identity, but attempts to manage her new one to her benefit. She recognizes that, if her co-workers and superiors knew who she "really was," they would try to get rid of her. In many respects, she is unable to exert much control over her new identity as her body slowly decomposes throughout the film. Her skin falls off and rigor mortis begins in her hands. To compensate, Patsy "masks" the smell of decaying flesh with perfume and even more makeup, bringing with it a different kind of (unwanted) attention from the curious janitor Kapotsky and Goodie, whose suspicions begin to grow.

Despite Patsy's transmogrification, her dating life has never been better, and here the film takes us through a comedic romp, often taking a bite out of the very gendered world of (hetero)dating. Since zombification, Patsy has become more attractive to men and takes advantage of this accordingly. After one particularly successful date with a co-worker, Patsy engages in some playful kissing, which in turn awakens her (cannibalistic) desire for human flesh, and she bites him hard on the lip. The date, not surprisingly, mistakes her lip bite for sexual lust, leaving him wanting more, yet she cannot go any further without risking her secret and her date's life. Meanwhile, Dox, frustrated by Goodie's repeated rebuffs at his sexual advances, starts to take an interest in Patsy (again). Goodie appears to use her sexuality as a powerful tool of negotiation. For her, marriage to a doctor equals social status and the possibility of promotion to head nurse. While Patsy can hardly contain her zombie cravings, Dox is shown displaying eerily similar desires as he constantly "gropes" Goodie, almost as if he is trying to "devour" her sexually. Here the film blurs the line between a zombie's hunger for meat and patriarchal constructions of a male sexuality expressed through aggression, objectification and a lack of respect. His own lack of personal and professional respect for Patsy is clear as he continuously makes sexual advances on Goodie at their place of employment (the hospital), despite her constant refusals. In an interesting role reversal, Patsy goes out with Dox, finally getting the attention she has been craving from her first love. But she is no longer the woman she once was and during dinner she watches in horror as he eats his dinner "like an animal," leaving her feeling disgusted and totally turned off. She gets the final revenge on the boy who once dumped her as she becomes the dumper this time. Her new zombie identity seems to have cured her, once and for all, of her feelings for Dox.

Not everyone is enamoured of the "new and improved" Patsy. Kapotsky and Goodie find out her secret. Kapotsky eventually confronts her and proclaims that she needs to be exterminated, but, before he can kill her, Patsy kills him first by ripping at his flesh. As he begins to reanimate into a zombie, she kills him again, this time for good, perhaps fearful that her secret won't "die" with him unless he is permanently dead. After killing Kapotsky, Patsy permits herself to feast on human flesh and starts using the hospital morgue as her own personal buffet. As the process of zombification quickens, so does her need for more and more human flesh, and she resorts to drugging patients in order to speed up the process of death. Certainly a commentary on the (failing) Canadian health-care system (i.e., patients become victims), Patsy's hunger eventually takes over the entire hospital, and more and more people become zombies. In the film's climax, Goodie has become the Final Girl, but she proves to be no match for Patsy, the ultimate femi-zombie. The film closes with a nod to Romero: the screen fills with zombies and we know there are no survivors. Patsy is truly victorious.

American Zombie, another independent horror film, was written by Rebecca Sonnenshine and Grace Lee, with direction by Lee.[1] By all accounts, *American Zombie* is an unconventional take on the horror sub-genre, combining documentary filmmaking techniques with horror to produce a mock-documentary about contemporary zombie life. Mock-documentaries "make a partial or concerted effort to appropriate documentary codes and conventions in order to represent a fictional subject" (Roscoe and Hight 2001, 2). The premise of the film centres on Grace (playing a version of herself) and fellow filmmaker John Solomon (also playing a version of himself) as they struggle to make a documentary about the zombie community. The film's backdrop is an alternative reality in which zombies coexist with "normal" humans. Due to scientific advances and knowledge of the zombie virus, zombies are viewed no longer

---

1   Korean American filmmaker Grace Lee is best known for her award-winning documentary *The Grace Lee Project* (2005), which documents her journey meeting other Grace Lees from around the United States and other parts of the world. Lee states on her website that, "Despite the differences in our ages and experiences and where we came from, it quickly became clear to me that there was a genuine sense of community among those of us interested in discovering our Grace Lee-ness (or lack thereof)." For more on Lee and her work, see http://www.gracelee.net/index.php.

as threats to society, but as a legitimate population with specific (medical) needs and issues. The filmmakers "document" the lives of four (high-functioning) zombies, but I focus specifically on the representation of the two female zombies: Judy, a shy vegan (!) zombie of Asian descent who fantasizes about marrying a human and having a family, and Lisa, a Caucasian zombie florist who preaches new-age spirituality but is haunted by her inability to remember how she became infected.

Lee and Solomon's "documentary" reveals an interesting world where zombies have become classified and contained by various institutions (e.g., medicine, capitalism), leading to inequality among different groups of zombies. According to the film's "medical experts," the zombie virus affects everyone differently. Some people become "feral" zombies, some become "low functioning" (i.e., speechless, slow), and the rest are labelled "high functioning" and can assimilate themselves into the living world. These pseudo-medical categories are also translated into social categories of class stratification. As the film progresses, it becomes painfully clear that zombies are not "just like us"; their "otherness" has become the basis for ongoing economic exploitation, as we witness in the sweatshops that profit from the labour of low-functioning zombies, who are literally unable to defend themselves. Ivan, one of the male interviewees, reveals to us early on in the film that zombies do not need to sleep or eat, which makes them an attractive labour force to be used and abused by disreputable businesspeople.

The film reveals another way in which zombies are exploited: they are an attractive niche market for the self-help industry and alternative medicines. During filming, we learn that zombies must carefully manage their bodies as they are in a perpetual state of disintegration and their initial wounds (the sites of infection) never properly heal. These wounds are a source of shame for Judy, who desperately attempts to construct an identity that hides her zombieness. We first meet her at her place of work, an organic food distributor. Later, in her apartment, she shows the filmmakers how "ordinary" her life is: she follows a vegan diet, she composts and she makes scrapbooks. Judy comments, "People have a lot of misconceptions about me, but I'm just like everyone else. I have hopes and dreams, hopes and dreams." As viewers, we are invited to question just how "normal" Judy can be, given our pre-existing knowledge of zombies. Yet her struggle for normalcy as human-like might also be a commentary on the links among ethnicity, shame and the desire for racial "normalcy" (i.e., attaining "whiteness"). Judy is doubly othered, for she is not only a female zombie but also a racially coded zombie, which is rarely portrayed and/or explored by filmmakers in the horror genre.

The film also offers a meta-critique of documentary film-making and its techniques when, during an extremely un-comfortable moment, John abruptly asks Judy if there is any human flesh in her refrigerator. Judy looks into the camera and thus at Lee (and us) as if confused and unsure of what to do. Grace later chastises John for his intrusive behaviour and line of questioning, calling his approach "stupid" and "insult-ing." Underpinning her comment is the (feminist) notion that the documentary filmmaker/subject relationship must be a re-ciprocal one founded on respect and trust. This view emerged as a critique of conventional documentary filmmaking (e.g., the observational approach and *cinema verité*) that claims to be objective and neutral yet can objectify and provoke subjects and even intrude on their lives, physically and emotionally, in the "quest for truth." Feminist and other critical documenta-rists and filmmakers have strategized to address these power relations between filmmaker and subject through alternative filming practices (see Waldman and Walker 1999).

American Zombie follows this critical style and engages with these tensions over how best to "capture the truth" through-out the film. John represents the objectifying (white, male) documentarist in his constant need to reveal the "money shot" (i.e., zombies do eat flesh!), suggesting that his search for the truth is clouded by a narrow perception of what it means to be a zombie. By refusing to see them as subjects, he reduces Judy and Lisa to the status of objectified other. Grace, unwilling to let John get away with such ignorant comments, embodies a (feminist) counterdiscourse, accusing him of reducing zombies to their (supposed) primary function. At one point, she says to John, "Stop essentializing zombies!" Grace not only offers a counterargument to his stereotypical beliefs about zombies, but also sets up the film itself as a commentary on the politics of representation within film. *American Zombie* invites us to consider how gendered and racialized power relations also structure filmmaking and audience reception.

Judy's desire for "normalcy" offers another interesting commentary on women's gender and racial identity. After the uncomfortable exchange in the kitchen with John in the previous scene, we see Judy sitting on the couch flipping through wedding magazines. She proudly states, "I can't wait to get married, settle down and have kids." Grace responds with a rhetorical question—"I didn't know zombies could have children?"—to which Judy abruptly interjects "adopt kids." To fulfill this fantasy of a pre-zombification life, Judy must find a human "Mr. Right"; in other words, her ideal mate is coded as a normalized other rather than a member of her community. Her desire for normalcy is made painfully clear later, during an extremely awkward and uncomfortable scene, when she tells the filmmakers that a human standing on the street is her boyfriend, but when she approaches him he brushes her off. Returning to the original interview scene, Grace asks Judy a difficult question: "Are you ashamed of being a zombie?" After a moment of silence, Judy responds, "It's just not something I want to advertise." Her aspirations speak to pervasive cultural stereotypes that portray Asian American women as "traditional," "docile," "passive" and "submissive" (Sandita 1997; Sun 2003). Moreover, Judy's desire to have a human (i.e., normal) mate might also speak to feelings of shame and/or internalization of the dominant culture's construction of harmful stereotypes about Asian men. Indeed, Grace's mockumentary offers an interesting and complex picture of women's negotiations of identity through the figure of Judy, yet these identifications are constantly in flux and malleable.

From this point, the documentary process becomes a site of revelation, as Judy's interaction with the filmmakers reveals her identity to be far more complicated than Judy wants us to believe. Her consumptive practices enable her to piece together an identity that allows for some semblance of normalcy while also containing desires that will most likely never be fulfilled. Indeed, the film asks us to question her beliefs, and

whether her strict adherence to the (human) feminine and racialized social script is really what Judy wants or if she uses it
as a prop to assimilate herself more easily into human society.
In other words, her attempts at cultural assimilation reveal the
performative function of femininity and racial identity, as her
repeated assertions that praise marriage and motherhood only
further illustrate how socially constructed such ideologies are.
Judy has learned how to adopt these ideologies to construct a
self that is acceptable to humans, that will (hopefully) mask her
zombieness, yet her decomposing body constantly reminds us
just how futile her efforts are. Viewers are invited to question
the definition of a racialized femininity in general as it circu-
lates in our dominant (white, patriarchal) culture. Judy might
be a zombie, but her investment in marriage and motherhood
is common to many women across all classes, races and ethnic-
ities. If her investments seem bizarre and outlandish, how can
we be sure that our own investments in these romanticized institutions are not also bizarre and outlandish?

Judy's story does not end there, though. Later in the film, Judy tags along with John and Grace as they venture out to the
much-loved but somewhat mysterious zombies-only festival,
Live Dead. The purpose of Live Dead is to celebrate zombie
culture and to provide a space for zombies to get together and
have fun. Judy, no longer isolated from other zombies, encounters her "people" for the first time; by the end of the festival,
she has made connections with other zombies, filling her with a
newfound sense of belonging. This change is further cemented
during a follow-up interview toward the end of the film, where
Judy has given herself a makeover: her new appearance is more
edgy and her apartment looks more "lived in." Her scrapbook
is full of pictures from Live Dead, she has quit her job ("I've just
been limiting my choices all this time"), and she now finds fulfillment and meaning within the zombie community.

As the filmmakers wrap up, they exchange goodbyes, at
which point Judy attacks John, turning him into a (low-functioning) zombie. No longer satisfied masking her zombieness
and buoyed by her participation in the documentary, she is unable to contain her desires. Judy finally comes to accept and
embrace her difference and no longer feels obliged to conform

to society's expectations or ill-informed perceptions of who she is and what she should be. Indeed, the last shot of Judy captures her giving John what he always wanted: the coveted "money shot." But, in an interesting reversal of subject positions, she becomes the aggressor, taking an active position, while he is "punished" for his relentless search for the "truth," a truth steeped in racial and gender stereotypes, as he was never quite able to look past the dominant perception of zombies as cannibalistic others. In the end, he becomes the victim and the object of her desires, thus completing her transformation from (the stereotypical) "passive" racialized other to empowered zombie subject. Sometimes a grrrl really does get her man.

Lisa, the zombie florist, artist and new-age spiritualist, also proves difficult to contain. Like Judy, Lisa is somewhat shy and reserved; when the filmmakers come to her home, she too seems intent on projecting a particular idea or vision of herself to the camera. Her zombie identity is funnelled through new-age spiritualism and self-help discourses that help her to overcome the emotional struggles she faces as a zombie (other). This representation invokes a rather familiar stereotype about the new-age, middle-class, hippie type coded as predominantly white and female. Whereas Judy initially tries to mask her otherness by isolating herself from the zombie community, Lisa appears to accept it. However, despite her attempts to belong, she seems haunted by sadness and never quite fits in with those around her. The only activity that seems to bring her any pleasure (even more so than her art) is floral arranging for funerals. She describes the dead as "the lucky ones." Such comments reveal an unsettled (zombie) self stripped of memory and forced to exist in the present. As Joel, a zombie activist in the film, notes at one point, "Zombies don't remember who they are. They're lost." Lisa epitomizes this sense of loss as she tries to get the filmmakers involved in a search for her past life.

As the film unfolds, Lisa becomes progressively anxious, especially when she learns that the filmmakers will not be following through with the search. During the wrap-up interview with Lisa, Grace and John discover that she has killed her neighbours. While waiting for the police to arrive, Lisa proclaims, "I did them a favour.... Now they'll never have to be zombies, ever. I don't want a sympathetic jury. Please, please make sure they give me the death penalty, please." As her violent behaviour belies her earlier declarations of a relaxed spirituality, the film seems to imply that these therapeutic discourses, especially when mediated through consumer culture, become empty clichés that merely help us to manage (and mask) our frustration and sadness with a culture that cares more about profit motives than people's mental and emotional well-being. As the police drag Lisa away, we hear her pleading with Grace to back her up, that her actions were rationally motivated: "I knew what I was doing the whole time.... Please don't let them lock me up forever.... They have to kill me!" Lisa, finally stepping outside her carefully managed zombie identity, shows us that zombification does not always lead to a sense of empowerment or freedom, as it does for Judy. Although Lisa never expresses a desire to be human again, not knowing how she became a zombie weighs heavily on her psyche, making it impossible for her to fully embrace her new identity, suggesting that identity is an ongoing process of negotiation, marked by precariousness and incompletion.

Both *American Zombie* and *Graveyard Alive* show a high degree of cultural and generic innovation, even as they are indebted to Romero's films, by pushing the boundaries of what audiences and fans have come to expect from the zombie film. Both films engage in a process of cannibalization, bringing together an eclectic mix of genres and filmmaking techniques that foreground the (female) zombie as a critical site for interrogating the struggles, anxieties and complexities of contemporary life for women. These images of female zombies have much to offer us, for they challenge not only monolithic conceptions of "woman" (i.e., passive), but also woman in representation. Moreover, they offer alternative channels for female visual pleasures that do not reside in mainstream women's genres (e.g., romantic comedies) and whose narratives most often centre on the (containable) female protagonist who "chooses," in typical postfeminist fashion, to invest in the dominant social order (e.g., marriage, motherhood). Unfortunately, such stereotypical visual pleasures are anything but soothing for women (like me) yearning for images of women who are utterly unapologetic in their desire to upset such conventions. This yearning has led me to literally take up and explore a female/feminine zombie identity through fan practice. In the next section, I explore the politics of this pleasure and its relationship to my feminist-fan identity.

THE Z WORD

I have been, and have walked with, a zombie. Seriously. On 31 October 2009, my partner and I spent the day transforming our bodies to resemble the living dead we so much adore, in particular the grey-green incarnations found in the Romero films *Dawn of the Dead* (1978) and *Day of the Dead* (1985). My zombie makeover complete, I set off into the night, only to find myself surrounded by other bodies excitedly performing various forms of zombie grotesque.

On that night, my bodily transformation enabled me to feel a sense of empowerment as I eschewed regular (non-blood-soaked) attire. I could purposefully reject dominant beauty ideals without being subjected to unwanted, judging stares. Early feminist horror film critics often derided the genre for victimizing women, but they rarely acknowledged the power some women might take from becoming grotesque, from cloaking themselves in monstrosity. I took great pleasure in the visceral responses to my bloodied body as people gazed on us with a combination of fascination, fear, horror, curiosity and even anxiety (though this didn't stop many of them from asking to take pictures of us; see Figure 17.1).

Figure 17.1. The Author as a Zombie Walk Participant.

Clearly, some people take great delight in being scared, in confronting realistic representations of horror's scariest monsters. It seems that, despite the many critics and fans who pan the living zombie as generically impure, creative festivals such as Hallowe'en continue to demonstrate a strong attraction to adopting a temporary zombie identity. We socialized with a surprisingly diverse range of zombies: zombie chef, zombie prisoner, zombie bride and groom, zombie business couple, and many a cigarette-smoking zombie! Moreover, the thousands of fans who participate every year in the annual Zombie Walk, held primarily in large cities throughout North America, certainly attest to the mass popularity of zombies, suggesting that the fans identify more with the zombies than they do with the survivors, even though they are considered the heroes and heroines. A quotation from *American Zombie* suggests, "We're here, we're dead, get used to it!" Yet this quotation is a play on the queer slogan used in Pride Parades around the world ("We're here, we're queer, get used to it") and enacts multiple meanings within the context of this discussion. Similar to its queer predecessor, the zombie slogan makes visible and brings awareness to the zombie's presence within popular culture; it highlights women's growing presence within the subculture as well as the zombie's queer status as neither dead nor alive but occupying an in-between space that refuses neat categorization. All of which prompts these questions: What is so seductive about the zombie figure? Why are some of us not content with merely "consuming" the zombie from a distance but feel compelled to step into their dead shoes?

Part of the pleasure I derive from masquerading as a zombie is symbolic. Zombification, for me, is akin to a process of transformation or becoming that allows me to explore alternative definitions and constructions of a gendered and racialized self that does not fit neatly into the categories "woman," "feminine" or even "feminist." The performative nature of zombie embodiment (as fan practice) challenges the idea that our identities are fixed or static. As feminist film scholar Annette Kuhn writes, "performance ... poses the possibility of a mutable self, of a fluid subjectivity" (1997, 200). Similarly, fan studies scholar Matt Hills states that, "By blurring the lines between self and other, fan impersonation challenges cultural norms of the fixed and bounded self" (2002, 171). Examples of female zombie fan performances can be found on a number of websites and groups sprouting up on the internet: Zombie Pinups

Calendar, Zombie Pinups Beauty Pageant, Night of the Stripping Dead[2] and the Barely Rotten Girls.[3] These groups illustrate how female fans' investments in, and engagements with, zombie culture are complex, even contradictory, and are made even more so due to negotiations in multiple and intersecting terms such as race, gender, class, ability and so forth. Within this context, fashioning a zombie self might also be viewed as a form of resistance and/or empowerment in a culture that insists on recycling the same images of women now imbued with a postfeminist sensibility that happily disavows feminist ideals as passé even as it appropriates discourses of "empowerment" and "choice" to narrowly (re)position us as primarily wives, mothers and, of course, consumers.

Indeed, rather than opening up more opportunities and avenues for women's self-expression and shining a spotlight on diverse femininities, postfeminist media culture has done its best to curtail such a revolution in gender representation. The female zombies in *Graveyard Alive* and *American Zombie* reject such limited notions of womanhood, instead revelling in their grotesque abjection and/or refusing to be controlled by feminizing, therapeutic discourses that attempt to contain and thus individualize women's angers and frustrations. Thus, these female zombification narratives, in conjunction with fan practices, open up spaces for women to intervene critically in and contest mainstream images of women; in the process, they/we become "active" participants in the production of alternative cultural discourses and representations, both on and off screen.

MY (FEMINIST) ZOMBIE LIFE

In this chapter, I attempted to contribute to the growing body of literature on zombie culture, focusing on the politics and pleasures of female zombies in the films *American Zombie* and *Graveyard Alive*. These representations are doubly important

2   The Zombie Pinups site archives the events listed above and can be found at http://www.zombiepinups.com/.

3   For more information, see http://www.facebook.com/pages/Barely-Rotten-Girls/99964487628.

not only for pushing the sub-genre's boundaries, but also for being the brainchildren of women writers and directors working in an industry in which women comprise a dismal five percent of the labour force in horror features (Lauzen 2007). Drawing on my personal experience as a zombie fan, I then explored the pleasures of zombie embodiment, or zombification, through fan performance, arguing that this practice holds complex and contradictory meanings for female fans. Female fans of horror (not just zombie films) are becoming increasingly visible, as the recently held Women in Horror Convention certainly attests to, along with fan blogs and zines such as *Day of the Woman: A Blog for the Feminine Side of Fear* (http://dayofwoman.blogspot.com/) and Hannah Neurotica's *Ax Wound Zine: Gender and the Horror Genre* (http://axwoundzine.com/blog/). Our growing subcultural participation further challenges (negatively) gendered perceptions of female horror fans as "inauthentic" and/or lacking in "fan cred" (Jancovich 2002, 475). As film scholar Isabel Pinedo asserts, "Critics who ignore the contradictory elements of the genre do a disservice to the complex readings of which audiences are capable" (1997, 133).

When discussions of women and horror do take place, especially within popular culture, the Final Girl character is often held up as a beacon of feminist hope in a postfeminist world. Where the postfeminist woman drinks martinis and compulsively shops, the Final Girl relies on her smarts and her courage for survival. I can certainly appreciate the symbolic justice meted out by the Final Girl and the sense of empowerment this conveys to female viewers. The Final Girl, presumably safe from the male killer(s), returns to her normal life to become a functioning member of the patriarchal-capitalist order once again. However, some of us would rather run from such containment. When I watch the "femi-zombie" on screen or step into her bloody, dirty shoes off screen, I am given a new life. I am undead, liminal and (super)empowered. I agree with *Newsweek* journalist Joshua Alston (2007) when he writes that "the Final Girl is no longer the only girl." He's right. There is indeed a new grrrl on the scene: the man-eating, uncontainable femi-zombie.

In the end, my critical musings on the significance of the female zombie on screen and as pleasurable fan performance off screen are based upon one feminist fan's experiences, and it would be worth exploring other women's experiences of such horrific transformations to gain a better understanding of why and whether other women find such images and "disguises" pleasurable. With the inordinate amount of attention that has been heaped on female horror fans recently, especially in the popular press, these discussions are inevitable. Until then, zombie grrrls of the world, unite!

REFERENCES

Alston, Joshua. 2007. "Bloody, Gross … Empowering?" *Newsweek*, 8 June. http://www.newsweek.com/id/34145.

Clover, Carol. 1992. *Men, Women, and Chainsaws: Gender in the Modern Horror Film*. Princeton: Princeton University Press.

Creed, Barbara. 1993. *The Monstrous-Feminine: Film, Feminism, Psychoanalysis*. London: Routledge.

Gaines, Jane. 1999. "White Privilege and Looking Relations: Race and Gender in Feminist Film Theory." In *Feminist Film Theory: A Reader*, edited by Sue Thornham, 293–306. New York: New York University Press.

Gill, Rosalind. 2007. "Postfeminist Media Culture: Elements of a Sensibility." *European Journal of Cultural Studies* 10, 2: 147–66.

Grant, Barry Keith. 1996a. "Introduction." In *The Dread of Difference: Gender and the Horror Film*, edited by Barry Keith Grant, 1–12. Austin: University of Texas Press.

———. 1996b. "Taking Back the *Night of the Living Dead:* George Romero, Feminism, and the Horror Film." In *The Dread of Difference: Gender and the Horror Film*, edited by Barry Keith Grant, 200–12. Austin: University of Texas Press.

Hills, Matt. 2002. *Fan Cultures*. London: Routledge.

hooks, bell. 1992. *Black Looks: Race and Representation*. Toronto: Between the Lines.

Jancovich, Mark. 2002. "'A Real Shocker': Authenticity, Genre, and the Struggle for Distinction." In *The Film Cultures Reader*, edited by Graeme Turner, 469–80. London: Routledge.

Kephart, Elza, dir. 2003. *Graveyard Alive: A Zombie Nurse in Love*. Bastard Amber Productions.

Kuhn, Annette. 1997. "The Body and Cinema: Some Problems for

Feminism." In *Writing on the Body: Female Embodiment and Feminist Theory,* edited by Katie Conboy, Nadia Medina and Sarah Stanbury, 195–207. New York: Columbia University Press.

Ladouceur, Lisa. 2005. "A Zombie Nurse in Love." *Rue Morgue: Horror in Culture and Entertainment* 48: 48.

Lauzen, Martha. 2007. "2006 Celluloid Ceiling Report." *Traction: The Magazine for and by Women in the "Industry."* http://magazine.women-infilm.com/Home/POV/StatisticalResearch/Reports/tabid/96/Default.aspx.

Lee, Grace, dir. 2007. *American Zombie.* Lee Lee Films.

Leverette, Marc. 2008. "The Funk of Forty Thousand Years; Or, How the (Un)Dead Get Their Groove On." In *Zombie Culture: Autopsies of the Living Dead,* edited by Shawn McIntosh and Marc Leverette, 185–212. Maryland: Scarecrow Press.

McLarty, Lianne. 1984. "The Limits of Dissatisfaction: Postmodernism, the Contemporary Horror Film, and the 'Problem' of the Feminine." PhD diss., Simon Fraser University.

Patterson, Natasha. 2008. "Cannibalizing Gender and Genre: A Feminist Re-Vision of George Romero's Zombie Films." In *Zombie Culture: Autopsies of the Living Dead,* edited by Shawn McIntosh and Marc Leverette, 103–18. Maryland: Scarecrow Press.

Pinedo, Isobel. 1997. *Recreational Terror: Women and the Pleasures of Horror Film Viewing.* New York: SUNY Press.

Roscoe, Jane and Craig Hight. 2001. *Faking It: Mock-Documentary and the Subversion of Factuality.* Manchester: Manchester University Press.

Russo, Mary. 1997. "Female Grotesques: Carnival and Theory." In *Writing on the Body: Female Embodiment and Feminist Theory,* edited by Katie Conboy, Nadia Medina and Sarah Stanbury, 318–36. New York: Columbia University Press.

Sandita, Sabrina. "Asian Fucking Stereotypes." In *A Girl's Guide to Taking Over the World: Writings from the Girl Zine Revolution,* edited by Karen Green and Tristan Taormino, 180–83. New York: St. Martin's Press.

Stacey, Jackie. 1987. "Desperately Seeking Difference." *Screen* 28: 48–61.

Sun, Chyng Feng. 2003. "Ling Woo in Historical Context: The New Face of Asian American Stereotypes on Television." In *Gender, Race, and*

Class in Media: A Text-Reader, 2nd ed., edited by Gail Dines and Jean M. Humez, 656–64. Thousand Oaks, CA: Sage.

Tasker, Yvonne and Diane Negra. 2007. "Introduction: Postfeminist Politics and Postfeminist Culture." In *Interrogating Postfeminism: Gender and the Politics of Popular Culture,* edited by Yvonne Tasker and Diane Negra, 1–25. Durham: Duke University Press.

Waldman, Diane and Janet Walker, eds. 1999. *Feminism and Documentary.* Minneapolis: University of Minnesota Press.

Weiss, Andrea. 1992. *Vampires and Violets: Lesbians in Film.* New York: Penguin Books.

Williams, Linda. 1984. "When the Woman Looks." In *Re-Vision: Essays in Feminist Film Criticism,* edited by Mary Ann Doane, Patricia Mellancamp and Linda Williams, 83–99. Frederick, MD: University Publications of America.

Wood, Robin. 1986. *Hollywood from Vietnam to Reagan.* New York: Columbia University Press.

AMERICAN HISTORY Z

DANIEL CHANGER

To date, there have been only a few "undead-denier" historians who have tried to write the zombie out of American history. However, from the "Bite Felt Round the World," to "Ghoulapalooza: The Real Thriller Tour," to Mr. Nibbles, the first ever space-walker (or "space-sloucher," as detractors insisted), zombies have been shaping American history from the get-go. And, perhaps save for some fringe theories such as Gerald Ford displaying symptoms of mild infection, zombies have plagued just about every modern presidency.

THE CUBAN ZOMBIE CRISIS
Of all the nail-biters of the Kennedy presidency, the Cuban Zombie Crisis had the world down to its cuticles. Since 1959, the United States and Cuba had been on a collision course after the revolutionary takeover of Cuba by Fidel Castro saw the dismantling of capitalism, Church and the craps tables. This was followed by the botched "Bay of Pigs" invasion of 1961 by Cuban expats—launched from and backed by the United States—in addition to many unsuccessful CIA assassination attempts on

Castro himself, including, but not confined to, the classic exploding cigar.

While deciding their next move, an American U-2 recon flight over Cuba of 16 June 1962 photographed what appeared to be a number of occupied zombie enclosures, more enclosures under construction and, more tellingly, rows and rows of inner tubes dotted around the Caribbean island. On viewing the images, President Kennedy hastily convened a select group of advisers, including his attorney general brother, Bobby. While many members agitated for a full-scale invasion to avoid an unstoppable flotilla of ghouls drifting toward America's eastern seaboard, the president was unsure.

Instead, JFK opted for a naval blockade (or, to be precise, a "quarantine") of Cuba from the zombie-laden cargo ships transporting the ghouls direct from the UZZR (Undead Zombie Zone of Russia) along with the prefab enclosures and commercial truck radials. Seeking broader support for his plan, the president requested and received backing from the Organization of American States (OAS). Then, on 22 October, the president delivered a televised address to the nation and the world outlining the quarantine and warning the Russians that zombies launched against any nation in the Western hemisphere from Cuba would be considered an attack by them on the United States "requiring a full retaliatory response."

As the blockade began, most Cuban-bound ships were turned back without incident. However, the situation appeared to worsen after another American recon flight confirmed that the zombies, along with the now-inflated tubes, were being herded toward the northwest Cuban coast. An emergency session of the United Nations Security Council was called for 25 October. There US Ambassador Adlai Stevenson challenged his Russian counterpart over both the existence and nature of the Cuban zombies. Not getting an answer, Stevenson famously told the ambassador he would wait for his answer till "there's no more roommates in hell" and went on to produce glossy, oversized prints showing both ghouls and hundreds of inner tubes lining the coast. (The bookish Adlai also noted the shape of the tubes—a torus—was also the "surface of a revolution"—a pun entirely lost in translation even after his exhaustive explanations.)

On the brink of war and facing mutual annihilation, an agreement was finally hammered out through a back channel when the Russian leader wrote directly to Kennedy. In return for the removal of the zombies, the United States promised never again to invade or interfere with Cuba and quietly to remove its Cold War troops stationed near the Russian border in Turkey. This compromise deal meant that the leaders of both Russia and America could save face—in every sense. The effort to empathize with the enemy was the apparent key to eventually ending the crisis. Unfortunately, it appeared that no one would go on to write it down as a reminder for next time.

VIETNAM AND THE ZOMINO THEORY

By the 1950s, the French had been in Vietnam for nearly a century. Attracted by the trade routes, resources and not-insignificant access to opium, the French had subdued the resident zombie population to the point that they could establish a permanent imperial colony there. However, by 1954, the ghouls were back with a vengeance, pushing the French south and finally forcing a complete *"bon voyage."* Seizing the moment, the United States began sending military personnel to the abandoned colony, both to establish a beachhead in Asia and to halt what was known as the "Zomino Theory."

The Zomino Theory (a contraction of "Zombie Domino Theory") was the US thinking at the time stating that, once ghouls took control of an area, it was only a matter of time before surrounding regions would also fall to zombieism—in this case ending with masses of undead slouching, rush-hour-like, across the Sydney Harbour Bridge. (Note that the theory is not to be confused with the proven effect that zombies do fall over much like dominos if aligned properly.)

These military personnel, or "advisors," initially made slow but steady progress, advising the zombies farther and farther north with a little help from their M14s, though, by the time JFK took office in 1961, previous years' gains were starting to be eaten away. Kennedy therefore decided to begin increasing

America's commitment, reaching sixteen thousand advisors by 1963. That figure would be the peak under his administration, as in November that year the dashing president was himself taken down by a direct shot to the brain, with the comparatively dour vice-president, Lyndon Johnson (LBJ), taking his place.

With JFK's full commitment to Vietnam questionable at the time of his death, the joint chiefs now took LBJ down their preferred path to a fast troop ramp-up. Apart from anything else, America had never felt the dishonour of defeat and wasn't about to start. Domestic opposition to the conflict was increasing, however, with May 1964 seeing the first major student demonstrations. Without formal declaration of war by Congress, the new administration couldn't escalate America's Vietnam involvement without a couple of iron-clad, watertight excuses. They came uncannily fast in the form of two US naval warships.

On a dark and stormy night in August 1964, the said warships claimed to have been attacked by zombies moving through the water at very high speeds in the Gulf of Tonkin to the east of Vietnam. These "zompidos," however, never actually reached their supposed targets—and what was later shown as just freakish weather patterns misinterpreted on radar was nevertheless enough to give LBJ the leverage to pass historic legislation through Congress. The "Tonkin Gulf Resolution" was significant in that it authorized the president to use military force in Southeast Asia without a congressional declaration of war.

A series of retaliatory airstrikes would eventually become "Operation Rolling Thunder," a three-year bombardment campaign targeting identified zombie hotspots, including jungle trails the ghouls used to attack from neighbouring Cambodia. However, as was widely known, bombing could only do so much. Unless there was a direct hit to a zombie's brain or full decapitation, the ghoul would get right back up on—or near—its feet and either walk, crawl or drag itself along with whatever appendages remained. So it was inevitable that, even with the airstrikes, LBJ was forced to send in ground troops to support the bombers for hand-to-head combat.

The increase in troop commitment meant that increasingly

more Americans were conscripted and methods of minimizing or completely avoiding the draft were quickly employed, from vocational rabbinate to the more extreme relocation to Canada. And, of course, if you had the connections of a Bush or a Quayle, the National Guard. For those who were drafted, nothing in their training could prepare them for the inhospitable jungle, where zombies proved so much harder to kill. Far from a shooting gallery, the triple canopy terrain provided the ghouls with the best form of protection short of a full metal helmet. To make it easier for a clear headshot, the United States embarked on a process of defoliation as early as 1961. Effectively crop-dusting forested areas to death with concentrated herbicides (most notoriously Agent Orange), by decade's end more than a tenth of all land had been affected. Unlike some of America's own troops, however, the undead did not suffer the ghoulish side effects of dioxin exposure.

Up until 1968, the American public had been the recipients of positively glowing reports and sunny optimism from the administration. Then came a major turning point in the non-declared war that officials simply could not downplay: coinciding with the lunar new year, a ghoul offensive of 31 January saw armies of undead suddenly show up at over one hundred US command centres simultaneously. Whether drawn by the moon or some distant memory, the hordes were beaten back by the troops without great loss. Nevertheless, it soon turned the tide of public opinion against the handling of the conflict.

On 31 March, LBJ made a televised address announcing a halt to unilateral bombing, having already knocked back a request for 100,000 more troops. He went on to stun the nation by declining to run for a second full term, having barely beaten peacenik Eugene McCarthy in the recent New Hampshire primary and with another charismatic Kennedy now eyeing the nomination. Ultimately, the Republicans won the White House that year—just—and one-time loser Richard Nixon was back on the promise of an "honourable end" in Vietnam. With a long timeline for troop withdrawal, opposition to the war again increased, with media reports now beaming unspeakable images into American living rooms. It escalated even further with the leaking of the "Pentagon Papers" detailing Nixon's secret carpet-bombing of neighbouring Cambodia and Laos. This, of course, was no secret to the Cambodians or the Lao.

In 1972, the Democrats campaigned to bring the troops home with the slogan "Return of the Living" accompanied by a detached zombie hand in the V peace sign. They lost the presidency but won control of both houses of Congress, giving them the numbers to later starve crooked Nixon replacement Gerald Ford of further funding for the conflict. That year also saw activist-actor Jane Fonda travel to Vietnam for a photo-op near some ghouls, claiming that, in spite of reports, they didn't in fact bite ... hard.

On 29 April 1975, the last of the US personnel were finally airlifted from the old French capital as the zombies swarmed into the city. A conflict spanning five presidencies, resulting in fifty-eight thousand American deaths, was finally over. In hindsight, and unlike the Cuban Zombie Crisis, one of the greatest US oversights was its lack of empathy. The zombies of this land were similar to yet fundamentally different from the Russian ones America was fighting in the Cold War. While their northern cousins would roam belligerently far and wide, those in Indochina had no history of straying from that sliver of land bordering the South China Sea. Even following the US withdrawal, the only areas that lived up to the dreaded Zomino Theory were neighbouring Cambodia and Laos, and probably as a result of the US secret bombings. In fact, as counterintuitive as it seems, in hindsight it might appear that the zombies of Vietnam just wanted to be left alone.

444 DAYS LATER

Unlike the zombies that it involved, the now infamous Hostage Crisis ensured that President Jimmy Carter's hopes of a second term were well and truly buried. His long fall from public grace began in 1977 when the ancient Middle Eastern nation of Iran began experiencing isolated zombie outbreaks. Initially put down by the military and notorious secret police of the US-backed monarch (and his ironically named "Resurrection Party"), over time these outbreaks increased, damaging both the nation's economy and more than a few refulgent images of its ruler along the way.

In the capital, America's embassy staff thought they were safe from the epidemic, mistakenly believing that as diplomats they had some sort of immunity. So, by the time prudence demanded they evacuate on 4 November 1979, the undead had managed to breach their embassy compound perimeter and only a handful managed to escape (fleeing the country as B-movie zombies, dressed by the Canadian embassy). The remaining fifty-odd diplomatic contingent, surrounded by hordes of undead, were effectively hostages in the main embassy building. And, with only a single exit to the street, they had unwittingly committed a classic zombie "what not to do."

Already perceived as weak at home, Carter planned an uncharacteristically brazen rescue attempt for 24 April 1980. Code-named "Operation Eagle Claw," it involved military aircraft placing a rescue team near the capital, using abandoned trucks to force a path to the embassy door, then driving the diplomats to a nearby soccer stadium to be airlifted to safety. Unfortunately, the mission shared the luck of many Carter initiatives: the military aircraft he deployed encountered a sandstorm just outside the capital and in the confusion two collided, killing eight crew members. Lacking the minimum airlift capacity for all embassy staff, Carter aborted the mission.

Announcing the "debacle in the desert" to a national television audience at 7 a.m. the following day, Carter himself appeared like death warmed up. Further rescue attempts were planned, but somehow, in spite of every effort Carter made, the remaining staff finally and incredibly managed to escape after 444 days, only moments after Reagan was sworn in at noon, 20 January 1981. This miraculous timing spawned more than a few conspiracy theories, which were somehow lost in the nation's new sense of pride and ascendancy. Not long after, the new administration would be merrily selling arms to their new friends in Iraq to fight their newly ravenous neighbours.

DAWNING IN AMERICA

Winning the Cold War would undoubtedly be the greatest of the Reagan legacies, just behind that of the gross national debt. The war had its genesis in the Russian zombie outbreak of 1916, which slowly reduced the once-great tsardom to a network of fortified towns and cities and put a swift end to the burgeoning socialist revolution. Marx himself could not have wished for a more complete elimination of the bourgeoisie and dismantling of the class system than the infected undead provided. Over time, however, this also meant that zombies, who generally went unchecked by the Russians, began wandering into Europe and eventually the West was forced to establish an "Iron Curtain" across the continent—a bit of Churchillian rhetoric for a barely contiguous front of barbed wire, interrupted by the occasional gun turret.

A band-aid measure at best, this soon proved inadequate, and the Cold War began in earnest, so called because of the time of year America and its allies would deploy troops near and sometimes into the UZZR in an effort to contain the zombie menace. Cold temperatures slow zombies down, none more so than the notoriously cold Russian winters, often freezing ghouls solid. This gave troops a greater advantage in culling an area, though they were left with the problem that a frozen zombie could go unnoticed, thaw out in the spring and begin the infection all over again.

Down the decades, little tangible progress had been made in the Cold War, with Russia seeing US attempts to push back the ghouls as internal interference. This view was also secretly shared by some American performing artists and writers, provoking concern that reached a fever pitch in the mid-1940s with the establishment of the congressional HUAC (House Undead Activities Committee) designed to 'name and shame' these crypto-cryptophiles. On 2 October 1947, Reagan himself had testified before this committee in his capacity as president of the Screen Actors Guild—as well as his roles in B-movies, such as Boy Meets Ghoul. Then a card-carrying Democrat, he defended the right of the zombieists to hold their views, stating that democracy was strong enough to take care of itself. But by 1964, he would be campaigning for Republican presidential candidate Barry Goldwater, who invoked dropping low-yield atomic weapons—or "Z bombs"—on ghouls in Vietnam.

Goldwater's landslide loss to LBJ nevertheless mobilized American conservatives, who by the mid-1970s swung behind Reagan's presidential bids; by 1981, he was president. Viewing victory in the long and seemingly unending Cold War as an exercise in literally outgunning the undead, Reagan authorized an unprecedented $1.5 trillion anti-ghoul weapons buildup, including the attempted development of a real-life light sabre under his dubious "Star Wars" program, along with the even more outlandish Ronald Raygun. Despite this flight of fancy, he was easily re-elected in 1984 with the feel-good "Dawning in America" campaign, and, while he continued to drive the United States deeper into debt, his strategy eventually succeeded: only months after leaving office in 1989, nation after nation east of the Iron Curtain began to be declared zombie free—with the UZZR finally able to have the stigmatizing "Undead," "Zombie" and "Zone" dropped from its name.

THE UN-DEATH PENALTY 1988

Late in his term as governor, Michael Dukakis was forced to deal with a small but sudden zombie outbreak in upper Massachusetts. But rather than ordering a shoot-to-kill clearing of the infected area, Dukakis ordered the capture of as many ghouls as possible and their subsequent transfer to a special quarantine facility just outside Boston. There an experimental "rehabilitation program" began. The incarcerated ghouls were exposed to certain stimuli from their pre-zombie existence in the hope that the "better angels of their nature" might be awakened—and that fast food would no longer mean McDonald's crew members running for their lives. Results were indeed promising. More than a few of the undead stopped grabbing for their "handlers" altogether and instead became more interested in what their lab-coated companions routinely brought them. From *Family Ties* episodes to games of "Mind Your Manners" to guitar-accompanied rounds of "Kumbayah," the zombies showed increasing signs of restraint and composure. One even managed a mumbled yet satisfying few lines of Psalm 23. The rehabilitation board finally gave its approval and on 6 June 1986 handlers departed separately with each of their ghouls for a weekend furlough, the first step toward zombie integration back into society.

The weekend came and went quickly, with all handlers and ghouls reporting back safely to the Boston holding facility by curfew—all except the mumbling zombie Billie. For, incredibly, while on furlough Billie had managed to give his handler the slip and ran amok, savaging a young couple before being taken down by police after a fairly one-sided chase. Despite this set-back, the governor did not shut down the program or change his stance in opposing the traditional zombie shoot-to-kill, or "un-death," penalty.

Handily winning the Democratic nomination in 1988, Du-kakis's campaign stalled as the Billie incident reared its ug-ly head. During the 13 October debate with George Bush Sr., journalist Bernard Shaw asked Dukakis point blank, what if it was his own wife who had been attacked by the furloughed ghoul. With classic Dukakis emotionlessness (or what detrac-tors called his "zombie heart"), the governor stated that, no, he would remain a lifelong opponent of the un-death penalty. His polling dropped five percent that night.

This was on top of the classic attack ads such as "Revolving Door," in which a line of ghouls moaned their way into a cage via a revolving door only to slouch straight back out again. An-other ad featured footage from an already botched PR stunt by Dukakis in which he entirely failed to ape a successful pho-to-op by British PM Thatcher to prove he wasn't a big softie. Instead of looking like tough, commander-in-chief material riding atop a zombie-killing tank, he was widely perceived as a giggly kid whose mommy let him go on the tank ride.

Needless to say, his popularity slumped seventeen points between the Democrat Convention and the general poll, which Dukakis lost to Bush Sr. For what was considered the dirtiest modern-day election, Lee Atwater, Bush's campaign manager, years later apologized to Dukakis on his deathbed, but only af-ter making the liberal governor promise to—should he show the slightest sign of reanimation—"paint the wall with [his] brains."

9/11 AND DOUBLE UMDS

The 1990s passed without any major zombie incident for the presidency, save for Bill Clinton's claim that the legal definition of sexual relations did not extend to a reanimated corpse. The new century, however, brought with it a major new twist on the traditional zombie threat—the *zomikaze*—that would have its first hideous outing in the 9/11 attacks on the mainland United States in a plan so devastatingly simple that it had been the plot of a best-selling paperback (whose film version has since gone into permanent hiatus).

On the morning of 11 September 2001, nineteen members of the known terrorist group Al-Qaeda slipped easily through airport security at Boston, Newark and Dulles international airports. Upon boarding four separate commercial airliners en route to the West Coast, the perpetrators quickly and quietly consumed vials of infected zombie tissue moments after the planes became airborne (and well before the more pedestrian airline food was wheeled out).

Within minutes, the terrorists had completed the ghoulish metamorphosis and completely overrun the cabin. Extensive use of airline blankets and "wake me for meals" masks ensured that the reanimation process went entirely unnoticed until it was too late, leaving one hijacker—the "designated driver"—to commandeer the cockpit in the ensuing pandemonium and fly the plane into the intended target. That fateful day both towers of the World Trade Center (WTC) were hit, along with the Pentagon, while another plane went down in a field near Pittsburgh, the attack being thwarted by passengers and crew. By afternoon, the US-based convenience store chain 7-Eleven was thanking the heavens the whole thing hadn't happened two months earlier.

Later, in what George Bush Jr. called "an interesting day," he learned of the first strike while heading for a photo-op at an elementary school in Florida. He learned of the second while reading *The Pet Goat* along with the kids. Never a fan of the cliffhanger, the president finished the book before being whisked off in Air Force One to a secure military location. The New York attacks were quickly identified as the work of Al-Qaeda, though Secretary of Defense Donald Rumsfeld was already looking at how Iraqi leader Saddam Hussein could be connected.

Of course, this was not the first attack on the WTC. In 1993, in a scene reminiscent of VW Beetle cramming, a Ryder rental van full of zombies was driven by foreign terrorists into the underground carpark of the north tower, where the ghouls were released. Thankfully, things didn't go according to plan, with only six casualties instead of the planned infection of the entire structure.

At 7 p.m. on 11 September, Bush addressed the nation, stating that the United States in its retribution would make "no distinction" between the terrorists and "those who harbour them" or between the quick and the undead. Reaffirming this on 20 September, he addressed a joint session of Congress, demanding that the Afghani Taliban government hand over all Al-Qaeda leaders "in [their] land." When the Taliban refused, the United States launched Operation Enduring Freedom: the invasion of Afghanistan.

Initially, America attacked covertly, using the CIA in conjunction with anti-Taliban warlords, later bringing in the US military. Many Al-Qaeda members fled to the east into the mountains and over the open border into Pakistan, including terror mastermind Osama bin Laden. However, the United States did manage to capture about three thousand—including those who had gone *zomikaze* in the fighting. Not knowing quite what to do with these captives, Vice-President Dick Cheney suggested they be sent to the US base in Guantanamo Bay, Cuba, and split into two areas for interrogation: "Camp X-Ray" for the living and "Camp Z-Ray" for the ghouls. The methods of restraining the two groups were identical, however: eyemasks, earcups and the notorious black headbags.

Then, in mid-October, with a ninety-percent approval rating, Bush called a press conference and suddenly accused Iraq of possessing the now famous "double UMDs" or "ultimate undead military devices" (UUMDs): a new superbreed of zombie destined for use against the United States and its allies. Despite his claim, however, the CIA could not turn up any evidence of *über*-ghoul development. So, when tenuous reports surfaced suggesting that Iraq might have imported barrels of radioactive nuclear waste from Africa, one could practically hear Cheney and Rumsfeld cracking the champagne.

Fast-forward twelve months and the paper-thin evidence of UUMDs had somehow become enough for Congress to hand the president a joint resolution authorizing use of US forces against Iraq. It didn't hurt Bush's case that the midterm elections were only weeks away and being "soft on ghouls" was never a big vote winner for either side of politics. However, at the behest of British Prime Minister Tony Blair, the president dispatched his ever-popular secretary of state, Colin Powell, to the United Nations in one final diplomatic push.

Powell would present America's case to the United Nations for joint military force in the face of Iraq's apparent breaches of the United Nation's own weapons inspection program, a hangover from the 1990–91 Persian Gulf War. Unknown to Powell at the time, much of the evidence provided for his presentation came from a single Iraqi defector in Germany code-named "Curveball," whom no one from the United States had met and whose stories of "mobile zombie labs" could not be corroborated by German intelligence. The presentation was reminiscent of Stevenson's in the Cuban Zombie Crisis, but without the one-liners or overall outcome. Left without un Security Council backing—and to avoid invading unilaterally—the United States was forced to cobble together a disparate "Coalition of the Living."

On 19 March 2003, Bush authorized hostilities at 8 p.m., after an ultimatum in which he gave Saddam and his sons forty-eight hours to leave the country. The Iraqi regime fell quickly to coalition forces as Saddam's statues were toppled, American flags were flown and missions were declared accomplished, but not a shred of evidence for a uumd superzombie program was uncovered from then until the present day. With critical military resources being diverted from Afghanistan, the United States is now struggling to "win the peace" in both nations, with *zomikaze* attacks now firmly established as an *Air Damocles* over the West's largely unprotected head.

CONCLUSION

Churchill once noted that history is written by the victor. That aphorism might once have been universally true, though in the struggle against the zombie it is written entirely by the victim, lest the ghoul recall how to use a retractable ballpoint pen.

That being said, the undead are generally accepted as victors only in the sense that they still survive. It is a singular blogosphere debate whether the zombie is actually a new species and, if so, whether it is the first ever to have devolved. Whether zombies are better adapted overall to their environment—beyond the elimination of tedious courtship from the reproductive process—only time will tell.

The United States, for its part, will probably face the challenge of zombies for many centuries to come. Although now more likely to fight the ghoul as a weapon rather than a wandering phalanx of cadavers, future presidents must do more than talk hope: they must deliver, ideally disarm and, far more important, decapitate.

ZOMBIES, DISABILITY AND LAW

JULIA GRUSON-WOOD

We must attend to both context and abstraction. (Wolf 1996, 5)

Zombies are the least palatable variety of the undead.[1] Although zombies and vampires are undeniably bound by the fact that they are both the living dead and share similar urgent, non-negotiable, gastronomic standards of various incarnations of cannibalism, where zombies and vampires "depart" is a matter of style, skin complexion, sex appeal and intelligence (among other things). Zombies do not look everlastingly youthful, they are not good in bed, they are not wise with five thousand years of undead living experience to draw from and they are definitely not personable. They will eat your arm, they will eat your brain, they will eat your baby and then you will assimilate.

The classic zombie has no free will, no mental capacity, no

1   In this section, when I discuss zombies, I am discussing the dominant notion of them as being mindless flesh-eating creatures. This portrayal of "a zombie" is what I refer to as "the classic zombie."

language, no community. The classic zombie is a mass of moving rot, clad with multiple open wounds and an insatiable hunger for human flesh. Classic zombies are deemed by human culture as agents of hell: distributing chaos and initiating genocide. Although zombies can be identified as prime creatures in which to examine the spread of outbreaks and infectious diseases (Smith? 2009), they are the apocalyptic embodiment of disease in and of itself. Disease, in its most extreme form, reverses what was once a generative life into a rapid process of deterioration until death; it consumes sentience and agency; and, as an irresistible contagion, it consumes others. The paradox of "disease" is that the strongest diseases are those most resistant to cures, most susceptible to spreading and most successful in wiping out their hosts. Accordingly, as much as zombies are indeed the living dead, they are, more than anything, survivors. It takes a really strong species not to be killed by death. On the contrary, death is the only thing that makes zombies "come to life." In a poignant symbolic sense, they are the representation of disease and a hyperbolic narration of the plagues that diseases wreak on human life.

Since they are spawned through human death, zombies hold a particular relationship with human culture and life. And all stages of modern human existence are intrinsically bound up with, and contextualized through, systems of law. Just as zombies have been situated as uniquely relevant creatures in which to address, examine and learn about the possible existence of unknown outbreaks and infectious diseases (Munz et al. 2009), so too do they lend themselves well to acting as a module in which to expose the systemic underpinnings, the ethics, convictions and conventions that inform the relationship between law and human existence.

This chapter addresses the legalities of zombies from within a legal context. In true zombie fashion, the chapter will be an act of chopping or bludgeoning three different bodies of knowledge: zombies, law and disability. To gnaw on the meat of these severed parts, the chapter is split into three sections.

ZOMBIES AND LAW: REQUIEM OF A CADAVER

The *Canadian Charter of Rights and Freedoms*, section 15 (1) and (2), asserts the following.

(1) Every individual is equal before and under the law and has the right to the equal protection and equal benefit of the law without discrimination and, in particular, without discrimination based on race, nation or ethnic origin, colour, religion, sex, age or mental or physical disability

(2) Subsection (1) does not preclude any law, program or activity that has as its object the amelioration of conditions of disadvantaged individuals or groups including those that are disadvantaged because of race, national or ethnic origin, colour, religion, age or mental or physical disability

This part of the chapter asks, if zombies existed as real creatures (un)living among us, which kinds of moral, ethical and sociopolitical issues would they bring forth to law (in this case Canadian law)? Where are zombies situated, what is their status, in relation to the legal system? Which responsibilities would the legal system have to the "lives" of zombies? And which challenges would zombies pose to various Western systems of law?

For example, how does capacity and consent law apply to zombies? In Canada, the *Health Care Consent Act, 1996*, defines a subject as capable if she is "able to understand the information that is relevant to making a decision about the treatment, admission or personal assistant service, as the case may be, and able to appreciate the reasonably foreseeable consequences of a decision or lack of decision" (2). Where do zombies fit in relation to this act? To be a capable person, one must first be a person. Are zombies people? What makes a life form a person? Is it agency? The capacity to think? Do zombies have the capacity to make informed decisions about their (un)lives, or are they all, in their very essence, incapable? And, if zombies are not considered people because they are a species perceived as incapable, does this not elucidate the crucial notion that incapable people are not real or full people?

Before biting off more than we can chew, let's explore whether or not zombies have the capacity to grant consent. (We will return later to the question of whether or not zombies are people or human.) Sure, they're the living dead and happen to feed off flesh and unfortunately are generally violent,

265

seemingly "absent-minded" and monosyllabic—usually they just grunt—and are highly contagious; does this always mean that every zombie can be defined by the sum of eat, eat, eat (and, by association, kill, kill, kill and spread, spread, spread)? I should remind the reader that zombies have also been represented as incredibly talented dancers (Michael Jackson's *Thriller*), which has to mean something. Right?

If dancing zombies aren't convincing enough for certain systems of law (in this case Canadian law) to believe that not all zombies are the same tired old antisocial, human-eating hell machines, what about the zombies of, say, *Shaun of the Dead* (2004)?[2] Although almost all of the drama of this British film is comically centred on the classic zombie outbreak that threatens to dish out the "Last Supper" of humanity, the ending of the movie supplies an alternative, nuanced perspective on zombies and what they might mean to human culture.

Shaun of the Dead begins on a satirical note, visually and sonically displaying its human characters as proverbial zombies. This part of the film expresses what I like to call the social constructivist notion of zombies, or "Zombies R Us," by exposing the ways in which the living often act and appear as though they are part of the living dead. Initially, it seems as though the film is telling us: life and death, po-tay-to/po-tah-to. But as *Shaun of the Dead* progresses, the whole zombie-human "thing" proves not so easy to work out. (Warning: the next few paragraphs are a spoiler.)

When zombies actually begin to appear and quickly overrun (or, rather, slowly overwalk) Shaun's city, we realize that they are just as introverted and hangry (hungry/angry) as they are purported to be—and definitely seem to go out of their way to find, eat and kill everyone. Shaun and most of his family and

2 In this section, I discuss a few zombie films, but I do so not from a zombie film theory perspective but as a mode of instigating engagement with the sociopolitical and cultural issues that I intend to probe in latter sections. I use film as a way to "get into" zombies as interesting figures that poignantly and singularly embody the realities and stereotypes, and mime the sociopolitical locations, of people with disabilities.

friends manage to fend off the living dead long enough for the military to arrive and blast the heads off the zombies in one final semi-automatic swoop, successfully saving the leftover scraps of the human race.

Back in his house after the *finis* of the zombie coup, Shaun cozies up with his girlfriend in front of the TV. Shaun, notorious at this point of the film for being an avid channel flipper, pauses on every station just long enough to catch what's on. Each channel is devoted to the apparently recent decision to live among the undead and integrate zombies into (British) culture. For instance, one channel features a woman on a talk show who decides to stay committed to her now zombie husband, who, yes, has to be chained up to restrain him from eating her, but other than this minor issue he remains the same guy she fell in love with. All of cable television is saturated with zombies living in the "everyday." Thus, where *Shaun of the Dead* is truly revolutionary is in its portrayal of zombies as individuals with personalities. All society needs is to put in place certain safeguards to prevent zombies from consuming illegal cuisine. The last scene of the movie stresses this point, with Shaun going out to his shed to visit his now zombie best friend, Ed, chained to the wall. Although Ed makes a haphazard attempt to eat Shaun, this is depicted in playful terms, and their relationship appears more loving than ever.[3]

Another interesting notion that *Shaun of the Dead* raises, surprisingly, is the idea of sociolegal liability. Since many zombies are innocent victims who have been bitten by other zombies, what is the legal responsibility of society to accommodate its zombie citizens who (un)live within its jurisdiction? Does the fact that a human who has non-consensually become a zombie mean that society suddenly can rightly and justly

---

3 Interestingly, Ed is repeatedly called a "moron" and an "idiot" in the movie and is notorious for his impersonation of an orangutan. After he becomes a zombie, he is locked away in a separate space like real-life intellectually disabled people in institutions. The included-yet-excluded divide of the zombies post-outbreak amid integration eerily resonates with the treatment that disabled people have experienced, and continue to experience, in Western culture.

lose all regard or evade all responsibility for this subject as, at the least, a citizen or, at the most, a mutated human being? Just as the government is responsible for generating a vaccine for H1N1, don't society in general and the legal system in particular have an obligation to support and legislate a search for an immunization or at least work on a way to ameliorate (think HIV cocktails or simulated insulin, but for zombies something like simulated flesh) the "deadly" aspects of zombieism, not just for the zombies themselves, but also for the sake of keeping the rest of society "safe"? In respect to safeguards and amelioration, vampires have "true blood." Being former humans and all, don't zombies deserve something of the same?

I wish to bring up a few more examples of zombies in film to address the legal complexities relating to what constitutes capacity and personhood. The films I discuss are not representational examples of zombies in cinema or brought forth to cite the discourse of horror/zombie film theory. Rather, the films I wish to engage with are based exclusively upon their relevance in terms of chewing on the legal complexities that zombies embody. In other words, this chapter takes zombies as real-life creatures. Although they exist only in fiction, I am viewing these films as if they are real life.[4] In saying all of this, the two remaining zombies-as-people "filmic" narratives I reference have to do with the theme of zombies in love. Because what could be more kitschily human than the capacity to love?

The most notable movie that features a zombie in love is, of course, *My Boyfriend's Back* (1989), in which teenage Johnny comes back from the dead to go on a date promised to him by his crush, Missy. That Missy's "alive" boyfriend is represented as a complete schmuck, while Johnny is portrayed as a very nice boy, proves wrong the general consensus that "good girls don't date dead boys." Score one for the undead! Although at first Johnny decides to stay home from the prom because he is afraid he might eat his date, he ends up going, tucking in his cannibalism long enough to have the time of his unlife. He and Missy are even crowned prom king and queen. Although most

4 Hence, film theory has no place in this chapter because here these films are viewed as instances of real life.

relationships do not usually have to deal with the literal urge to gnaw on one's significant other's flesh, every relationship dishes out particular and unique ethical and emotional dynamics. And I implore you: tell me of one teenage romance that is not torn with the overpowering cravings of destruction and consumption?

Gay Zombie (Simon 2007)[5] is another zombie-in-love film that features a queer zombie, Miles, who goes to West Hollywood to "find himself" and ends up falling in love with non-zombie Todd. Miles finds a nice group of friends who help him cover up his increasingly visible rot and encourage him to follow his heart, and the viewer learns to love this remarkable gay zombie back. However, before long, Miles too finds himself wanting to eat Todd all up. This is the moral dilemma of being a zombie in general, but especially of being a zombie in love.

In arguing for the possibility that not all zombies (as seen on TV[6]) are incapacitated, voidal hell machines, I should point out that most humans also feed on animal flesh (that has been killed by humans themselves); carry diseases and bacteria that can be highly contagious; and often display the masculine monosyllabic (watch any Vin Diesel movie for proof, not to mention carnage). Unless these features disqualify the average human from her status as a legal citizen, a zombie who has not yet bitten should not be discriminated against on the basis that she is undead. In fact, denying a zombie legal rights based on the stereotype that her "race" is known for biting could arguably be in violation of section 15 of the *Charter*.

Films such as *Shaun of the Dead*, *My Boyfriend's Back* and *Gay Zombie* work to prove, without reasonable doubt, that not all zombies as a species are incapacitated (mindless, soulless, evil) non-individuals. *Theoretical Exclusions* states that "everyone is subject to the law" and that "the law treats everyone

---

5 Not to be confused with the YouTube homophobic spoof of *Gay Zombie* that compares homosexuality to a zombie outbreak and makes "manly" men suddenly talk with a lisp, comment on outfits, develop "limp" wrists and start necking.

6 Reminding the reader once again that text is all we have in regard to the existence of zombies.

the same as legal equals" (Cormack 1999, 23). If a zombie has not broken the law in any way but is denied citizenship rights or ends up getting decapitated, then this should constitute a *Charter* violation because this zombie is being judged not on her own behalf, but as a representative of her (sub)species. Thus, any zombie who is denied the right to vote, work, own, marry, *et cetera*, could feasibly claim legal discrimination (under section 15.1 of the *Charter*). Live and let (un)live, people.

DIE ANOTHER DAY: IN MEDICAL SCIENCE, THE UNDEAD ARE ALIVE AND WELL

Other obvious barriers for zombies in pursuing legal citizenship rights are that they are (1) dead and (2) not generally perceived as part of humanity. To broach the legalities of "undeadness," it is important to ask a couple of questions. What defines the human species? Are zombies human? All zombies were once human, for all zombies exist only through human bodies and selves. The obvious differences that set zombies apart from human identity are that they are cannibals and not alive. But is this legally enough to claim that zombies are not human?

Admittedly, the whole cannibal thing is unfortunate and presents a serious barrier to zombies receiving citizen rights. However, as stated before, I do think it is up to governments and other social bodies to try to contain zombies long enough to either cure the condition of zombieism or to find a way to substitute flesh with some other nutritionally valuable and satiating simulated substance. Let's imagine, for the sake of this argument, that the flesh-eating issue has been dealt with. If this were the case, then where would the status of zombies as archetypically withdrawn and legally dead leave them in relation to human identity, legal citizenship and equity rights?

In a contemporary Western culture saturated with medical science advancements, enhancements, inventions and interventions that literally halt the dying from dying or transform the dying into the living (think pacemakers and life-support systems), what can be said to define life? Is it the ability of an individual to stay alive or the ability of non-living substances (i.e., technology) to keep a human system up and running? As

Mark Pauline so eloquently states, "The true marriage of human form and technology is death" (Gray 2001, 107). David Brin echoes Pauline's sentiment, noting the trend of scientists who believe that in this contemporary Western culture, which exists in a warp speed engine of techno-futural intervention, life and death are merely outfits that stopped being perceived as a steel-toe reality about the same time spray-painted metallic Doc Martens went out of style. Brin explores the meaninglessness of the category of death among scientific quests to pursue human cryonics. The hope of cryonics is to enable a reality in which an individual could be in control of turning on life and death like a cell phone. Amid the proliferation of techno-science in this contemporary Western culture, Brin ponders, "what will it mean to be 'dead' in the future?" (Gray 2001, 107).

The present liminality that technology brings to the traditionally opposed states of alive/dead is further discussed by Chris Hables Gray (2001). Gray details contemporary medical organ donor culture as informed by a researcher named Linda Hogle. In both Germany and the United States, Hogle observed the ways in which death was actively being reconstituted and recontextualized with terminally ill patients who elected to donate their organs. Nurses would provide company and encouragement to the patients while they were still alive. Yet, once their hearts and lungs failed, a team of medical specialists would rush into the room, bringing with them high-tech, life-sustaining machines and drugs to keep the body of the "single dead" subject alive. The specialists, machines and drugs would be used to retrieve the organs while the brain was still alive and the body was functioning. When the brain "died," this was considered to constitute "double death." It was not until the organs began to decay that they would consider the subject to be "triple dead." It is at the point of triple deadness that organs can no longer be harvested. Hence, the enterprise of organ donation exclusively depends on, and is generated through, this state of undeadness. As Gray articulates, "the line between living and dead, human and not human, has never been vaguer" (2001, 108). In this statement, Gray expresses how the ethical complexities and confusions regarding life and death are deepened when the individuals who receive the "alive" organs are saved through the powerful liminal space of undeath. It is only through the particular paradoxical dynamic of the aliveness/deadness (or the once or twice deadness) of the organ donor that the organ recipient is able to live.

The last example I will cite regarding the confusion that techno-culture brings to the distinction between categories such as life and death is the story of a woman called Janet, who, in the twenty-third week of pregnancy, died of an aneurysm (Gray 2001). At the hospital, the same medical staff who confirmed her death confirmed that her baby was still alive. The hospital decided to devote life-sustaining machines as well as a team of nurses to care for Janet and her baby until birth was possible. Although Janet was declared legally "dead," her hair, nails and baby grew, and nurses said she could hear music, as evidenced by her changing heartbeat. Even though Janet was legally dead, all those around her felt that her "soul" was still there and that she was somehow, somewhere, still alive.[7]

What would have happened if Janet had suddenly come back to life? What if she had squeezed her hand or groaned? Would she still have been a human, or would she have been considered part of another species? Hearts momentarily stop beating, sometimes for longer than it takes for some people to become zombies, and the individual who is successfully resuscitated does not tend to be classified as "not human," even though he was, for an instant, legally "first or second dead." If having experienced death does not classify one as being "not human," and being undead plays an important and significant role in sustaining or generating life (as elucidated by Janet and organ donors), then zombies' status as undead should not necessarily mean that zombies are not human.

That alive-dead people are capable of spawning life from within them demonstrates how we are indeed in a stage of our evolution in which life and death are ambiguous, somewhat beside the point, and will ever more become quaintly

---

7 It is interesting that, though those caring for Janet and her baby all felt she was alive, she was taken off life support as soon as the baby was delivered. If she could physically react to music, I wonder why there wasn't further investigation of other ways in which Janet might still have been alive.

anachronistic. As technology improves, the undead will continue to give life to others and there will be increasing possibilities for the undead to exist among the living. To be human might always begin with being alive, but might be techno-medically sustained far past one's actual expiration date. In a world of emerging "heart-beating cadavers" (Gray 2001, 109), the animation of the third dead might soon snuggle right into the definition of what it means to be human. Perhaps modern Western culture is striving toward a reality in which alive and dead are obsolete distinctions, passé binaries, eclipsed by the possibilities of the continual ability to be animate. And, if this is so, then humanity is defined not by one's status as alive, but by one's ability to function. If this is the case, then zombies are not separate from humans, but merely a niche form of humans. How would this relationship between "human" and "zombie" transform the treatment, attitude and legal approach toward those whom reality bites?

NOT DEAD YET: DISABLED PEOPLE AS LEGAL ZOMBIES

What is the age of consent for a zombie? And how does this shift when considering that some zombies have been converted yesterday and others have awakened from many years of eternal slumber? Does the cause of zombification create a new category with respect to age and consent or one's status as a legal citizen? What happens when, for example, a brain-dead mother is killed by her daughter? Is this a murder, mercy killing or compassionate homicide? Can a zombie claim wrongful rebirth? If so, who is held responsible? The parents of the zombie? The government?

I ask these questions because, if you replace the word *zombie* in the above sentences with the words *disabled person*, you will elucidate the legal confusion that surrounds the life and the human/person status of people with disabilities. Hence, this section of the chapter explores how zombies are legally analogous to disabled people when confronting the law as they characterize the central issues of legal placelessness[8] that

8 The notion of "placelessness" and disabled people was articulated by my friend and classmate Laurence Parent, who wrote about disability, publiclessness and placelessness.

273

people with disabilities experience in the context of Western law. As Ruth Enns puts it, "Disabled activists across Canada and around the world have exorcized a number of the demons that had isolated them and made them feel like a collection of defective body parts, less than fully human" (1999, 1).

A good example of what Enns is referring to is the case *R. v. Latimer* (2001). In the trial, Laura Latimer claimed that her daughter Tracy's "birth was way sadder than her death," that she "lost Tracy when she was born," and that this was when she "grieved for her" (Enns 1999, 14). To Laura, Tracy was born dead and remained so for the entirety of her life. Enns examines how the defence in the Latimer trial worked to construct Tracy as the sum of burdensome, suffering victim, as an empty mutilation of dependency that constantly fed on the time and energy of her parents, needing them for every task (primarily eating and excreting) and consuming every ounce of life from those around her.

Contrary to the classic zombie that eats human flesh, disabled people who require assistance to eat, sleep and go to the washroom are framed as individuals who feed on the lives of their caregivers, eating away at their very quality of life. As Enns states (1999, 11), "Sitting, eating and doing things unassisted have nothing to do with pain, but dwelling on them worked to dehumanize Tracy, to show that her brain was so damaged that she could not even recognize people, then she herself was not a person and could never have been anything but a burden." Enns continues to explain how this depiction worked to reinforce the notion that "death was preferable to life" because Tracy was implicitly rendered "sub-human and her murder something less than murder."

Victoria Woodhull, a public figure in the woman's suffrage movement in late-nineteenth-century America, shared Mrs. Latimer's sentiment, describing her "half-idiot" son, Byron, as "a sad and pitiful spectacle [roaming] from room to room, muttering noises more sepulchral than human." Woodhull expressed her misery: "Where ever I go, I carry a living corpse in my breast, the vacant stare of whose living counterpart meets me at the door of my home" (Richards 2004, 74). Woodhull and the discourse surrounding the Latimer trial articulate how physically and/or intellectually disabled people have tended to be considered as real-life zombies.

Philosopher and animal rights activist Peter Singer is (in)famous for his dehumanization of subjects who have intellectual disabilities. Singer not only claims that he would give his speculative intellectually disabled child up for adoption because, plainly, he is "the kind of person who wants" his "children to be children" (Denton 2004), but also he vouches for their use in scientific testing in replacement of animal testing. In fact, testing on disabled people has actually happened. In the twentieth century, Dr. Ewen Cameron conducted brainwashing experiments on institutionalized children in Montreal that were funded by the US Central Intelligence Agency (CIA). These experiments robbed these children/patients of their memories and sometimes their complete established personalities (Enns 1999, 5). Hence, not only were these children already perceived as being void of person status, void of the central features that classify aliveness (in choosing to conduct these experiments on them in the first place), but also their initial zombification was increased and reinforced by tampering with their minds so that they had little to no connection with their life experience or personhood. Adding to the historical trend of depersonalizing disabled people as symbolic of their status as part of the unliving is the repeated evidence that children housed in medical or rehabilitation institutions were not only involuntarily sterilized, stripped of the ability to give life, but also referred to by room and bed number instead of name (Enns 1999).[9]

A disability activist group called Not Dead Yet highlights the strikingly similar legal equivalencies between zombies

9 Although I point out the negative aspects of law and people with disabilities, law has made some moves toward accommodating people with disabilities. I justify my negative discussion of law because the legal system is mostly awful and insufficient in terms of accounting for, accepting and protecting the rights and equity of people with disabilities. Usually, I would note the positive aspects of the legal system in reference to disabilities, but zombies either exist or do not exist and the tacit systemic ethos of law in Western culture is that disabled people are zombies.

and disabled people. Not Dead Yet began in 1996 to challenge the legal categories of assisted suicide, compassionate homicide and mercy killing that impose a "deadly double standard for people with disabilities" (Not Dead Yet 2010). Not Dead Yet argues that these disability-specific death/killing-related laws tend to support the ethos that (1) disabled people are sociolegally treated as if their existence is reduced to embodying some kind of worthless and disposable living death, and that (2) disabled people receive more legal support in dying than they do in living.

The focus of Not Dead Yet, other disabled activists and critical bioethicists is not necessarily to argue that it is unjust and ethically wrong to acknowledge that some people want to die, or that issues related to dying and killing are not morally and emotionally complex, but to shift the discussion toward quality of life and social inclusion.

Currently, in Canada, disabled people experience the highest rates of poverty and unemployment, and the lowest rates of education (In Unison 2000). In popular media, disabled people are generally represented as charity cases, victims, monsters or asexual. Alternatively, they are presented as heroes just because they manage to complete tasks that would define any non-disabled person as "average" (Garland-Thomson 2001). Many stores, buildings, residences, public transportation facilities and educational institutions are inaccessible to individuals with many forms of disability. Ubiquitous inaccessibility creates social limitations that reduce one's opportunity to live among the living, compelling one to feel hurt, pain, depression, anger, humiliation and alienation. As Tom Shakespeare states, "a narrow focus on impairment and suffering ... risks obscuring the social-contexts which often determine the quality of disabled people's lives, in particular the availability of independent living and civil rights protections from exclusion and discrimination" (2006, 118). Certainly, there are cases on this sometimes lonely and unrelenting Earth in which the "possibility of death can be life-enhancing" (141). But so can the possibilities of life itself.[10]

10 Or, as Johnson states, "Choices are structured by oppression. We

The same sorts of issues raised by the concept of zombies in relation to citizenship rights, rule of law, and laws relating to suicide, murder, sex, marriage, voting, capacity and consent are gnawingly similar to those faced by people with disabilities. Disability has turned murder into mercy killing; incited debate over the right to assisted suicide and compassionate homicide; instigated a little something called "wrongful birth"; reconceived the ethics of prenatal testing; and generally situated intellectual disability as a means to fine-tune what it means to be a human individual and a rights-bearing subject in the "eyes" of the law.

To reinstate the meat of my metaphoric evocation: disabled people are zombies, legally speaking, because law has considered, and often continues to consider, subjects with so-called disabilities to be part of the living dead. As a study conducted for the Victorian Office of the Public Advocate elucidates, "workers were unclear about what constituted a crime against a person with an intellectual disability" (Young and Quibell 2000, 750). Disability ruffles up the very basis upon which the rule of law is founded, for the concepts of autonomy, individuality and a life worth living are complicated by the lives of disabled individuals. Why else has it (not so) historically been legal to lock disabled people up (Parmenter 2001), sterilize them (Asch 2001), bar them from voting (Baynton 2001), generally consider all sexual relations to constitute "rape" (how can the living dead consent to sex?) (Stefan 1993) or condone paying adult working subjects $1.25 an hour if they are employed at a sheltered workshop (how can the living dead produce the same quality of work as the really living?) (Wong 2002)? The law is a system created for and about the living, and the legal construction of what it means to be alive casts disability into a liminal space of undead.

Another interesting way to examine the relationships among law, disability and zombies is by exploring how the category of

shouldn't offer assistance with suicide until we have the assistance we need to get out of bed in the morning and live a good life. Common causes of suicide—dependence, institutional confinement, being a burden—are entirely curable" (2003, 57).

intellectual disability has been applied strategically to all other marginalized groups to create zombies out of them as a way legitimately to deny citizenship rights (Baynton 2001). Newcomers, women, Aboriginal people, economically disenfranchised people, people of colour, queer people, people who enjoy a few drinks (lest we forget the temperance movement!) and physically disabled people have all been labelled intellectually disabled (and/or "degenerate") at different points in time as a way to justify oppression and deny legal citizenship. Being charged with an intellectual disability has been perceived as a legitimate reason to legally disenfranchise only because so-called intellectual disability itself is perceived as a "condition" that ideologically converts the very human status of a person into that of a living death. After all, the prime trope that characterizes a zombie's personality is lack of personality, intellectual emptiness, barren mind. This seems to explain their will to eat humans, their moral blankness and their ethically easy disposability.

In "Disability and the Justification of Inequality in American History," Douglas C. Baynton (2001, 33–34) provides another historical account of how medical and scientific diagnoses of intellectual inferiority and mental illness were implemented as a tool to disenfranchise, oppress, and dehumanize women and people of colour. Women were perceived as irrational, excessively emotional and physically weak; a mentally, emotionally and physically disabled version of the white male norm. Similarly, racialized people and immigrants were perceived as prone to feeble-mindedness, mental illness, deafness and blindness.

Pro-slavery movements used mental illness and incapacity to justify and frame the perpetuation of slavery as morally and ethically salient. In 1851, Dr. Samuel Cartwright described two types of mental illness specific to African Americans.

Drapetomania was a "condition" that caused slaves to run away. The origin of this illness was rooted in certain masters' tendency to become "too familiar" with their slaves. Masters who treated slaves as equals threatened the very constitution of the African American since "the need to submit to a master was built into [their] very bodies ... written into the physical structure of his knees, being more flexed or bent than any oth-er kind of man" (cited in Baynton 2001, 38).

Dysaesthesia aethiopus, the second African-American-spe-cific disease, was described as a desire to "avoid physical work and generally to cause mischief," otherwise known as "rascal-ity." African Americans, proponents of slavery stated, were in-ferior to all whites except those who were deformed, idiotic, insane or "otherwise incapable" (cited in Baynton 2001, 38). As a race marked by intellectual and mental disorders as well as other forms of disability, African Americans needed to be over-seen and governed by non-disabled whites to contain the out-break and ward off further degeneration that would occur if given the opportunity of freedom (Baynton 2001, 38). Thus, the classification of African Americans as innately mentally inca-pable—and the contextualization of their attempts at escape and resistance as signs of illness—were ways to deny agency, power and self-determination to subjects wanting their rights to freedom.

In the nineteenth century and early twentieth century, wom-en's suffrage became a point of societal contention. Like Afri-can Americans, Baynton explains, those who opposed women's suffrage justified their prejudice by claiming that women were inflicted with two different strands of intellectual disorder. The first disorder was generalized: women were inflicted with men-tal disabilities that made them weak and their nervous system would fester if "exposed to the rigors of political participation" (cited in Baynton 2001, 42). As Grace Goodwin stated, "The suf-fragists who dismay England are nerve-sick women" (cited in Baynton 2001, 42). The second illness was much like the first, though the focus was on contagion. The emancipation of wom-en would cause all women to overuse the brain, which would cause "neuralgic, dyspeptic, hysterical, menorraghic, dymenor-rhoeic ... and other derangements of the nervous system" (cit-ed in Baynton 2001, 42).

Rachel P. Maines also discusses how, in the late nineteenth century, "as many as three quarters of the female population were 'out of health'" (1999, 55). All forms of sexuality that did not promote the archetypal heterosexual family model were pathologized, perceived as symptoms of mental degeneracy and evidence of hysteria. At this time, the standard medical view of curing this mental disorder was marriage.

All of this is to say that ascribing degeneracy, mental disability and intellectual disability carries the social and legal power to justify the disenfranchisement of social groups at times of inequity. This is not to promote the notion that having what is considered to be a mental or intellectual disability is in any way inherently negative, but to demonstrate the ways in which it is conceived as negative: conceived as rife with the power to dehumanize so much so as to revoke and deny a person his or her legal rights.

LAW AS ZOMBIE MAKER

Law creates zombies out of human individuals by perceiving them as part of the undead. The legal system in Canada has continually perceived disability as an infectious disease that needs to be identified, contained and destroyed. Legal enforcements such as the sterilization act, IQ testing, prenatal screening, genetic testing, residential schools, mercy killings, compassionate homicides, marriage laws, age of consent, education systems and rehabilitation laws have all been used to deny humans their right to be alive, turning them into one of the living dead. In other words, disabled people are not zombies, but law ideologically aligns them with the fictional tropes that mark zombies. Law does this by repetitively defining people with disabilities as not fully human or alive, existing in a liminal space somewhere between animate and in the grave. If we consider disabled people as half-heartedly human, their opportunities to live are systemically decapitated.

Rather than law being a system that identifies, controls, contains and prevents the epidemic of the living dead (disabled people) from infiltrating human culture, law itself creates and spreads this very notion. In this sense, law itself is a zombie that infects human individuals with the idea that they are part of the undead. Law summons the fictional tropes of the zombie to the disabled person—and this fiction, in turn, infects social relations.

It is a well-known "fact" that the only way to kill zombies

and prevent the destruction of human civilization is to hit them hard and decapitate them (Munz et al. 2009). I take this bludgeoning of the zombie literally,[11] as a totalizing deconstruction, as an act of ideological beheading. Hence, in tracing the origin of the spread of zombieism in culture as the legal system, I argue that the gavel needs to be "hit hard and hit often" (as Munz et al. 2009 so eloquently state) for the notion of the living dead to be killed once and for all. The legal construction of what it means to be alive needs to be completely decapitated to find a "cure" for zombies, for disabled people to live among the living.

DONE LIKE DINNER

Let us return to the gnawing query: can zombies be said to be legal persons/individuals? To answer this question, we must first answer another: What is an individual? To be an individual, does one have to possess abstract qualities, such as agency, intellectual thought, language and so on? Or is being an individual a requirement of being part of the human species? These inquiries slice open centuries of debate. According to certain important thinkers, "human" is exclusively defined by embodying the "essential" ability to think. For instance, John Locke described a "person" as "a 'thinking' intelligent Being, that has reason and reflection, and can consider itself as itself, the same thinking thing in different places" (cited in Parmenter 2001, 270). Locke continues to compare the animal intellect to that of the "idiot," insisting that "human" is distinct from and above these two categories. Or, in the words of Shakespeare, "What a piece of work is man! How noble in reason! How infinite in faculty! The paragon of animals" (cited in Parmenter 2001, 269). In the age of technological impurity and political ambiguity, it is hard to know which qualities have staying power as those that represent the core of what it means to be a human person. However, the line that one sits on in relation to whether or not zombies can be people too is likely to reflect whether one thinks a disabled subject—specifically an intellectually disabled

11 And perceive it as the ultimate irony.

subject—can also count fully as a human and accordingly deserves the legal opportunity to live her life as if she is part of the living.

In one way or another, reality bites. And when it does, people still ought to have the base respect of being cultivated, valued and recognized as moving examples, as enacted instances, of life.

REFERENCES

Asch, Adrienne. 2001. "Disability, Bioethics, and Human Rights." In *Handbook of Disability Studies*, edited by Gary L. Albrecht, Katherine D. Seelman, and Michael Bury. Thousand Oaks, CA: Sage Publications.

Babalan, Bob, dir. 1993. *My Boyfriend's Back*. Written by Dean Lorey.

Baynton, Douglas. 2001. "Disability and the Justification of Inequality in American History." In *The New Disability History: American Perspectives*, edited by Paul Longmore and Lauri Umansky. New York: New York University Press.

Canadian Human Rights Code, R.S.O. (1985), c. H-6.

Cormack, Elizabeth. 1999. "Theoretical Excursions." In *Locating Law: Race, Class, Gender Connections*, edited by Elizabeth Cormack. Halifax: Fernwood Publishing.

Denton, Andrew. 2004, 4 October. "Professor Peter Singer." Episode 62 of *Enough Rope*, 4 October, ABC TV. http://www.abc.net.au/tv/enoughrope/transcripts/s1213309.htm.

Enns, Ruth. 1999. *A Voice Unheard: The Latimer Case and People with Disabilities*. Halifax: Fernwood Publishing.

Federal, Provincial, and Territorial Ministers Responsible for Social Services. 2000. *In Unison 2000: Persons with Disabilities in Canada*. Hull, PQ: HRDC.

Gray, Chris Hables. 2001. *Cyborg Citizen: Politics in the Posthuman Age*. New York: Routledge.

Health Care Consent Act, S.O. (1996), c. 2, Schedule A.

Johnson, Harriet. 2003. "Unspeakable Conversations." *New York Times*, 16 February. http://www.nytimes.com.

Maines, Rachel P. 1999. *The Technology of Orgasm: "Hysteria," the Vibrator, and Women's Sexual Satisfaction*. Baltimore: Johns Hopkins University Press.

Munz, P., I. Hudea, J. Imad and R.J. Smith? 2009. "When Zombies Attack! Mathematical Modelling of an Outbreak of Zombie Infection." In *Infectious Disease Modeling Research Progress*, edited by J.M. Tchuenche and C. Chiyaka. Hauppauge, NY: Nova Science Publishers.

Not Dead Yet. 2010. http://notdeadyetnewscommentary.blogspot.com.

Parmenter, T.R. 2001. "Intellectual Disabilities: Quo Vadis?" In *Handbook of Disability Studies,* edited by G.L. Albrecht, K.D. Seelman, and M. Bury. London: Sage Publications.

R. v. Latimer (2001), 1 S.C.R. 3.

Shakespeare, Tom. 2006. *Disability Rights and Wrongs.* New York: Routledge.

Simon, Michael, dir. 2007. *Gay Zombie.* Written by Michael Simon.

Smith?, Robert. 2009, 18 August. http://www.nowpublic.com/strange/zombie-attack-must-be-dealt-swiftly-says-professor-robert-smith.

Stefan, Susan. 1993. "Silencing the Different Voice: Competence, Feminist Theory, and Law." *University of Miami Law Review* 47.

Wolf, Susan M. 1996. *Feminism and Bioethics: Beyond Reproduction.* Oxford: Oxford University Press.

Wong, Sophia Isako. 2002. "At Home with Down Syndrome and Gender." *Hypatia* 17, 3.

Wright, Edgar, dir. 2004. *Shaun of the Dead.* Written by Simon Pegg and Edgar Wright.

Young, A. Damon and Ruth Quibell. 2000. "Why Rights Are Never Enough: Rights, Intellectual Disability, and Understanding." *Disability and Society* 15, 5.

THE ZOMBIE PARADIGM

HELEN KANG

The following events are entirely fictional. None of the names, except appropriately referenced authors, pertain to actual people.

The events of February 2012 conjure up a multitude of confused images. It is almost too early to contain the memories of the events in manageable stories that we can tell and retell so that we can command some mastery over the chaos. The events are still fresh in public memory and in the memories of all the individuals who were affected by them, which is to say every person within range of international travel and media reception. All we "know" for now is that words such as *nightmare, apocalypse, the plague, Armageddon* and *pandemic* currently circulate as though they mean the same thing, at least in the English-speaking parts of the world affected by the events.

One word in particular entered our collective consciousness in ways that it hadn't before: *zombies.* It's a word that had resided in the pop cultural sub-genre of horror and science fiction to describe the once-human figure doomed to an eternal hunger for human flesh and blood. When we started to use the word *zombie* to describe the events of February 2012, something happened in our cultural consciousness. Every word has a history and carries with it a baggage of meaning as it travels across cultural domains. When *zombies* emerged out of the fictional world of horror films and entered news media, biomedicine and public health to give description to what was otherwise indescribable, the word created a bridge between fictional and non-fictional worlds. And when *zombies* joined with the words *disease* and *outbreak* to name this unnameable, incomprehensible thing as *zombie disease* and *zombie outbreak,* these words had specific and profound consequences.

You, reader, who managed to survive February 2012, might be puzzled, even enraged, that I have the audacity to speak of meanings, images and culture at a time like this. I, too, am a person of this world. I have been deeply affected by the chaos, both as a victim and as a witness. I, too, have used the words above to describe the events in my futile attempt to make sense of the absurdity of what I saw. But I am also a critical cultural studies scholar, and my immediate reaction is to jump into analysis of what I see and hear and do not see and hear. Yet the unfathomable number of those who died, the kinds of deaths they experienced and the degree of trauma suffered by those who survived make it almost impossible, morally unthinkable, to call for an analysis of symbolism, metaphor and imagery.

Yet meanings matter. How we represent the events of February 2012 matter. Because, when we represented them with images of zombies, diseases and outbreaks, the meanings associated with these words shaped our perceptions of these events and the people involved. These perceptions in turn informed how everyday people reacted to someone foaming at the mouth and dragging his feet on the street. These perceptions informed how scientists agreed to name the "cause" of the "disease" as acute necrotic virus (ANV), which is transmitted by biting and results in massive cell death in a human body. These perceptions informed how journalists and public health workers told the public about which "symptoms" to watch out for in others and how the military justified forced quarantine of tens of thousands of people. And these perceptions will inform how we decide to look back and assess how we reacted as a society to these events.

Diseases and illnesses are not just about health and medicine, though the latter tends to have a lot of authority on the matter. The work of historian Sander Gilman (1985, 1988a, 1988b) and philosopher Susan Sontag (1990) has shown that disease, or being diseased, has always been linked to perceptions of moral integrity and moral degeneration. To be diseased is to be feared, to be blamed or to be pitied (depending on one's moral standing), to be pushed out, to be contained for fear of infecting others, or to be "othered." "Other" is a term used to describe social groups who are not considered to be part of the "norm," which is racially white, Christian, heterosexual, male, middle class and able-bodied. Through histories of colonialism, racism, homophobia, sexism, classism and ableism, these social traits have gained dominance so that individuals who possess them not only have power, but are also considered morally superior. Alternatively, those who are other to this norm are considered morally suspect. Being diseased also tends to fall under the category of other as being associated with moral degeneration.

The naming of a disease is an important part of creating the cultural line between norm and other. Twenty years ago, groups of gay men in major cities in the United States died of unknown causes; then similar symptoms were identified in intravenous drug users who were generally urban, poor and racialized. Before the names AIDS and then HIV became the official names of this illness, several informal names circulated that took on an explicitly moral tinge: "gay disease," WOGS or "Wrath of God Syndrome" and GRID or "Gay-Related Immunodeficiency." It was not only everyday "ignorant" people who used these names, but also medical researchers who published in medical journals and doctors at hospitals, people whom we expect to be completely objective and neutral. These names simultaneously drew on existing stereotypes of gay men and intravenous drug users as morally degenerate and further amplified these discriminatory sentiments by linking the illness to being a certain type of person rather than a series of activities that lead to infection. These moralizing tendencies lingered in the names AIDS and HIV and had profound social, economic and political consequences. In the United States, the religious right found moral justification in HIV/AIDS to demonize what were perceived as "deviant" behaviours and systematically to deny care and support to those most affected by the early wave of the epidemic, leading to countless deaths.

The social, moral, cultural, political and economic impacts of HIV/AIDS have been vast, and prominent scholars in cultural studies have engaged with these effects over the past two decades. One of the central questions that they have grappled with concerns the processes by which a disease, such as HIV/AIDS, is named. Paula Treichler (1988, 1999) and Cindy Patton (1990) in particular have extensively examined news media, public health and biomedical discourses on HIV/AIDS to untangle the complex processes by which the names HIV and AIDS, as well as the meanings and knowledges associated with them, emerged. The authors pay attention to power struggles, ambiguities, controversies, conflicts and uncertainties along the way in the conversations among journalists, scientists, doctors, patients and activists that over time were lost and forgotten. These forgotten stories remind us that, when we name a disease in a way that draws on notions of "otherness" and "deviance" from the social "norm," news media can become a vehicle for mass panic and scapegoating, that scientific "facts" are grounded in interpretations and cultural meanings, and that how we define symptoms and identify who is afflicted draw on and amplify pre-existing stereotypes.

The literature on cultural studies of HIV/AIDS can provide us with the framework and tools with which to understand and analyze the recent events of February 2012. These events are now simply called "zombie outbreak," "zombie epidemic" and "ANV outbreak," but we must remember that these are shorthand forms that mask a multitude of complex and conflicting stories and representations. The simplicity and increasing ubiquity of these names and associated "symptoms" can hide the fact that the processes whereby we came to understand the condition were full of uncertainties and ambiguities, not just in news media and perceptions of everyday people, but also in scientific research, public health and the military. A disease is not just about medicine, health or science but also about social and cultural struggles over how a disease is named and then taken up to reinforce moral boundaries between those who are at fault and deserve to die, and those who are innocent and deserve sympathy or protection.

THE BIRTH OF THE ZOMBIE

The first high-profile use of the word *zombie* is attributed to the medical journalist Caroline Peters from the *New York Times*. In an article on 3 February 2012, which appeared on page 5 of the main section, she quoted an interview with Dr. Dan Morgan, a clinician at New York Downtown Hospital:

> The patient is in a comatose state but still has full motor function. He can walk and move his arms. He also retains certain basic physiological functions, such as the need to expel urine and feces and the need to eat and drink. But the patient can't judge what is edible and what is not. One patient in our emergency ward chewed on a metal bedpost for hours overnight and completely destroyed the right side of his teeth and gums. It was incredible. A normal person wouldn't have been able to stand the pain. They are like zombies. They move, make noises and eat, but the lights are out inside.

The headline for this article read "New Disease Makes People into 'Zombies.'" The caption beneath a close-up of the patient's ravaged jaw, which took up the top half of the front page, read "'Zombie' patient eats bedpost. 'A normal person wouldn't have been able to stand the pain,' says Dr. Dan Morgan at New York Downtown Hospital." This story marked the beginning of media frenzy over "the zombie disease." The combination of the words *disease, zombies* and *normal* with images of visibly sick people made this article not only strictly a medical story, but also a moral one. To talk about what is normal means to refer to what is abnormal. Gilman (1985, 1988a, 1988b) has argued that these ideas are as much about morality as they are about health. His extensive work on the history of representation of illness, such as syphilis, tuberculosis and HIV/AIDS, shows that illnesses in Western culture have always been associated with moral judgments about the conduct and innate qualities of the person who is afflicted. The "zombie disease" was no exception.

English newspapers quickly jumped on the word and "zombies" began to appear in headlines within a matter of hours across the globe. Newspapers such as the *Globe and Mail* and the *National Post* in Canada retained the quotation marks around this fictional word as if reluctant to indulge in fantastic imagery to describe what was quickly becoming a public health catastrophe. Within forty-eight hours of the word's first appearance on the cover of the *New York Times*, the quotation marks were dropped altogether in the majority of English national newspapers, as though it was now an indisputable fact that people were turning into zombies. Soon afterward, zombie disease, zombie outbreak and zombie epidemic became part of the daily repertoire of news broadcasters, such as CNN in the United States, the BBC in Britain and the CBC in Canada.

An early preoccupation in the news coverage of February 2012 was to ascertain the origin of the disease. It was as though, if we can find where it comes from, then we can automatically gain control of it. Gilman (1988a) and Treichler (1999) have explained that the impulse to find out who or what "brought" a disease into the nation is more about the need to place blame for the disease than about medical problem solving. Two distinct stories of the origin of the zombie disease circulated in the media: Haiti and contaminated meats from East and Southeast Asia. These stories were also about placing blame and punishing those who were deemed "guilty" of spreading the zombie disease to the rest of the world.

Haiti has historically been linked to the zombie and voodoo, but the recent earthquake disaster amplified the fear of the origin of the zombie in Haiti. Some media reports linked extremely impoverished and unhygienic living conditions in the aftermath of the earthquake with stereotypical ideas about primitiveness and barbarism of the "Third World," suggesting that Haitians cannibalized one another, leading to the spread of the zombie disease, which was "encoded in their genes." Alternatively, recent scares with H1N1 combined with the epidemiology of the avian flu, resulting in stories about contaminated meats from Asia, again suggesting stereotypical notions of dirt-iness and barbaric livestock-farming practices. These images of barbarism and backwardness are age-old myths that framed non-Western, non-European places and people as inferior to white Europeans to justify colonial conquest and imperial rule. In February 2012, these mythical images were invoked to create sensationalistic stories about the origin of the zombie disease, with severe economic and political consequences: wealthy na-tions stopped sending relief aid to Haiti and ceased importing meats from Asian countries in acts of economic and moral pun-ishment for the "guilt" of spreading the zombie disease.

The media stories in February 2012 uncritically combined cultural myths and pseudo-scientific explanations to talk about the events, especially when they put zombies and disease to-gether to create a media shorthand: zombie disease. The term circulated so widely that it became taken for granted, unques-tioned and incorporated into common-sense knowledge, even before biomedicine and science formulated their own theo-ries. On 9 February, the *Ottawa Citizen* published an article on the mathematical model of the zombie outbreak. Previously, a group of mathematicians at the University of Ottawa (Munz et al. 2009) had produced what was conceived as a playful model of the spread of a hypothetical zombie outbreak. For the math-ematicians, the fictional "communicable disease" had pre-sented interesting parameters that are absent in nature: those who died from the disease "returned" to become new vectors of the disease. Upon its publication, this academic article had received widespread attention in news media in the English-speaking world, including the BBC, the CBC, the *Wall Street Jour-nal* and the *Ottawa Citizen*.

The article was part of a broader resurgence of the zombie trope in the popular cultural imagination: novels such as *World War Z* by Max Brooks (2006) and *Pride and Prejudice and Zom-bies* by Seth Grahame-Smith (2009); films such as *28 Days Later* (2002), the remake of the 1978 classic *Dawn of the Dead* (2004) and its parody *Shaun of the Dead* (2004); and video games such as the *Resident Evil* series (1996 onward) and the *Doom* series (2003 onward). Kyle Bishop (2009) explains this resurgence by pointing out that the zombie theme resonates with post-

9/11 cultural consciousness in the United States, namely the fear of disasters such as viral outbreaks and terrorism. Munz et al.'s (2009) article was part of this cultural play: part horror, part comedy and part intellectual musing. However, shortly after the *New York Times* article appeared with the first reference to zombies, the article became the explanatory guide of the outbreak. By the end of the second week, it reached the hands of every journalist, policy-maker and public health worker in Canada.

Munz et al. (2009) directly drew on zombie films to come up with their formulae and parameters, which in turn were now being used to inform journalism and health practices. The immense popularity of this article beyond scientific circles shows how seeing the events of February 2012 as a zombie outbreak blurred the lines between fiction and reality. Zombies of Romeroesque horror films became the primary lens through which the events of February 2012 were imagined, told, conceptualized and problematized. The imagery became the single paradigm that dominated how all the different stories of this illness were to be told, including scientific explanations.

BIOMEDICAL UNCERTAINTIES

It is unclear how many who were infected actually recovered. The different avenues of transmission are also unclear. In fact, because the outbreak was so sudden and so recent, there is insufficient clinical research on this event to make any reliable findings or comprehensive countermeasures. Scientists and doctors know so little about it that even the transmission theory of the disease is just that, a theory. It is unclear where the belief originated, but biting was the most commonly perceived way that people became sick, an idea that quickly gained momentum. The predatory biting zombie was terrifying and grotesque but also already familiar through popular horror movies. In the midst of chaos and confusion, this imagery gave people something they could identify with and hold on to.

But as the very first media report of the incident in the *New York Times* suggests, the afflicted person bit random things, which included other people but also objects and even his or her own body. Yet what was overly highlighted in media stories were people biting other people as the "cause of the disease." It did not help that afflicted people had chewed on their own flesh and had lesions all over their bodies, adding to the terrifying image of the flesh-eating zombie. The news media and public health officials immediately latched on to the notion that the "infectious bite" from a predatory zombie was the primary, if not the only, way that one could get sick. But there were many other hypotheses that circulated in biomedicine about the causes of the illness that were unknown to the general public. The name ANV, or acute necrotic virus, which we now take for granted as the indisputable cause of the zombie disease, was in fact the result of intense competition among scientists who vied for the prestige of naming the new illness.

In Canada, the Centre for Disease Control (CDC), in conjunction with Health Canada, hosted an emergency symposium on 10 February 2012 at St. Paul's Hospital in Vancouver, British Columbia. There was considerable political squabbling over where the symposium should take place. McMaster Hospital, a teaching hospital known for cutting-edge research, and McGill University, a university medical school with considerable prestige in Canadian medicine, also vied for the honour of hosting the monumental event. But St. Paul's was chosen and, though the exact reasons were unclear to the press, my contacts in the biomedical community, who participated in the symposium, informed me that it was because of the prevailing belief, mostly from urban legends and recent outbreaks of H1N1, that the zombie disease originated from East and Southeast Asian livestock imports. This speculation made Vancouver a potential point of entry of the epidemic into Canada; a ground zero, so to speak. Vancouver has always been notorious for being the entry point for illicit drugs and "illegal" immigrants to Canada, making it a particularly vulnerable location that needs to be defended.

I was able to get hold of the symposium proceedings through my contacts, including a video recording of the roundtable discussions in which various disciplines went head to head on who would get to define the biomedical phenomenon. At the end of a very dramatic three-day discussion, acute necrotic virus was decided on as the technical biomedical term. The long process by which the symposium participants arrived at these terms, however, is far from straightforward or even purely "scientific." Naming something as a disease means much more than giving a definition to a condition. It means framing a phenomenon in scientific terms, giving biomedicine the ultimate authority on what it is, learning how to identify it and determining how to stop it. Once a phenomenon is framed in biomedical terms as a disease or a condition, the battle is on over which biomedical discipline, which laboratory and which team of scientists will be credited with its discovery, the ultimate reward for scientific work. Hence, naming ANV was as much a political struggle as it was a pursuit of scientific explanation.

The name ANV reflects the battle between two "camps" led by immunology and virology. At the beginning of the talks in Vancouver, immunologists held the reins. A team represented by Dr. Emily Chan from Dalhousie University proposed that environmental irritants, such as pollution and GMO foods, particularly corn and soy, cause a severe auto-immune response that attacks the central nervous system and ultimately the brain. Their argument was supported by molecular geneticists, who further elaborated that the auto-immune response was the result of genetic predisposition, which was aggravated or "triggered" by environmental factors. Hence, this group of scientists diverged from the prevalent belief that it is a communicable disease transmitted through a human bite that punctures the flesh. The immunology-genetics camp jointly proposed gene therapy in conjunction with immune treatment. The union of immunology and genetics made sense at the time because the same genetics lab team had previously "discovered" the asthma gene. For the geneticists, an auto-immune link to the activation of the gene meant a new direction for research as well as the ability to tap into a larger pool of research funding that included both genetics and immunology. An environmentally aggravated illness was an argument that would have been popular at the time, when climate change was already a growing concern, resulting in Kyoto Agreements and green movements across the globe. The immunology-genetics camp pointed out figures for recovery rates and proposed dietary monitoring and isolating environmental pollutants.

Virologists at the symposium, led by Dr. William Goldman

from the University of Toronto, vocally opposed the immunology-genetics explanation. They proposed instead that an
extremely virulent viral infection caused premature and sudden cell death on a full-body scale. Drawing on peripheral research on the effects of spider venom seen to cause necrosis
(premature cell and tissue death), which was controversial and
deemed inconclusive among toxicologists, the virologists argued that this viral toxin was similarly transmitted through a
bite. There was no representation from toxicology at the symposium to refute this argument. The virologists drew on media
reports of biting and images from newspapers and broadcast
news as "evidence" alongside grainy, microscopic images of in-
distinct viral particles. Despite questionable findings, the notion of the infectious bite was immensely popular and, by the
end of the second day of the symposium, the name acute necrotic virus was born. It was as though a "zombie paradigm"
had taken hold, pushing out all complexities and any hypotheses or findings that contradicted the theory of a viral disease.

Although the transcripts of Dr. Goldman's arguments contained repeated references to the "necrotic virus" and even the
"zombie virus," no virus had yet been isolated. Treichler (1999)
draws on the works of science-studies scholars Bruno Latour
and Steven Woolgar to remind us that, even when research or
"evidence" is lacking, simply using a name, such as the virus or
the zombie virus, can eliminate all uncertainties and make it
into a "fact." The virologists drew on this semi-fictitious zombie virus to claim that a virological model of the epidemic was
much more sound than an environmentally triggered genetic auto-immune disease. They pointed out that the immunology-genetics argument contained too much uncertainty with
no concrete measures or findings and was based upon inconclusive data on the effects of GMOs on the immune system.
However, a viral model of the illness was equally based upon
inconclusive data. This camp argued further that gene therapy would take too long to research, without the guarantee of a
cure, when time and scientific speculation were luxuries. They
accused immunology of not doing "hard objective science" and
instead indulging in science fiction. Yet the virologists themselves drew on a media-invented notion of the zombie virus to
make their claims. Canadian feminist science studies scholar

Sheryl Hamilton (2003) explains that scientists often use the term "science fiction" in a derogatory way to discredit the work of their competitors.

Once the virological model of the disease was more or less agreed upon, Dr. Goldman and his team of virologists quickly called for the development of a vaccine against the (yet unknown) virus to prevent further infection, a proposal met with significant enthusiasm in the symposium. Nowhere in the transcripts was there any mention of developing a treatment or cure for the toxic infection. The original focus on treatment by the immunology-genetics team was replaced by an overwhelming emphasis on prevention. Instead of treating those who were already afflicted back to health, the emphasis was placed on preventing those who were still healthy from becoming zombies. Through the vaccine, biomedicine could provide the means to create a safe distance between those who were already sick (the other) and those who were not (the norm), a prospect that was attractive to policy-makers and public health representatives at the symposium, who showed the most positive response to the vaccine.

Left undiscussed at the symposium were the rare documented cases of people who had recovered after "turning." Instead of exploring the possibilities of recovery and treatment through these cases, they were dropped, and all remaining efforts went into discussing vaccine development. It was as though in the zombie paradigm, which seemed to prevail even in biomedicine, you can't conceive of treatment and recovery, only prevention. Zombies in popular films do not recover from their death-like state. They are the living dead, with an emphasis on "dead." The only way out is not to get bitten in the first place or to protect yourself from the zombie "venom" with a vaccine. By week four in February 2012, over ten million people had died, according to the World Health Organization (WHO), an estimate that continues to rise every day as more and more bodies are recovered in remote places, such as northern Canada. What is not evident in these figures is that a significant number of these deaths have less to do with ANV than with factors related to mass panic: starvation, psychological trauma and physical assault.

CONFUSED TERMINOLOGY AND MORAL PANIC

We're just doing our job. We're just protecting the innocent victims. We'll do whatever it takes to contain this thing and bring it under control. This is a national emergency. Heck, it's a world emergency. It's irresponsible for these activists to talk about human rights. These people have no idea what we're dealing with everyday on the ground. These zombies are not people. At least not anymore.

—Richard Johnson, Chief of Emergency Medicine,
Glendale Hospital, Calgary, Alberta

In the days that followed the infamous *New York Times* article, "zombie stories" flooded the headlines of newspapers and evening television news. People were stricken with mortal fear as they watched on television everyday Joes and Janes turn into walking comatose bodies for unknown reasons. The number of these bodies seemed to grow exponentially, but more recent reports by the WHO revealed that the actual "transmission" rate was lower than journalists made it appear. The number of newspaper articles and news segments on zombie stories grew much faster than did the actual number of people who "turned." Media zombies went more viral than the virus itself.

In a climate of acute uncertainty and heightened fear, the Centers for Disease Control (CDC) and the National Institutes of Health (NIH) churned out press releases by the dozens on the latest identifiable symptoms of what was fast becoming called the zombie disease or the zombie virus by the media, scientists and the everyday person on the street. The long list of symptoms was a confused collection of at-times contradictory behavioural and physiological characteristics. Here is a list that I saw on the CDC website on 14 February 2012, which I captured as a JPEG image on my computer:

Possible manifest symptoms of infection:
- a high fever followed by sudden extreme cooling of body temperature;
- an uncontrollable desire to eat (including things that are inedible);
- an uncontrollable desire to bite (including self and other people);

- foaming at the mouth or inability to control saliva (drooling);
- insomnia;
- loss of speech;
- ulcers and open sores on face, back, arms, legs and torso;
- an unusually slow and sloppy gait (dragging of the feet);
- ignorance of hygiene and other social mores;
- moaning, murmuring and other unusual speech patterns;
- sudden loss of body weight;
- unusually high amount of sleep;
- unusual bursts of uncontrollable anger;
- abnormally high feeling of mental and psychological stress;
- cataracts or eye infections;
- propensity to bruises and bone fractures;
- severe mood swings; and
- anesthesia to pain (e.g., bone fractures).

The list changed daily, even hourly, by the third week after the *New York Times* story was published. People checked the websites of the CDC, the NIH and local health ministries like they checked websites for weather, flooding the bandwidth and crashing the mainframes on a daily basis. Regardless of the fact that the reality of the zombie virus or its "symptoms" was debatable, public panic was palpable.

The list above combines symptoms that you might experience when "infected" with symptoms that you can identify in someone else. Hence, the purpose of the list was confusing and ambiguous. Was it intended for people to use to diagnose themselves and seek a health professional accordingly? Or was it intended for people to diagnose others in order to avoid them? From a public health perspective, both are equally viable routes of health promotion and preventative education. If people monitor their own symptoms and those in people around them, then it is easier to prevent the spread of infection and avoid a pandemic. The CDC's "List of Zombie Symptoms," as it was commonly called, was meant as a guide for citizens to take precaution and seek a health professional if necessary. However, everyday people used the list to focus primarily on the visible symptoms of others, especially strangers whom they encountered in public spaces such as buses, streets, malls, schools and other places where large numbers of people gather. Fear of contracting the zombie virus combined with a list of ambiguous, untested and inconclusive symptoms resulted in mass panic and paranoia.

Patton (1990) has argued that media consumers interpreted HIV/AIDS coverage in complex ways that were not always straightforward or intended by media producers or health educators. Media information about symptoms, transmission or HIV antibody tests did not directly lead to changes in public perception or behaviour. However, media and scientific "information" on HIV/AIDS was far from objective to begin with. It reflected and amplified existing social perceptions of "abnormal" sexuality and "illicit" drug use but couched them in the language of objectivity and neutrality. The words *symptoms of infection* for ANV were the CDC's attempt to frame the behavioural and physiological traits as objective medical measures of disease. Yet the symptoms themselves were already saturated with social and cultural values of what is deemed a "normal" biological and social human.

The words *abnormal* and *uncontrollable* painted the picture of a person who is unstable, out of control, socially inept, *et cetera*. References to lack of hygiene, talking to oneself and dragging one's feet while walking fell neatly into existing social and cultural images of the homeless and the mentally ill, whose poverty and mental states already marked them as other. The CDC's list of symptoms drew on ambiguous yet highly moralized notions of what is socially normal, acceptable and desirable as a way to define what is normal in terms of the disease. This semantic confusion between signs of social mores and of health, coupled with an existing array of negative images about the homeless and the mentally ill as unclean, irrational and animal-like, resulted in a mass moral panic that anyone who "looked" homeless and/or mentally ill was automatically a zombie who would, with scientific certainty, bite you and kill you.

DANGEROUS SLIPPAGES AND ANGRY MOBS

The imagery of the ANV patient, or zombie, did not emerge in a cultural vacuum. Since the summer of 2009, the Conservative federal government in Canada has pushed for the elimination of safe-injection sites for intravenous drug users. These sites constitute public health measures to prevent the transmission of HIV and other bloodborne infections by sharing dirty needles. As part of the harm-reduction model of HIV prevention in intravenous drug use, these sites provide clean needles and space for safe injection (away from the streets) under the supervision of a health professional. The model does not impose on clients to go "cold turkey" and instead tries to minimize the risks of HIV transmission in drug use. These injection sites are located in major Canadian cities, such as Toronto, Montreal and Vancouver, and have been subject to controversy, particularly from moral and religious conservatives.

In October 2009, the Conservative federal government took the matter to various provincial supreme courts and tried to gain voters' support for the elimination of these sites, drawing on stereotypical images of "homeless drug addicts" to make public statements such as "We must not let tax dollars be used for these junkies to shoot up in the streets." The debates around the safe-injection sites were already old material on national broadcast news and newspapers when the events of February 2012 hit. By the time the CDC's list of symptoms became common knowledge, Canadians were already familiar with the stereotypical image of the homeless drug addict. In the case of ANV, drug addiction, homelessness and mental illness came clashing together with the zombie virus.

In the height of "media AIDS," Gilman (1987) demonstrated how the cultural imagery of syphilis in the early nineteenth century shifted onto the imagery of HIV/AIDS in the 1980s. Although HIV is not strictly a sexually transmitted infection (STI), because of the strong cultural and moral association between the viral infection and sex, particularly "abnormal" gay sex, HIV/AIDS was culturally framed as a venereal disease. Prior to HIV/AIDS, syphilis had been the most lethal STI and was associated with deviant and amoral sexual behaviour, particularly in women (including sex workers) who transmitted the infection to unsuspecting men, thereby corrupting them both morally and physically. This moral implication of syphilis as a venereal disease was so strong that, even when it became treatable with the discovery of antibiotics, the imagery of amoral sexual behaviour that leads to disease did not fully disappear. Gilman argued that, when HIV/AIDS appeared, it replaced syphilis as the next lethal venereal disease, and the imagery of syphilis "slipped" onto HIV/AIDS and found new variations: gay sexuality, prostitution, intravenous drug use and "African heterosexuality," which became perceived as abnormal due to stereotypical images of primitiveness.

In the case of ANV and debates over safe-injection sites in Canada, we saw the imagery of the morally suspect and unclean homeless person who is mentally ill and who uses intravenous drugs "slip" onto the imagery of the ANV patient or zombie. On 21 February, the *Toronto Star* reported how an "infected zombie" had a "fit of uncontrollable rage" in the underground subway and attacked people "while foaming at the mouth." The "situation was brought under control" by "brave bystanders" who were later quarantined and then praised for their heroism. What the article didn't tell was how these bystanders beat a homeless man to death because he was inebriated and could not stand properly, a story that was later reported on a small local alternative news website. In another case of mob violence, the *Georgia Straight* reported that a schizophrenic woman was beaten to death at a suburban park by a group of parents when she approached the playground full of young children while talking to herself.

These terrifying stories of regular people turning into angry mobs didn't appear in major newspapers or on broadcast news and tended to appear in independent, local and alternative press, if they appeared at all. I found many more stories on personal blogs and Facebook posts of photos and videos of group beatings, but they were pushed to the periphery by frightened people and sensationalist media. We have yet to see the full ramification of the image of the morally suspect intravenous drug user who visits the safe-injection sites transformed into the uncontrollable, violent and infectious ANV zombie. We cannot forget how, in the United States in the 1980s and 1990s, the religious right found ammunition in HIV/AIDS to condemn and control "abnormal" sexualities and the "uncontrollable" addictions of the urban poor. The conservative agenda of the Reagan administration further fuelled the moral panic, denying care to those dying of AIDS, education to prevent the spread of infection and research to develop treatments.

In the aftermath of the ANV outbreak in Canada in February 2012, I can only imagine how the moral conservatives in this country will take up and use the zombie disease to condemn some of the most vulnerable and disenfranchised people in our society. Instead of identifying economic inequalities and colonial violence, and turning to improve social security, housing and health care as solutions to homelessness, mental illness and addiction, we as a society might become a giant angry mob, ready to corner, imprison and kill. In fact, we already began to do this during the height of the ANV outbreak in the form of military-controlled quarantine camps.

QUARANTINE AND "STATE OF EMERGENCY"

> What about the people who are not infected? Who are scared and in hiding? What about *our* rights? The survival of mankind [*sic*] is at stake here.
>
> —Jennifer Madison, Human Liberation Front (HLF)

Very few of us who survived the events of February 2012 knew about the quarantine camps all across Canada and the United States. In Canada, these camps first began as detainment zones in hospital wings, expanding to entire hospitals and then to makeshift housing in remote rural areas. What began as a series of emergency public health measures quickly dissolved into militarized quarantine zones, complete with barbed wire, surveillance cameras and guards armed with automatic weapons. At first, people went into hospital isolation voluntarily because they were either afraid that they were infected or afraid of infecting their loved ones at home. When rumours spread of the deplorable conditions and inexplicable deaths at these camps, the rates of voluntary quarantine diminished while the rates of infection escalated.

The US federal government issued a state of emergency, enlisting municipal police and military soldiers to round up infected zombies (also called "zombie hostiles," mostly the homeless and the urban poor) by force if necessary, even before they demonstrated full-blown symptoms. Under pressure from the US government, the Canadian federal government quickly followed suit. Both American and Canadian militaries instituted a complex series of hurdles for security clearance at the camps, making it impossible for journalists and health-care professionals to enter the camps to document what was happening inside them and to provide desperately needed medical care. The situation was war-like and these camps resembled military prisons. Indeed, both governments called it a "war against zombies."

In 1989, Sontag cautioned that, when we use military metaphors, such as "the war against AIDS," to describe a society's reaction to an illness, we invoke the belief that, during a war, social ethics and principles can be sidelined to deal with an "emergency" situation. Not only is excessive (military) spending seen as a trade-off in war, but also civil liberties and the protection of the rights of citizens go out the window. According to the symbolisms of war, the military and the nation, those who become infected also become "guilty" enemies of the state, while those who are not yet infected become the "innocent" people whom the state must protect at all costs, which include the cost of the lives of the infected. Hence, the dichotomy between the "guilty diseased" and the "innocent healthy" feeds into and amplifies the binary between norm and other, turning people into us and them, and justifying the claim that we must protect ourselves from them at whatever cost.

Tens of thousands died in these camps in the name of the "war against zombies" all across North America and little is known about what exactly caused these deaths. Due to this uncertainty, these numbers are not tallied into the calculation of the total death toll due to the ANV outbreak. When journalists and health-care workers entered these camps after the outbreak had subsided in early March, they discovered bodies that showed signs of extreme trauma, which included bites but predominantly starvation, malnutrition, stabbing, rape, beating and other acts of extreme violence. Some of them were the bodies of children and infants.

Several journalists who took "pilgrimages" to these quarantine camps recently embarked on a series of exposés in major newspapers across North America, calling on the Canadian and American militaries to provide formal explanations. Their defence is slowly making its way into news media and includes references to "state of military emergency," "zombie hostiles" and "zombie terrorists" that draw on the rhetoric of "the War on Terror" to assume that the sick were the guilty enemies who threatened the state and its citizens and whose disease/guilt justified the violent actions of the military. By turning the victims of ANV as well as state violence into hostiles and terrorists, both national militaries attempt to legitimize their attacks on citizens.

The militaries also claim that the "zombie infectants" were not human by medical definition and were therefore not subject to human rights or constitutional rights. One of the most vocal supporters of the military is the militant vigilante group called Human Liberation Front (HLF), which took it on itself to hunt and kill zombies as part of its constitutional right to bear arms and protect itself. The current string of lawsuits against the American and Canadian militaries faces the difficulty of having to defend that those who died at the camps or otherwise in the hands of the military were, in fact, human. It is as though we are starting with the fiction-based definition that "zombies are not human" unless found otherwise; those who died in the camps were already guilty of threat unless the prosecutor can prove that they were, in fact, still human and therefore innocent. We find ourselves back to square one: those who died were others because they were already zombies, which meant they were no longer human, as opposed to those of us who survived because we were still human. This moralizing rhetoric of guilt and innocence based on disease is now mapped onto definitions of human versus non-human in a court of law as families of those who died in the camps try to find acknowledgement of injustices and as the militaries argue that the violence was justified as defensive actions to protect citizens.

Gay activist Richard Goldstein (1989) reminds us that the social contract is an agreement between citizens and their government that individuals will relinquish some of their rights as individuals for the welfare of the community as a whole. As social beings, we tend to see ourselves not just as isolated individuals but also as part of a community, a family and/or a nation, and we sacrifice our own needs for the greater good of the whole. Goldstein argues that not all citizens enjoy equal protection or equal expectation to sacrifice themselves. Those who are perceived as other, outside respectable, "normal" society, are expected to forgo this protection and sacrifice their individual rights. Twenty years ago, intravenous drug users, sex workers and gay men were expected to control their "deviant" behaviour or expect to be controlled by the state for the greater good of "normal" society. In February 2012, if you were homeless, poor, mentally ill or an addict, then you expected to be suspected of ANV infection and expected to be quarantined for the greater good of "normal" society. In this logic, any casualties or losses of individual rights were a "fair trade-off" for the good of the whole. For us now, this seems to mean that we can be fine with knowing that tens of thousands died horrific deaths while living in subhuman conditions under forced military quarantine.

Or can we?

LIVING AFTER DEATH

> I don't recognize anything or anyone anymore. Nothing is the same. Nothing will ever be the same. It makes me sick to my stomach. Sicker than when I first saw someone get bitten.
> —Sophie O., social worker at St. Paul's Hospital

I have always wondered when watching films about the end of the world, be it due to human-instigated disaster (e.g., nuclear war, biomedical research gone wrong) or natural disaster (e.g., comet impact, climate change, disease outbreak), when you begin the story with the end of the world, how do you end the story?

What happens to the people who survive? I ask the same question for us now in the aftermath of February 2012. Which nightmares will plague our dreams? How will we manage to maintain healthy and trusting relationships? How will we deal with conflict, one that is more complex than good versus bad, innocent versus diseased, that requires something different from imprisoning people or hacking them down with an axe? How will we make sense of the bizarre play of chance that made us into survivors while countless others died horrific deaths? What does life mean in the aftermath of so much death and living death that never seemed to end? When does life mean more than surviving? Will it ever mean something different?

We might all have opposing reactions to the events of February 2012. Some of us are angrily seeking answers from our governments. Some of us just want to forget because it is too painful to remember. Some of us want to heal, rebuild and move on. And some of us are mourning the loss of loved ones. Whatever our individual reaction, all of us are stricken with the inability to disassociate ourselves fully from those who died. I could have been bitten instead of my friend who was standing beside me. I could have been beaten to death by a mob when I staggered home drunk after a party. I could have been taken to the camps. I could have stopped people from being beaten or being dragged away.

In all of our diverse reactions in the aftermath of February 2012, the events of the month remind us that how we decide collectively and individually to tell the story of what happened will be extremely important. When we as journalists, doctors, scientists, public health workers, politicians and everyday people decided to call this inexplicable phenomenon the zombie disease, there was mass panic. Representing the events as the zombie disease through news media, public health and biomedical research gave this name truth status, making it impossible to entertain other possible explanations. Every word or image has a cultural history and baggage beyond its immediate meaning. When we merged zombie with disease and outbreak, the popular cultural image of the predatory, flesh-eating monster was automatically perceived to be the "cause" of the spread of this condition of living death. And when we called certain social and physiological traits associated with being poor, homeless and/or mentally ill a list of zombie symptoms, and then waged a war against zombies as a way to deal with the events, we further marginalized, oppressed and violently killed some of the most vulnerable people in our society. All of these words and images combined to create a climate of mass panic and extreme moralizing about who deserves to die because they are zombies and other, and who deserves to live because they are "normal."

We must be cautious about how we represent the events of February 2012 in newspapers, medical journals, history books, novels and other records hereon. The images, words and stories that we use to remember the events will deeply inform how grievance cases against militaries will unfold, what the citizenry will demand from its government, whom we define as victims and therefore deserving of retribution and peace, and what we identify as worthy of healing and rebuilding for the future.

We must not rely on a humanist utopian notion of the "human story" to pull us out of this trauma into a place that is more comfortable, safe and palatable than the nightmare we just lived. The very idea of "human" was turned on its head and put into question, with lethal consequences. Everyday people succumbed to a strange and inexplicable condition of living death. Other everyday people became an angry and frightened mob that turned on individuals without hesitation or due process. We might want to tell the story of how the things that make us human were lost and of the death of innocence, but none of us was truly innocent when we came up against this thing. We all conformed in one way or another to the description of the zombie outbreak that resulted in mass panic and extreme moralizing.

What we must do, collectively and individually, is never forget the things that we'd like to forget. We must never forget how sensationalist news media fuelled the panic about the unknown phenomenon and how so many of us believed it. We must never forget how a health emergency was used to further marginalize and oppress the disenfranchised and how many of us did nothing about it. We must never forget that the military forcibly quarantined people *en masse*, without a transparent process, resulting in the deaths of tens of thousands. We must never remember any of this as an acceptable reaction by a state or society. We must continually ask ourselves difficult questions. What are our beliefs and values as a society? What are we willing to risk and sacrifice, how far are we willing to stretch the social contract, and what does this willingness say about us? Ultimately, what kinds of individuals, what kinds of communities and what kinds of societies do we want to become? And we must remember that, when we answer these questions in our stories, representations and memories, we do so with honesty, self-reflection and great difficulty.

REFERENCES

Bishop, Kyle. 2009. "Dead Man *Still* Walking: Explaining the Zombie Renaissance." *Journal of Popular Film and Television* 37, 1: 16–25.

Boyle, Danny, dir. 2002. *28 Days Later.* DNA Films.

Brooks, Max. 2006. *World War Z: An Oral History of the Zombie War.* New York: Three Rivers Press.

Gilman, Sander. 1985. *Difference and Pathology: Stereotypes of Sexuality, Race, and Madness.* Ithaca: Cornell University Press.

———. 1988a. "AIDS and Syphilis: The Iconography of Disease." In *AIDS: Cultural Analysis/Cultural Activism,* edited by Douglas Crimp. Cambridge, MA: MIT Press.

———. 1988b. *Disease and Representation: Images of Illness from Madness to AIDS.* Ithaca: Cornell University Press.

Goldstein, Richard. 1989. "AIDS and the Social Contract." In *Taking Liberties: AIDS and Cultural Politics,* edited by Erica Carter and Simon Watney. London: Serpent's Tail.

Grahame-Smith, Seth. 2009. *Pride and Prejudice and Zombies.* Philadelphia: Quirk Books.

Hamilton, Sheryl. 2003. "Traces of the Future: Biotechnology, Science Fiction, and the Media." *Science Fiction Studies* 30, 2: 267–82.

Munz, P., I. Hudea, J. Imad and R.J. Smith? 2009. "When Zombies Attack! Mathematical Modelling of an Outbreak of Zombie Infection." In *Infectious Disease Modeling Research Progress,* edited by J.M. Tchuenche and C. Chiyaka. Hauppage, NY: Nova Science Publishers.

Patton, Cindy. 1990. *Inventing AIDS.* New York: Routledge.

Snyder, Zack. 2004. *Dawn of the Dead.* Strike Entertainment.

Sontag, Susan. 1990. *Illness as Metaphor; and, AIDS and Its Metaphors.* New York: Doubleday.

Treichler, Paula. 1988. "AIDS, Homophobia, and Biomedical Discourse:

An Epidemic of Signification." In *AIDS: Cultural Analysis/Cultural Activism*, edited by Douglas Crimp. Cambridge, MA: MIT Press.

———. 1999. *How to Have Theory in an Epidemic*. Durham: Duke University Press.

Wright, Edgar, dir. 2004. *Shaun of the Dead*. Studio Canal.

DIARY OF A LANDSCAPE ARCHITECT

LISA MACDONALD

SEPTEMBER 14

I'm sitting at my desk, and there's ripped-up trace paper everywhere, ink and graphite smeared on everything, stale coffee tipped over next to me. My eyes are burning. I feel exhausted and sick, I've been here all night, and I'm utterly apathetic. The only difference between now and the times I've felt exactly this way in studio or trying to produce something—anything—to meet a deadline at work is that right now there's a half-eaten corpse next to me.

We're in my office right now; we made it here about eleven last night. All along, I've been second-guessing my decision to bring us here, because our small office, in this part of town, isn't exactly defensible. And the zombies have obviously already been through here. I don't want to examine any of the destruction here too closely, 'cause I'm afraid that I'll find some familiar office apparel on some torn-up piece of meat that was a co-worker.

But I think it's worth it to have come here. I used to joke about this place being a fire-trap, with roll after roll of dusty paper piled everywhere. But *all* of it—other than the rejected design concepts and proposed landscape plans not built yet—is survey after survey and floor plan after floor plan of buildings[1] and developments and neighbourhoods in this city—or what's left of it. After the disaster last night, we have to find a place to go that we know like the backs of our hands.

Yes—so, what happened last night is that our hideout was breached. It was horrible.

In the beginning, when things first started to get bad, everybody was still trying to go to work and keep our economy going and all that, as though it were some kind of a fucking snowstorm or something. The high-density residential area was already overrun, but that didn't affect management, so we thought we could keep things together. But no time at all after the single-family homes started to be invaded, the office towers emptied out. Single-family homes in the "safe" neighbourhoods were the first to go. Windows on the ground floor = zombies smashing through and eating your kids' brains in front of you.

I was renting a flat in a nice neighbourhood. I just panicked and more or less found myself chased into the downtown area—which is funny 'cause I didn't consider it "walking distance."[2] I found a good spot on the twelfth floor of some

1 My companions were surprised at how much information we had about the insides of buildings, being *landscape* architects. I think like most people they assumed we plant pretty flower gardens. I pointed out that the outdoor environment has to respond to the program and appearance of the inside of a building, and vice versa in some cases, so of course we'd have to know what's going on inside a building too. Then, for the record, I explained that we also design lots of other environments, such as parks and plazas and roadways and athletic facilities and streetscapes, and we do inventory and analysis and master planning and public consultation, and we work with engineers and planners and.... And then it became obvious that they weren't paying attention anymore.

2 We were taught in school that city dwellers will typically perceive x number of kilometres as being acceptable walking distance; beyond that, they will seek other means of transportation or select a new destination. There's such an assumption of choice in that standard. I

office building where I met the rest of my new human companions. Lucy and Fatima had barricaded a bathroom on the sixth
floor; they had both worked there once and came out looking
for food. I think Jack had been contemplating the collapse of
modern civilization for some time and had been able to store
up a lot of portable supplies and gear. Daniel had been mess-
ing around with radios listening for news when they found him
on the tenth floor, so they thought he'd be useful. They took me
in because they came to see that the spot I'd chosen was the
most comfortable and secure: two solid walls, full view of every entrance, lots of options for potential escape routes, well lit
with comforting natural light and a great view through the windows of the whole entrance forecourt of the building. When
they realized how great it was and we agreed to hole up there
for a while, I remember I mumbled something about "prospect
refuge,"[3] but nobody was paying attention.

We were as settled as anyone is nowadays and were starting
to chat when Lucy noticed movement below in the entrance
plaza outside. Some of the zombies were pursuing their exhausted prey in from the street. We were so far above that the
humans' painfully exaggerated movements seemed sickening-
ly wasteful next to the zombies' shuddering movements. They
were just running so hysterically.

I knew a while back I was becoming life-savingly desensitized to everything around me, but when I was staring down
at the plan-view of destruction I was getting a little ill at how
analytical I had become. I remember seeing the raised barricades—planters and decorative walls—advance and darken,
and the many ramps and stairs into the plaza recede until I was

thought about whether or not I believed there was a standard for the
maximum distance I'd run screaming in terror from zombies before
deciding to lie down and give up.
3 This is the principle that people fundamentally prefer spaces
where there are good views of the surrounding area, and opportunities to hide and take shelter. This principle seems even more significant in my experience of space now that there are shambling,
flesh-eating creatures running around everywhere.

looking at something like a figure-ground analysis.[4] The paving pattern was rectilinear and square; it seemed like a graph or an arcade game in which I was watching them all fail to navigate the exits and get overtaken and consumed.[5] I was hearing the gasps of the others but was half in a daze when they pulled me toward one of the exits, which, by pure luck, ended up being only somewhat zombie infested, so we were able to dispose of them. Computer games might have desensitized me to danger, but at least I get a deep sense of triumph out of destroying a vaguely human monster opponent.

We then made our way to a clear side street, and no one had any idea where to go. Out of desperation, I pushed to come here to the office as a place to collect ourselves and maybe find some base information that could prove helpful.

So now we've arrived, and I've piled up what's left of the papers and plans throughout the office. The plotters[6] are smashed, and the area where the server was kept is mostly burned anyway, so there's no point in digging up any digital drawing files.

By looking at this information, I should be able to figure out a plan of where we should go, and what we should do when we get there, but I'm looking and nothing is coming to me. But it's okay; I'm still in the "inventory and analysis" stage. Something will show up.

4 These are the diagrams in which buildings or obstructions and empty or accessible spaces are rendered black and white to show the spatial relationships among the objects and voids in an environment. Very useful to understand the proportions of a space or analyze and plan traffic and movement patterns.

5 This particular plaza had unfortunately been designed with a change in grade and raised planters that effectively "orphaned" the street—a plaza ought to feel like a separate space from the street, but not cut off from the street. This failure in design resulted in, among other things, poor navigability.

6 These are large printers we have in the office. Originally, plotters referred to printers specifically for vector-based graphics, but we just apply the term to any big printer that is equally capable of producing photo prints as CAD line drawings.

SEPTEMBER 16

Now that we have a destination, stealth is the order of the day. It's amazing that everything that used to make me feel safe now makes me feel vulnerable and vice versa. We've started travelling at night 'cause the zombies don't seem to have the best vision, so we have a bit of an advantage. I figure it's 'cause they don't blink very often, but Lucy also pointed out they don't really protect their eyes much at all. Even so, we're instinctively avoiding areas that are well lit. I'm not a lighting designer, or an electrical engineer, but I've had the occasion to lay out some lighting before and the attention we paid to avoiding blocking light or creating hotspots is driving me crazy now. I'm amazed there's still electricity, let alone that it's so hard to avoid uniformly lit areas as we make our way through the city. I feel the same way passing through a square or a pedestrian mall now as I used to feel about walking through a narrow dark alley in the non-zombie-infested world.

But, yes, we are making progress. After some thought about what to look for in a refuge from zombies, and some sifting through the drawings I found in our old office, I settled on this new office building on the other side of the greenbelt. It's a government facility and there are some security features to the design, but not so many that the drawings are classified, so the place won't be locked down or anything. And, unlike most, this building might not be filled with mangled corpses, 'cause it isn't finished yet and wasn't even in use. In almost every building project, the landscape design is among the last things to be implemented, and we've just started on this one; the last time I was at the site the workers were just completing the finishes on the building.

We're doing well for food because we spent the night passing through a mixed-use neighbourhood[7] that had a lot of food

---

7 These are neighbourhoods or developments where there are residences and commercial buildings and institutional facilities and all sorts of things in the same area instead of being isolated in one area of a city. It's good for raising population density and reducing sprawl, but as a landscape architect I just like it when people get out of their cars and walk around, which they do more when there's a shop or a park or

shops. It was pretty bad there. So many things I used to think of as desirable in the built environment make me so uneasy now. Pedestrian-oriented streetscapes with trees and benches and bicycle racks. All designed to be useless to hide behind, but perfectly good at obstructing the quickest escape route. This area was beautiful and animated once. Now its desirability as a place to "live, work and play" made it basically a zombie farmers' market. Fresh, locally grown humans, now in season.

It's not that the zombies are hard to outrun; most of them just shuffle along. But when there are so many people in one area, it attracts a lot of zombies and they just overwhelm you with numbers. It's obvious from how mangled the corpses are that these people were swarmed and not stalked.

One poor guy had obviously done pretty well for himself before the zombies got him. What's left of him is grasping a picket he ripped off a nearby decorative fence. I stopped to look at it closely. I'm familiar with the product: a cast aluminum pre-fabricated modular fence. It's cheaper than cast iron and fairly tough. This one must have been previously vandalized for him to get the picket off so easily.[8] He did pretty well with it: stabbing some of the zombies through the eyes from the looks of it. But there were too many it seems. There's not much left of him....

SEPTEMBER 17

I'm so lucky not to be travelling alone. While I was standing

a job within walking distance. People tend to notice more about their environments then, and I get to design to a human scale.

8 In selecting site furniture for a place, we have to give a lot of thought to the amazingly creative ways people will try to destroy it. The manufacturers put so much effort into making things scratch-proof, easily cleaned of paint, impervious to solvents, strong enough to resist bending and breaking. And the fasteners! They have to be theft proof, so some guy with some tools from home who fancies a new bench in his backyard can't run off with it, galvanized so they won't bleed rust all over the place, strong enough so they can't be broken off by humans, but with enough give that, if someone hits a tree guard with a car, the bolt will break and not the guard.

over that body on the street yesterday, contemplating welds
and fasteners and how I'd design that streetscape if I knew
then what I know now, a pack of zombies came toward us from
a formerly pleasant side street. They were moving toward us at
a good clip, and I might not have noticed them in time if Daniel
hadn't grabbed my arm and pulled me into a run. They were doing that typical zombie groan, but I couldn't hear them 'cause
the tree I was standing under still had lots of leaves, which
were rustling in the breeze.[9]

We ran and ran, but between the half-eaten humans on the
ground, the abandoned, out-of-fuel cars in the parking lane[10]
and all over the street, we were tiring quickly. When another group of zombies came in from an entrance to a courtyard
off the street, we were almost cut off and starting to lose our
heads.

Dan led us down a side street, and the entrance to it had
been closed to traffic from this street, so there was a barrier
curb and bollards, with only a couple of paths with depressed
curbs. Luckily for us, there were enough zombies chasing us
now that, when they all pushed into this bottleneck, it slowed
them down enough that we were able to increase our lead a bit.

9 I hate trees now. I think of how I used to push and plan for each
square metre of clear space below grade to put as many of those damn
things in as possible, whining to get cables and ducts and conduits
and pipes pushed under the roadway to clear space for tree roots—
which would need elaborate underground structures and special soils
to grow in so that paving over top wouldn't compact the earth to the
point where the tree would die for lack of water and air. I used to gripe
about people carving or breaking the trees we'd spent so much time
and tax money getting planted, how people didn't appreciate how
positive the urban forest is for us, and how difficult it is to get them to
grow at all in all the concrete and salt and pollution we throw at them.
Now, this damned, distracting rustling makes me want to burn them
all. These trees were also obviously carefully specified to have no
branches below 1.8 metres or so, so they're not even of any use to hide
behind. Damn that standard.
10 Parking on the street: supposed to be good for traffic calming.
Hmmmph.

We were coming into an older neighbourhood with fewer con-
dos and townhouses and no shops, so the carnage thinned out
a bit, too.

As we continued to flee, it became clear we were outrunning
the zombies, so we started to calm down a bit and slow our
pace to something less exhausting. I could think clearly again,
and I realized that this older neighbourhood, with its outdat-
ed standards for universal accessibility, was far less navigable
for zombies than the brand-new developments we'd passed
through. Looking at the heavy cross-slope on the narrow side-
walks, the high, uneven curbs and the heaves and cracks in the
concrete itself, I thought again of how difficult and frustrating
getting around must be for the disabled. I hoped at least that
all the careful grading I'd done over the years to meet accessibility standards would have helped some people with mobility problems to flee a little more easily. Contrasting values in
building material and way-finding cues we'd planned wouldn't
mean much to zombies, but hopefully some of the visually impaired people out there were able to find escape routes more
easily.

This is a dangerous line of thinking. When I start to think
about how many dead people I've seen, and what's going to
happen long term even if we do find a way to get rid of these
zombies, I usually try to stop thinking again immediately. I wonder if there will still be records of my student loans;
wouldn't mind so much if those were erased. But I suppose
if they were, so would my degree and all the steps I've tak-
en toward my certification: getting my "stamp."[11] Maybe, in a

---

11 Landscape architecture in my area is regulated under a *Name Act* in
the provincial legislature, meaning the title is conferred by a govern-
ing body to which one must apply to use it. In my area, you're required
to write a series of exams administered by a pan-North-Ameri-
can organization and undertake practice supervised by a licensed
professional for a set period of time before you can apply for full
membership—once you've finished your bachelor's or master's degree in landscape architecture, of course. Once you are a full member,
you must adhere to the standards of the organization. In many cities,

post-zombie world, I could gain professional credibility from designing with all my new experience of navigating a zombie-ridden environment. I could rewrite all the design standards to optimize zombie fleeing. There would be a lot to rebuild and people would probably think about the built environment in a whole new way. And the courts would take a long time to set up properly again, so I wouldn't have to worry about liability and errors and omissions insurance[12]—haha!

SEPTEMBER 18

The first thing I'd do in my new post-zombie built environment is push for more green space! Particularly naturalized green spaces.[13] We reached the green belt last night, and there are a few zombies in here, but they have a really hard time with the uneven terrain and the obstacles. They get themselves all tangled in vines and snagged in thorn bushes, really quite messed up. And while we're no longer enjoying the advantage of speed over the zombies, thinking critically and planning one's route make a huge difference in the pursuit. We've been able to build a fire, which also lends a sense of security and comfort.

Although I feel comfortable in here, I'm still focused on getting through and making our way to the unfinished government office complex I had set as our original goal. Not everyone in the group feels this way. Jack loves it in here and is navigating us beautifully and making us all comfortable. He's all for setting up some sort of camp here and waiting for some resolution

approval for permits for many types of construction projects requires the "stamp" of a licensed landscape architect.

12 There would be a whole new set of dangers included in a "slip-and-fall" suit: your faulty drainage pattern caused water to collect, ice to form, and my uncle slipped and was devoured by zombies!

13 By this I mean areas that had pre-existing, naturally occurring vegetation or an area that was deliberately and artificially "reforested." We do some reforestation work: small specimens of native plant species planted at high densities with some understorey plants. It's assumed that some of them will die, but the general result is intended to be similar to a natural woodlot.

to the zombie problem. I think Lucy and Fatima are inclined to stay, as well; the prospect of leaving the shelter of these woods isn't that appealing to me either. But I can't help wonder how we'll do when it starts to get colder.... I'm also not entirely confident that there'll be any successful resolution to the zombie issue anytime soon, and I'd like a proper building for shelter when there's snow on the ground.

It's difficult, though. As long as we were all moving and all focused on getting to a particular point, we had a focus that kept us from noticing the discomfort and terror of our situation quite so much.

Just as the sun was coming up, we found ourselves engaged in an increasingly irrational and irritable argument about the direction we should take. It was difficult. Everything we'd gone through had frayed all of our nerves, but it had also made us dependent on each other to a certain extent. So we were all feeling that urgency to come to a consensus. I was getting heated in my advocacy for keeping to the original plan when I was reminded of a cheesy saying from our studio classes early on; I think one of the professors used it in the context of the value of critique of one's work: don't be married to an idea. I fell silent and left Daniel to argue the point and considered whether I was arguing because I had one idea in my head and couldn't escape it or because it actually was the best course of action. I'm practised in selling my point. Professionally, a common task is to sell an idea to a client or to the public,[14] but usually I

14 Public consultation is a big part of most large infrastructure projects and really any large-scale project in which there are identified stakeholders who aren't necessarily the specific end users or those holding the purse strings. These can be open houses where design concepts and graphic presentation materials are displayed for information purposes, or interactive workshops where people are invited in and set to developing guiding design principles, or even the rudiments of form. The ones I've been involved with have varied from overwhelmingly positive experiences in which there are group hugs at the end and people leave feeling as if they're on the verge of solving the world's problems through design solutions, to events where I've been more or less called an idiot by the participants, who have refused to engage and actively work to discourage others from contributing.

have pretty pictures to help me do so. Right now, though, I had to back up for a second and determine whether my point was worth selling. Looking around and seeing the early signs of autumn in the trees and noticing the smell in the air tipped me in favour of human-built shelter for a long-term refuge. Was there value in lingering in the woods? I thought there wasn't. If the building we were headed toward proved unsuitable, it could take a while to figure out where to go next.

I pinched a yellowing leaf[15] off a nearby shrub and held it up. Visual aids! Never fails. We'll rest for the day and keep going later at night.

SEPTEMBER 21

I'm sitting in a windowless, unfurnished room, with white walls, beige carpets and a whiff of new-building off-gassing in the air. Heavenly. I'm cozy in here with Jack and Lucy. Dan and Fatima are off investigating the bowels of this building to see which other resources we can scare up. The sense of security is euphoric.

When we left the woods last night, we felt instantly agoraphobic crossing the fields. We had to travel through a newish subdivision next, and we could see the segments of the identical roofs curling over the hills. When we made our way into the streets, our anxiety got worse. The circuitous roads are great for lowering traffic speeds and discourage motorists from passing through, which can increase crimes of opportunity, but they're hell to navigate. Same with the strongly similar appearances of the houses. However, as we walked along, I was pleased to see that some effort had been made to "green" the development. There were more street trees planted than the bare minimum required by the city for new developments,

---

15 I feel here like I should instantly trot out the botanical name of the plant and all pertinent characteristics of it. But I'm a landscape architect, not a horticulturalist or a botanist. I know some landscape architects who are brilliant with plant identification, and most of us can identify the most popular street-tree species, but the least devout member of my parents' garden club knows more about plant material than I ever will.

and some ambitious individual had designed bio-swales for the boulevard.[16] And thank goodness he or she had. The bio-swales worked amazingly well at tripping the zombies that burst out of the backyards of some of the houses about ten minutes after we entered the subdivision. It was amazingly consistent: as we raced down the middle of the street, zombies would appear from the side yards, lope toward us in the centre of the road, step into the bio-swales and flop face first onto the ground. It would have been comical if (a) they didn't get right back up again, in some cases with fresh injuries that contributed to their already unpleasant appearance, and (b) other zombies weren't coming right behind them, sometimes using the earlier ones as bridges over the bio-swales or managing to find a driveway that led them right to the road. In general, these zombies were in better condition than the ones we had encountered in the city core (probably fresher), and we were getting concerned as more and more of them appeared. We knew that eventually we would tire and they would overtake us, but we finally spilled out onto a main road that, thankfully, I recognized from the route I had planned to our current hideout. I couldn't have told you how long we ran if I hadn't had drawings for that road, clearly marked with station points every ten metres. I remembered that to the west, as we left the new subdivision development, the road maintained its grade while the land around it sloped away and when we paused for breath at one point—a creeping horde of zombies advancing toward us in the distance—I explained my plan. In another five minutes

16 Bio-swales are one of the many design tools used to deal with stormwater run-off in areas with a lot of impermeable surfaces. Rainwater that hits asphalt or concrete in subdivisions like these usually runs into retention ponds or, in some cases, storm sewers. Both are expensive to build and maintain, and there are fundamental problems associated with forcing rainwater to absorb into the group in only certain areas in terms of groundwater recharge. Bio-swales are like ditches along the side of the road into which water can flow and seep into the ground or be absorbed by the plant material put there. I've worked on the designs for a few of them, but they're problematic in our climate since we tend to salt the roads heavily in cold weather, which is terribly toxic to most plant material.

or so, the sides of the road dropped away behind the guard rail, and we hopped over and skidded down the steep slope to the railway line that passed under the main road. We ran along it to the north, pausing in the shadows of some scrubby trees that had sprung up nearby. We were gasping and shaking, and we could barely move as we watched the zombies approach. The first of the group that had seen us slip off the road made their way onerously around or over the guardrail, but were unequal to the uneven surface of the tufty, unmown grass and the steep 3:1 slope.[17] They slid and stumbled and tripped each other, and those that weren't seriously slowed down by injuries (zombies don't feel pain, but it's still hard to get around on a dislocated knee) seemed to be seriously disoriented by the fall. We were quiet in the trees and out of the light, so even though one or two continued to make their way toward us it seemed to have been a random choice, and we were able to sneak away without pursuit.

But we were so tired. We were stumbling, and I felt sick to my stomach and clammy with a slimy sweat from the fear and exercise. We briefly bickered about stopping in the trees for a rest, but we were so close that I urged everyone to keep going.

And we finally arrived! We turned a bend in a new-looking, virtually empty road and found the building, almost finished but still with some of the protective film over the windows. A pristine building sitting in an unfinished landscape: the rough grading complete and the tire tracks from the construction vehicles still imprinted everywhere. I stared out over the totally black, dried mud that spread outward from the base of the building to the trees around it and my exhausted brain started to fill in the picture with the design I had completed months

---

17 In grading exercises, the steepness of a slope is usually expressed by a percentage or a ratio. In this case, a 3:1 slope indicates that, for every three units of measurement you travel horizontally, you rise or fall one unit vertically. 3:1 slopes are often the steepest allowed because any steeper and they can't be mown, erosion can occur and plant material has a difficult time establishing itself. These aren't usually areas intended to be regularly travelled by people, since it would be hazardous for them and the traffic would contribute even more to erosion.

earlier for the site. A large parking lot to the right, with islands and street trees, and paved paths clearly indicating the entrances to the building. Everything smooth and clean and easily navigable. To the left, groupings of trees in a park-like setting, with lawn and picnic tables and shade structures placed informally among them. Smooth paths leading to a network of trails in the woods. A soccer field and a volleyball court behind. A standard, simple landscape for a large office building, full of spaces for employees to relax and work off steam at lunch and after hours.

As soon as my mind's eye had completed the picture, it started to dissolve and was replaced with a new vision of what could be there. A secured perimeter with deep gullies at the steepest possible slopes. Further in, places for crops and large, bare, unmown areas that are easily surveyed. There would be a clear expanse immediately around the building but, beyond, a heavily planted buffer of dense shrubs and vines to trip and slow the zombies. Designed to be high enough to disguise movement around the building itself, but not so high that movement beyond it would be unnoticeable from the top floor of the building. The perimeter would be well lit, but not the area within the planted buffer, so that the observed are obvious but the observers are not. The roof would be an intensive green roof—with greenhouses to grow fresh fruit in the winter! Paths to the building would be direct, but with gates that could quickly be closed by the pursued, directing the chasing zombies to either side, where they would be forced into a hostile environment of thorn bushes, uneven terrain and steep slopes to slow them. Visions of zombie-proof construction details were flashing across my eyes as we beat the door down and walked into our new home.

Glancing over the pages of this short journal, I'm reading a fairly clear record and analysis of a zombie-ridden landscape. All of the observations I've made are design problems waiting to be solved. Hopefully, there will be a solution to the zombie problem. Whether we eradicate zombies completely or simply restrict their activities to certain continents, if we survive, then their appearance will have altered irrevocably how we view our environment.

CONTRIBUTORS

Matt Bailey (matthew.bailey@mq.edu.au) is a historian working in the Department of Modern History, Politics and International Relations at Macquarie University, Sydney, Australia. He researches retail and urban history as well as developments in consumer culture. Matt recently completed his dissertation on the history of major shopping centres in Australia.

Melissa Beattie (tritogeneia@aol.com) holds an MA in archaeology for screen media from Bristol and a BA in classics from SUNY Buffalo. Her current projects include the cataloguing of the Ianto Memorial in Cardiff Bay, co-editing and contributing to the conference proceedings *Whoniversal Appeal: An Interdisciplinary Postgraduate Conference on* Doctor Who *and All of Its Spin-Offs; Time, Unincorporated 3: Writings on the New Series* (co-edited by Robert Smith?); and several other works relating to science fiction and classical reception. Her PhD studies, at Cardiff University in media studies, examine the connections between televisual epic, national identity and *Torchwood*'s fan audiences.

Arnold T. Blumberg (the14thdoctor@yahoo.com) is sorry if he omitted any of your favourites; there are, after all, about six hundred zombie movies out there, so it's hard to cover everything in one chapter. He is the co-author of *Zombiemania: 80 Movies to Die For* (Telos Publishing), an exhaustive guide to zombie cinema from 1932 to 2005 in which he does cover everything. In the fall of 2010, he launched a course on zombies in popular culture at the University of Baltimore (where he earned his master's and doctorate) that garnered international media attention. He also teaches a course in comic book literature at the University of Maryland Baltimore County. To *Doctor Who* fans, he's the co-author of the *Howe's Transcendental Toybox* series of *Doctor Who* merchandise guides from Telos, the designer of other Telos books, including *The Target Book*, the author of "Stolen Days" in *Short Trips: How the Doctor Changed My Life* and "Mardi Gras Massacre" in *Short Trips: Indefinable Magic*, and the *Doctor Who* DVD reviewer for IGN.com. He has written numerous books and magazine articles on comics, genre film and pop culture history. He has an occasionally out-of-date blog at www.atbpublishing.com. His home is not nearly as zombie proof as he'd like it to be.

Daniel Changer (dan.changer@gmail.com) is a writer and political satirist living in Australia. Starting out in editorial cartoons, his later work impersonating the then prime minister, a self-described "Lazarus with a triple bypass," provided the perfect segue into this world of the living dead.

Sasha Cocarla (scocarla@gmail.com) is a PhD candidate with the Institute of Women's Studies at the University of Ottawa. Her primary research interests focus on gender, sexuality, cultural analysis and theories on the abject/grotesque and the ways in which all of these topics are framed and represented within film and popular culture. She is also fascinated by the prospect of reclaiming spaces and subverting dominant ideologies in fun, playful and sometimes horrific performative ways.

Tony Contento is a cell biologist and lecturer working for Iowa State University in the Department of Genetics, Cell and

Developmental Biology. His current research involves the study of macroautophagy in plants in response to abiotic stresses. He is also working on a study of negative gravitropism in *Arabidopsis* seedlings for NASA. He spends his free time in Ames, Iowa, working with the Cub Scouts of America; writing textbooks, fiction and screenplays; blogging and editing WikiAnswers; creating stained glass windows and *objets d'art*; and mushroom hunting with his family and their two corgis. His weapon of choice when stalking the undead is his homemade aluminum katana or a slingshot loaded with either lead shot or paintball pellets filled with a fast-acting sedative. He can be contacted in his suburban, zombie-proof compound via email at tonycontento@gmail.com.

Harris DeLeeuw (Harris.DeLeeuw@btinternet.com) is the pen name of a strategic intelligence analyst with over ten years of experience in three countries: Australia, the Netherlands and the United Kingdom..She has been trained in counterterrorism intelligence analysis and has led a team similar to the SIAG in an exercise testing the capability of strategic intelligence in such an event. She has also been involved in a SIAG-like team during a real emergency situation. Her chapter is an amalgamation of approaches typical of Australian, European and North American criminal intelligence analysis, but is embellished with factors drawn from experience often forgotten in the textbooks.

Julia Gruson-Wood (juliagrusonwood@gmail.com) is completing her master's degree in the Department of Critical Disability Studies at York University in which she dedicates at least ninety percent of her attention to examining science fiction from the perspective of species variability. In addition, Julia is working as an administrative assistant for anesthesia, which allows her to do cool things such as watch surgeries and give CPR to startlingly humanoid robots. Before pursuing her graduate degree, Julia worked as a full-time short-story-writer-slash-waitress. Before that, she completed her undergraduate degree in cultural studies at Trent University. Pre-postsecondary education, Julia grew up as a figure-skating Toronto kid and went to SEED alternative high school, where she was taught to cultivate the value of being different. One day, Julia hopes to return to writing fiction monogamously. This is her first time writing about zombies. And she really, really liked it.

Sean N. Francis (francism@dukes.jmu.edu) is a senior biology major at James Madison University. Sean enjoys travelling and hopes to optimize his travel itinerary in order to minimize the opportunity for zombie interaction.

Marina Levina (mlevina@memphis.edu) is an assistant professor in the Department of Communication at the University of Memphis. Her research focuses on critical studies of science, technology and medicine, network and new-media theory, visual culture and media studies. She has published work on health information technology, personal genomics, biocitizenship, affective labour, networks and globalization, and visual culture's engagement with scientific and medical research. Recent publications include an edited collection, *Post-Global Network and Everyday Life* (Peter Lang, 2010); a chapter in the volume *A Foucault for the 21st Century: Governmentality, Biopolitics, and Discipline in the New Millennium* (edited by Sam Binkley and Jorge Capetillo, Cambridge Scholars Publishing, 2009); and articles in the *Journal of Science Communication* and in *Spontaneous Generations: History and Philosophy of Science and Technology.* Currently, she is working on a book manuscript titled "Life as a Virus, Life as a Code: Science, Culture, and Regulation of Difference in the Global Network" and article-length works on health information technology, cyberfeminist practices and affective biolabour in online patient forums. She is an avid fan of monster and horror narratives and has written numerous articles, chapters and opinion pieces on the critical meaning of monsters, especially their connection to scientific and medical cultural anxieties. She has also repeatedly taught a very popular course on monster films. She blogs at www.biocultures.blogspot.com.

Lisa MacDonald (lmmacd@gmail.com) is a landscape architect living and working in Ottawa, Ontario. She was an unlikely candidate to write a composition about zombies and landscape architecture, having spent most of her life irrationally terrified of the former and completely ignorant of the latter, but she has been working for some time on facing her fears and lessening her ignorance. Between writing the first draft of her composition and doing the final edits, she acquired her full membership in the Ontario Association of Landscape Architects. She spends most of her free time reading, playing the violin and tripping over domestic animals.

Sarah McHone-Chase (sarah.mchonech@gmail.com) is the information delivery services librarian of Northern Illinois University, specializing in interlibrary loan and document delivery. She has published and presented primarily in library disaster planning, but she has also published numerous encyclopedia articles on subjects as diverse as Mother Jones (the person and the magazine), Djuna Barnes, intellectual property, the Haymarket Riot and bicycles. In 2006, she was among the American Library Association's first group of emerging leaders. For several years, Sarah has suffered from zombie nightmares, which have only strengthened her resolve to find ways to combat them.

Caitlin V. Johnson (johnsocv@dukes.jmu.edu) is a reluctant senior mathematics major at James Madison University. Caitlin is interested in attending medical school to create a vaccine for those affected by a zombie bite.

Helen Kang (hhk3@sfu.ca) is a doctoral candidate in sociology at Simon Fraser University. Her dissertation examines the development of morality in the Canadian medical profession using Pierre Bourdieu's concept of invested disinterestedness. Her research and teaching interests include feminist cultural studies, social studies of science and technology, critical pharmaceutical studies, and studies in visual culture. She is also interested in community-based research, particularly in relation to art, culture and community building.

Philip Munz (pmunz@connect.carleton.ca) has been an avid zombie connoisseur since *Night of the Living Dead* scared the popcorn out of him as a teenager. He recently completed a master's in applied mathematics at Carleton University, where he co-authored (with Robert Smith?) the groundbreaking paper on mathematical modelling of zombies. He currently spends his time researching the undead—without the help of any government funding—and has dreams of becoming zombie fodder in some upcoming blockbuster zombie flick.

Natasha Patterson (ndp@sfu.ca) is a doctoral candidate in the Department of Gender, Sexuality and Women's Studies at Simon Fraser University, British Columbia. Her work is included in *Zombie Culture: Autopsies of the Living Dead.* In addition to her fascination with zombies and horror, she researches and writes about reality TV, celebrity culture, postfeminism and feminist research methods.

Jen Rinaldi (jenrinaldister@gmail.com) is a doctoral candidate in the Department of Critical Disability Studies at York University, expecting to graduate in 2011. She is writing her dissertation on reproductive decisions and genetic impairments. Jen completed her master's in philosophy at the University of Guelph in the summer of 2007, where she defended and published her thesis *The Point at Which the Canadian Same-Sex Marriage Policy Should Be beyond Deliberation.* At the University of Windsor, she graduated with great distinction in 2005, earning a combined honours degree in philosophy and classical civilizations.

John Seavey (jseavey_mn1@comcast.net) is a writer from the Twin Cities whose work has appeared in a wide variety of publications from short-story anthologies to gaming sourcebooks to ... well, to books of academic essays about zombies. He is perhaps best known for his "Storytelling Engines" column, which ran at Xenagia.com, Comics Should Be Good, and at his own blog, Fraggmented (http://fraggmented.blogspot.com). In his spare time, he works.

Kate Small (smallkt@netspace.net.au) is an adult educator based in Melbourne, Australia. She writes and develops training programs for staff and has run numerous training workshops for people transitioning to new systems. Although she only teaches adults, she can report that the zombie-like quality of students extends across all age groups.

Adam Smith (adambensmith@hotmail.com) is a freelance intellectual from the Indiana corn country. He studied political science in Chicago and political theory in Toronto. After spending several years in East Asia, he set up shop in Portland, Oregon. He spends his days there writing an eclectic mix of non-profit grant proposals, articles on financial education policy and pretentious fiction.

Robert Smith? (rsmith43@uottawa.ca) is a professor of mathematics who spends his classroom time teaching biologists at the University of Ottawa. The result is a math class for students who hate math. Consequently, they are more akin to terrified survivors running in fear from zombies than zombies themselves. He is the author of *Modelling Disease Ecology with Mathematics* (which isn't nearly as scary a title as it sounds) and the co-editor of two books in the *Time, Unincorporated: The Doctor Who Fanzine Archive* series from Mad Norwegian Press. He's also a world-renowned biomathematical modeller of infectious diseases (and zombies), but there's a chance you already knew that.

Lynne M. Thomas (lynnemthomas@gmail.com) is the head of Rare Books and Special Collections at Northern Illinois University, where she is responsible for popular culture special collections, which include the papers of SF authors Robert Asprin, Tamora Pierce, Elizabeth Bear, Kage Baker and Jack McDevitt, as well as significant collections of dime novels and popular historical children's literature. She has published scholarly articles about cross-dressing in dime novels, maintains the blog Confessions of a Curator and co-authored *Special Collections 2.0*, a book about Web 2.0 technologies and special collections in libraries, with Beth Whittaker of the University of Kansas (Libraries Unlimited, 2009). She is also the co-editor of *Chicks Dig Time Lords*, a Hugo-award-winning essay collection celebrating women in *Doctor Who* fandom and the production of the series (Mad Norwegian Press, 2010).

Anthony Tongen (tongenal@jmu.edu) is an associate professor in the Department of Mathematics and Statistics at James Madison University. His research interests include mathematical biology, materials science, numerical analysis, mathematical modelling and anything else that is fun and math-related. Anthony also enjoys time with his family, church-related activities and sports. His new claim to fame might be writing an article on zombies without ever watching a movie with zombies!

Philippe Vachon (pvachon@connect.carleton.ca) is a student at Carleton University currently working to finish a computer science degree. His interests include image processing and photogrammetry; he has a perverse love of hardware reverse engineering, which takes up a substantial amount of his spare time. When he's not found in his natural habitat, he can be seen wandering in the parks and forests surrounding Ottawa searching for signs of zombie infestation in the wildlife of the city, photographing whatever he can find. After a hard day of work protecting humanity, he can then be found anywhere overpriced scotch is sold.

Anthony Wilson (anthonyrwilson@hotmail.com) keeps himself busy with any number of things. By day he is a schoolteacher in Inner London, in the evenings he runs a variety of musical theatre performing groups for children and adults, and by night he writes things down. If nothing else, this keeps him off the streets. Anthony has been involved in the performing arts for over twenty years, and he has directed or musically directed more than one hundred musicals. He also composes music and his work has been played on national radio. He is a regular contributor to the online *Doctor Who* guide *The Cloister Library* (with Robert Smith?). He has also contributed to a number of anthologies (including Mad Norwegian Press's *Time, Unincorporated* series) and has written an online guide to A-level music technology for Northamptonshire County Council. He currently lives just outside London. He has never been attacked by zombie hordes but might well have taught them on occasion.